Praise for *Re:Imagin*

"All around us the old stories are failing, crumbling in the face of lived experience and scientific reality. But what stories will replace them? That is the subject of this crucial book: helping readers to tell irresistible stories about deep change–why it is needed and what it will look like. The Story-based Strategy team has been doing this critical work for fifteen years, training an entire generation in transformative communication. This updated edition of *Re:Imagining Change* is a thrilling addition to the activist tool kit."
   ~Naomi Klein

"Indigenous peoples around the world are on the frontlines defending our rights and fighting for ecological and climate justice. We are offering powerful stories reawakening humanity to its relationship and responsibilities to defend the rights of Mother Earth. But how can we strengthen our voices and make our calls for change heard? This book offers strategies for our movements to creatively build the power to guide society toward a more just and sustainable future for all."
   ~Tom Goldtooth, *Indigenous Environmental Network*

"Once upon a time, left-wing activists thought being right was good enough, but the past decade has seen a more elegant and effective understanding that you need to be a lot more if you want to win. Center for Story-based Strategy's guidebook to being that *more*–smarter, more engaging, more subversive, more powerful–should be in every activist's hands and imagination. It's a great toolkit for change."
   ~Rebecca Solnit, *author of numerous books including* The Encyclopedia of Trouble and Spaciousness, Men Explain Things to Me, *and* Hope in the Dark

"CSS shows us that if organizing is the muscle of social movements, and strategy is the brain, then story is the heart and soul. CSS's methodology combines the power of story together with strategy to serve grassroots organizing and build powerful, unstoppable movements. And it's working! From climate justice to low-wage workers; from anti-militarism to migrant rights; story-based strategy is amplifying our voices and deepening our impact."
   ~Gopal Dayaneni, *Movement Generation Justice & Ecology Project*

"Yo organizers! Stop what you are doing for a couple hours and soak up this book! We know the importance of smart 'issue framing.' But *Re:Imagining Change* will move our organizing further as we connect to the powerful narratives, stories and memes of our culture."
   ~Chuck Collins, *Institute for Policy Studies, author of* Born on Third Base, 99 to 1, *and other books about economic inequality*

"There is an African proverb that says, 'Until the story of the hunt is told by the lion, the story of the hunt will always glorify the hunter.' Similarly, for frontline communities, it is too often others who are framing the narratives of the systems, policies, and practices that hold sway over our lives. Through *Re:Imagining Change*, the Center for Story-based Strategy provides tools and pathways to put community framing, stories, and vision at the center of the transformation that is necessary to transition from systems and structures characterized by extraction and domination to regenerative, cooperative, resilient communities."

~*Jacqui Patterson*, *director, Environmental and Climate Justice Program, NAACP*

"Our stories are powerful enough to change the world, particularly when we know how to put them at the center of our organizing and direct action campaigns. That's why *Re:Imagining Change* is an essential how-to manual. Its accessible framework walks activists through the process of aligning transformative storytelling with movement building, organizing, and action. It is a critical resource for any community that is fighting for justice. Don't find yourself on the frontlines without it!"

~*Sharon Lungo*, *executive director, The Ruckus Society*

"Story-based strategy is integral to winning the fight for social, economic, and political power for Black people. On the front lines of civil and human rights, we're not only fighting for our lives but for the right to own our experiences and our stories, too. As we battle long-standing, mythological narratives about Blackness and Black people, many of which lead to prejudicial legislation and deadly policing, we'll use tools like this book to equip our organizers with narrative strategy that advances us to a more equitable and just world for all people."

~*Shanelle Matthews*, *director of communications for the Black Lives Matter Global Network*

"*Re:Imagining Change* is worthy of praise. As an introduction to story-based strategy, the book offers organizers and advocates a new and necessary way to understand and transform the impact of stories on our public life."

~*Malkia Cyril*, *executive director of the Center for Media Justice and cofounder, Media Action Grassroots Network*

"Knowing how to knock on doors, organize community meetings, and plan a street protest is no longer enough. Today's activists need to know how to generate symbols, tell stories, and tap into popular dreams. *Re:Imagining Change* is THE handbook for fighting on this cultural terrain."

~*Stephen Duncombe*, *author of* Dream: Re-Imagining Progressive Politics in an Age of Fantasy

"*Re:Imagining Change* is a one-of-a-kind essential resource for everyone who is thinking big, challenging the powers that be and working hard to make a better world from the ground up. This innovative book provides the tools, analysis, and inspiration to help activists everywhere be more effective, creative, and strategic. This handbook is like rocket fuel for your social change imagination."

~*Antonia Juhasz*, author of Black Tide: the Devastating Impact of the Gulf Oil Spill: The Tyranny of Oil; and The Bush Agenda

"We are surrounded and shaped by stories every day, sometimes for better, sometimes for worse. But what Doyle Canning and Patrick Reinsborough point out is a beautiful and powerful truth–that we are all storytellers too. Armed with the right narrative tools, activists can not only open the world's eyes to injustice, but feed the desire for a better world. *Re:Imagining Change* is a powerful weapon for a more democratic, creative, and hopeful future."

~*Raj Patel*, author of Stuffed and Starved and The Value of Nothing: How to Reshape Market Society and Redefine Democracy

"This is a groundbreaking book to mark up, share with friends, and keep within arm's reach of activists. The analysis and case studies you hold in your hand are tools to shift paradigms and raise ruckuses! Please try this at home."

~*adrienne maree brown*, author of Emergent Strategy: Shaping Change, Changing Worlds and Octavia's Brood: Science Fiction Stories from Social Justice Movements

"Brilliant and invaluable. Lakoff introduced the progressive movement to the power of framing. Canning and Reinsborough take framing to a far more powerful level and provide practical tools essential to the success of every progressive organization that seeks to bring forth a world of peace and justice. It gets my highest recommendation."

~*David Korten*, board chair of YES! magazine and author of The Great Turning and Change the Story, Change the Future: A Living Economy for a Living Earth

"This powerful and useful book is an invitation to harness the transformative power of stories by examining social change strategy through the lens of narrative. *Re:Imagining Change* is an essential resource to make efforts for fundamental social change more enticing, compelling, and effective. It's a potent how-to book for anyone working to create a better world."

~*Ilyse Hogue*, president, NARAL Pro-Choice America

2nd Edition

Re:Imagining Change

How to Use Story-based Strategy to Win Campaigns,
Build Movements, and Change the World

Patrick Reinsborough and Doyle Canning

Re:Imagining Change—How to Use Story-based Strategy to Win Campaigns, Build Movements, and Change the World
Copyright ©2010, 2017 Patrick Reinsborough and Doyle Canning

2017 Creative Commons Non-Commercial License
This work is licensed under the Creative Commons Attribution-NonCommercial-ShareAlike 4.0 International License. To view a copy of this license, visit http://creativecommons.org/licenses/by-nc-sa/4.0/.

ISBN: 978-1-62963-384-8
Library of Congress Control Number: 2016959584

Editing and Book Design by Jess Clarke, Christine Joy Ferrer, and Merula Furtado from Reimagine! Movements Making Media,
www.reimaginerpe.org.

Cover by John Yates/stealworks.com

10 9 8 7 6 5 4 3 2

PM Press
PO Box 23912
Oakland, CA 94623
www.pmpress.org

Printed in the USA by the Employee Owners of Thomson-Shore in Dexter, Michigan.
www.thomsonshore.com

This book is dedicated to everyone everywhere
who has ever dreamed of a better world and
had the courage to move toward that vision.

"If you want to build a ship, don't herd people together to collect wood and don't assign them tasks and work, but rather teach them to long for the endless immensity of the sea."

–Antoine de Saint-Exupéry

"No necesitamos pedir permiso para ser libres."

–the Fourth Declaration of the Lacandon Jungle Zapatista Army of National Liberation (EZLN)

Re:Imagining Change

CONTENTS

Story-based Strategy Campaign Model Chart   xii

Foreword to the 2nd Edition   xiii

Introduction to the 2nd Edition   1

I   Why Story

1.1   The Narrative Animal   8

1.2   Hacking at the Roots   10

1.3   The Era of Outdated Stories   11

1.4   Movement as Narrative   13

1.5   From Improvement to Innovation   17

1.6   The Story-based Strategy Approach   19

II   Narrative Power

2.1   Truth vs. Meaning   23

2.2   Narrative Thinking   26

2.3   Narrative Power Analysis   27

2.4   Setting the Frame   31

2.5   Designer Stories and the Branded World   33

2.6   Memes   36

2.7   Power and Mythology   39

2.8   People-Power and Narrative   40

2.9   Creation Myths of the United States   42

2.10   Control Myths & Memes   44

2.11   Narrative Filters   47

2.12   The Elements of Story   48

III   Winning the Battle of the Story

3.1	Building on the Cornerstones	53
3.2	Beyond the Story of the Battle	57
3.3	The Battle of the Story	59
3.4	Framing the Conflict	62
3.5	Creating Narrative Frames	64
3.6	Amplifying Compelling Characters	67
3.7	The Drama Triangle	71
3.8	Imagery: Show, Don't Tell	73
3.9	Foreshadowing	76
3.10	Challenging Assumptions	79
3.11	Designing a Framing Narrative	82
3.12	Action Logic and Meta-Verbs	86

IV   Points of Intervention

4.1	Social Change as Intervention	91
4.2	Point of Production	93
4.3	Point of Destruction	94
4.4	Point of Consumption	96
4.5	Point of Decision	97
4.6	Point of Assumption	98
4.7	Reframing Debates	100
4.8	Offering New Futures	103
4.9	Subverting and Creating Spectacles	105
4.10	Making the Invisible Visible	110
4.11	Repurposing Popular Culture Narratives	113
4.12	Brand-Busting	116

V   Changing the Story

5.1   Strategic Improvisation   121

5.2   *Case Study*
      Greenpeace: Save the Whales   123

5.3   *Case Study*
      Rural Vermont   125

5.4   *Case Study*
      Protect Our Waters   129

5.5   *Case Study*
      Coalition of Immokalee Workers   133

5.6   *Case Study*
      #Healthy Hoods   136

5.7   *Case Study*
      Our Power: A New Climate Narrative   142

**VI   Navigating Crisis and Transition:
      A Call to Innovation**

6.1   Beyond Talking Points   149

6.2   The Slow-Motion Apocalypse   151

6.3   Psychic Breaks   153

6.4   Turning Moments into Movements   155

6.5   Narrating Change   157

6.6   A Movement of Storytellers   160

Endnotes   163

Glossary   179

Further Reading   185

Gratitude and Acknowledgments   194

About CSS   197

About the Authors   198

Story-based Strategy Campaign Model

Strategy Development

Narrative Power Analysis

Action

Reflection

Battle of the Story (deconstructive)
- What are the stories we need to change?
- Use narrative power analysis to deconstruct with elements of story
- Identify underlying assumptions
- Are there larger mythologies of the dominant culture that we must challenge?

Battle of the Story (constructive)
- Use narrative power analysis to apply elements of story and construct our story
- How does our story target underlying assumptions in the dominant story?
- What are our shared values and assumptions?

Cornerstones: Identifying Targets & Audiences
- Targeting Institutions: What institutions are implicated in the problem?
- Targeting Decision Makers: Who can give us what we want?
- Audiences: Who are we talking to and what do we want them to do?
- What do we need to know about our audiences? What are their narrative filters?

Design: Framing Narrative & Action Logic
- Synthesize your campaign's narrative
- Memes: How do we encapsulate our story?
- Viralization: What are the venues, networks, cultural currents, media environments, or spectacles where our meme could spread?
- Action Design: Tactics? Scenarios?
- R & D: Creativity, experimentation, testing
- Group preparation for action

Social Movement Building

Ongoing Practices
- Building networks & alliances
- Leadership development
- Skill & capacity building
- Monitoring narratives & (re)assessment
- Self & community care
- Celebration!
- Reflection and innovation

Cornerstones: Visioning & Campaign Goal Setting
- What do we really want?
- What are the incremental steps to get there?

Evaluation
Is there evidence that:
- Our memes are spreading?
- Framing has shifted?
- We met our organizing and alliance-building goals?
- We have influenced the target?

Intervention
- Identify physical points
- Identify points of assumption
- Intervention tied to goals (organizing, persuasion, pressure on target, etc.) and appropriate for group capacity
- Interventions launch/repeat core memes

Results?
- Success!?
- Story has changed?
- Goals met?

Shared Problem or Issue Identified

Constituency Organizes
- Research
- Power analysis
- Outreach & education
- Organizing

For specific tools & resources visit: storybasedstrategy.org

Re:Imagining Change

FOREWORD TO THE 2ND EDITION

By Jonathan Matthew Smucker
February 2017

Stories are never neutral. At its fundamental level, a story is an assertion—either a reinforcement or a contestation of our interpretations of reality. And today, the contest between competing narratives to explain the present state of our world has never felt so consequential.

Over the past 15 years, the Center for Story-based Strategy (formerly *smart*Meme)—an organization on whose board I have the honor of serving—has used the tools in this book as the basis of their prolific training and partnership work with some of the most dynamic campaigns and creative movement leaders in the United States. Thousands of change-makers have utilized these narrative tools to strategically reframe important social issues and win campaigns.

In these pages, you will read about the battle of the story: a contest over the meaning of unfolding events and social reality. While progressive change-makers have utilized this conceptual tool to shift sentiment on particular issues, we can also examine larger-scale societal shifts through this lens. In the unique political moment in which we now find ourselves, the battle of the story has suddenly scaled up to epic proportions.

On issue after issue, the narrative landscape is dramatically shifting, as pressure mounts and fault lines give way. Today, the whole dominant narrative itself seems to be up for popular reconsideration. It's on.

Now, when a student struggles with the question of whether or not to stay in school because the price is a lifetime of debt, she is less likely today to see her situation as a private matter. Similarly, when a family faces foreclosure, or when a town's public library or post office is shuttered, more and more people are making sense of such events through a new emerging story—not one of personal shortcomings, but of public crisis. Grassroots social movements have been central in inventing the vocabulary that is helping society re-narrate the present political reality. Classic elements of a story have been introduced into the popular lexicon: villains like Wall Street and the "one percent."

Or consider the narrative about climate. Today as so-called natural disasters hit with ever-increasing frequency, again we find that the story is changing. By telling a different story, environmental justice groups are exposing the real impacts of the climate crisis, connecting affected communities to each other, pushing their members forward as protagonists, and naming the greed-driven fossil fuel corporations and culpable public officials as villains.

And consider narratives about race in the United States. When a Black man is shot by police, we are no longer able to see this as an isolated incident. No. It is part of a bigger narrative that reverberates across the country as millions take to the streets to raise our voices collectively to assert that Black Lives Matter—and to foreshadow a world where this is true, while we organize to make it so.

These shifts in popular meanings create the cultural and cognitive conditions that can facilitate on-the-ground political organizing. Antonio Gramsci used the term "articulation" to describe a kind of narration of political alignment. Political contenders—from social movements to political parties to individual leaders—articulate a shared story about why things are the way they are; stories about blame and stories about solutions. By "articulation" Gramsci meant the process of conjuring—bringing into being—the social forces necessary to achieve the political task at hand. As you can read in Chapter II, he was especially interested in how "common sense" is always itself a political achievement, typically normalizing, naturalizing, justifying, or even invisibilizing status quo power relations. As organizers and movement builders, one of our central tasks is to change the common sense. That's what changing the story is all about.

Yet for Gramsci this wasn't just about hitting on the perfect message. Articulation was not merely a rhetorical move, but it involved a ground game. Rhetoric, symbols, and stories are essential instruments for striking a popularly resonant chord. But we also have to organize the people our stories engage into an empowered political force. As *Re:Imagining Change* argues, we must not naively imagine that sparking social transformations is merely a matter of communications savvy. Rather it behooves us to recognize narrative strategy as a critical complement to any grass-roots organizing effort. The story-based strategy approach outlines how well-crafted stories that communicate a cohesive set of strategic frames can dramatically boost the impact of advocacy, protest, and organizing.

We must remember that power relations are not just a matter of force, but also of meaning and legitimacy. When Beyoncé celebrates Black Power in a Super Bowl halftime show or Colin Kaepernick kneels during the National Anthem, these brave acts enkindle a shift in symbolic power. These interventions are so important because history suggests that shifts in symbolic power always precede shifts in structural power.

Today, we find our nation and, indeed, our whole world at a cross-roads. In the United States, as in many other countries, the story that the political establishment has been telling about its own legitimacy now rings hollow with a critical mass of the populace. This constitutes what political scientists call a crisis of legitimacy. In the midst of such crises, new political challengers emerge from the margins to offer new stories. When the high priests lose their authority, prophets emerge from the wilderness with visions of a path forward. And where prophets emerge, so do false prophets. This explains the simultaneous popularity (amongst portions of the U.S. public) of both the Tea Party and Occupy Wall Street, and of both Bernie Sanders and Donald Trump. Both poles offer new stories: new premises for political alignment, even for the basis of society, its values, and its aspirational horizon.

It is striking that both progressives and reactionaries have to navigate the same narrative terrain, but the meanings and consequences of their stories could hardly be further apart. Both narrate a vision for "the people" and both point fingers at "the establishment," but one punches up at structured injustice while the other punches down at the most vulnerable people in society. One "we" is inclusive—seeking to expand who is included in that aspirational phrase We The People—and the other is exclusionary, seeking to close borders and shut people out.

We need stories that can win this battle. We need stories with protagonists with whom people can identify—who invite our intended audiences to join them and enter the story as agents of change. We need stories with compelling villains who help us grasp the true nature of the dangers and threats we face. We need stories that foreshadow the world that we know we can build together.

But most importantly, in order to grapple with these strategic imperatives, we need the conceptual tools to weave what CSS calls narrative power analysis into our efforts for social, economic, and political change. Fortunately, this book introduces vital concepts and frameworks to meet this need. I suspect many readers will eagerly apply them.

The sharp insights and clear methodologies that fill the pages of this book have emerged through dynamic pedagogical processes within and in relation to social movements. It is exciting that this revised and expanded new edition reflects new learnings back to the movements from which they were learned. I know that many movements and changemakers will find something useful to their work in this book.

These are exciting but dangerous times, ripe with many possible futures. So much depends on the capacity of grassroots people-powered social movements to wage and win the battle of the story. In the years ahead, stories will play a central role in determining how we see ourselves and the path society ultimately takes. That is why we should all embrace *Re:Imagining Change*'s artful reminder—as true today as ever—that we hold the awesome and transformative power to change the story.

Jonathan Matthew Smucker is the director of Beyond the Choir and has worked for more than two decades as a grassroots political organizer and strategist. He is the author of Hegemony How-To: A Roadmap for Radicals.

INTRODUCTION TO THE 2ND EDITION

As the poet Audre Lorde reminds us, "There are no new ideas. There are only new ways of making them felt." Indeed, what could be less new than the power of story? Storytelling is a foundation of human culture and has always been central to successful social change campaigns and movements.

In that spirit we humbly offer gratitude to the generations of movements for justice, dignity, and ecological sanity that have come before us. Both authors have roots within the Irish diaspora, a community that values the power of a good story (and we take some pride that the modern term "slogan" comes from the ancient Gaelic word for battle cry), but this book synthesizes insights from across the canon of social change strategy: from Alinsky to Zapatismo; from critical pedagogy to advertising, branding, and communications; from grassroots organizers on the frontlines to scholars at the Harvard Kennedy School. The story-based strategy methodology weaves elements of many strands of social change practice together—community organizing, nonviolent direct action, strategic communications, alliance building, power analysis, advocacy campaigning—into a new tapestry for strategic thinking and creative cultural intervention.

We offer a specific gratitude for the insights we have gained from the traditions of pan-Indigenous resistance, organizing, and storytelling across the Americas. Our thinking has been particularly impacted by the ideas and practices of Mexico's EZLN, popularly known as the Zapatista movement. Often called the first "postmodern revolution," the Indige-nous-led 1994 uprising was launched on the first day of the North Amer-

1

ican Free Trade Agreement and revealed the power of spectacle, symbol, and narrative intervention to challenge the pathology of the neoliberal world order. Zapatismo's rallying cry for a "world where many worlds fit" helped spark global networks of resistance and transformation that continue to animate a diversity of initiatives resisting oppressive monoculture in all its forms.[1]

Story-based strategy is an evolving approach, which continues to be innovated by practitioners in numerous sectors. The framework catalogues practices that have always been part of transformative victories, while updating the timeless art of social change storytelling for the contemporary context. These tools and techniques have been codified through the collective inquiry, experimentation, and application of a community of change-makers connected to the Center for Story-based Strategy (CSS), a movement strategy project founded in 2002 to explore narrative as an arena of control, contestation, intervention, and potential transformation. This book builds upon that powerful foundation.

This initial inquiry was premised on three simple assumptions that continue to underpin the broader story-based strategy approach:

1. *We live in a unique time in the history of our planet, which requires that we fundamentally shift the political, economic, and cultural systems that structure our lives.* The current globalized economic model based on extraction and exploitation is on a direct collision course with the life support systems of our planet. At the time of this writing, concentrations of atmospheric carbon dioxide are at 406 ppm and rising, well above what scientists tell us is the safe level.[2] Not coincidentally, this very same system is concentrating wealth and power in the hands of the few, at the expense of democracy, human rights, and the welfare of most people on the planet. At the time of this writing, eight men own more wealth than the 3.6 billion people who make up the poorest half of the world's population.[3] Needless to say, a system this unjust is increasingly unstable and therefore requires increasing repression, militarism, and social control to maintain itself, hence the rise of the far right and neofascism. At the time of this writing, the United States has just inaugurated an authoritarian, demagogue, billionaire reality-TV star as its 45th President. Practically, this means understanding that the systemic roots of our shared problems transcend single issues to connect all the issues: if we are fighting to restabilize the climate, we also must push for racial justice; we can't stop wars without standing with underpaid workers to transform our economy. In the words of the slogan popularized by the 2014 People's Climate March in New York City: "In order to change everything, we need everyone!"

2. *Social change happens when ordinary people come together to organize with a shared purpose as part of a broad-based social movement.* The his-

tory of human progress shows us that when people get organized we can overcome powerful, entrenched forces and catalyze extraordinary changes—end oppressive institutions, win new rights, redistribute resources, topple dictators—and expand the realm of what is politically possible. We believe the most lucid analysis of social problems comes from those who are directly affected by them and that people-powered movements led from the frontlines of impact are the most reliable drivers of systemic change. Our practice is rooted in the understanding that moments of historic social confrontation that advance freedom and justice are not random events that "just happen." Rather, these confrontations are engineered or harnessed by strategists embedded in social movements who understand the power of narrative to shape public understanding and manifest political power through collective action. This book is designed to support today's organizers as we actively struggle to reshape the course of history.

3. *In order to change systems we have to change narratives.* To resonate beyond their core supporters, movements must communicate larger narratives persuading a critical mass of society that fundamental change is not only possible, but urgently necessary. Narrative is a key arena of struggle and contestation: a powerful tool of liberatory social movements, but also a weapon for maintaining elite control or unleashing reactionary waves of bigotry and violence. Particularly in the 21st-century United States, where the apparatus of narrative control has reached new levels of sophistication (consumer culture, corporate propaganda, political manipulation, and full scale information warfare), social movements need better tools to contest the narratives preventing systemic change and tell our own stories about what is actually possible.

CSS's initial efforts in the early 2000s generated some preliminary frameworks to understand and harness the power of narrative. Trainings, creative experiments, and direct support for grassroots movements and mass actions organically grew into partnerships with organizations to experiment with and apply the ideas in practice. Over the subsequent decade and a half, CSS has partnered with hundreds of leading grassroots organizations to frame issues, build alliances, and win campaigns. CSS has trained over 5,000 organizers and community activists, and since 2011, has convened an annual five-day advanced training for practitioners. Out of these years of applied experimentation, the story-based strategy methodology documented in this book has been created, tested, and implemented at scale.

When our work began, we often encountered skepticism in the institutional world of nonprofits, professional advocates, and social change philanthropy. Many perceived narrative as a specialist pursuit, an afterthought, or even a distraction from lobbying decision-makers with well-reasoned, fact-based appeals. All too often progressives succeed in winning the battle of the facts only to lose the battle of the story, let alone the broader war of ideas. We are heartened to report that in recent years these dynamics have begun to shift. In the time since launching the organization (2002), to the release of the prototype version of this book as a widely downloaded online manual (2008), to the publication of the first edition (2010), to the arrival of the second edition of this book (2017), the interest in narrative and story has grown exponentially. At the time of this writing, people of conscience from all walks of life are mobilizing to fight back against a new U.S. regime whose rise to power was driven by memetic appeals to fear, racism, xenophobia, and misogyny. We believe now more than ever, that strategies for contesting narrative power, as articulated in this book, have a foundational role to play in both resisting the Trump regime and broader efforts to transform U.S. society.

The past 15 years have been a time of accelerated change, forcing society to navigate seismic shifts in information technology, communications, and media. Collectively, the end of the broadcast era amounts to a transformation in the political economy of representation, a change that everyone, including social movements, is still racing to keep up with. It was recognition of these emerging changes that informed CSS's original interest in virality and memes—self-replicating units of culture that can carry ideas and narratives with them as they spread (as discussed in Section 2.6).

The original name of the organization—the *smart*Meme Strategy and Training project—was inspired by the role that well-crafted and strategically deployed memes could play in spreading transformative ideas and scaling social movements. Over time the name of the organization changed to more accurately reflect the broader focus on the story-based strategy methodology. Nevertheless, it has been exhilarating to see what we previously called "meme campaigning" reach profound new levels of impact in recent years with the resurgence of distributed organizing driven by social media. From #BlackLivesMatter, to climate mobilizations, to the struggle for migrant rights, powerful new models of decentralized movement building are highlighting the role of narrative in unleashing networked constituencies to act and shift the discourse around entrenched issues.[4]

CSS's years of experimentation have only deepened our initial suspicions regarding the transformative potential in narrative social change strategies. As we've learned over the years, there are always more ideas to explore, more stories to tell, and more interventions to imagine.

Using This Book

Re:Imagining Change is a resource for people who want to create positive change and shift our society toward a more just and sustainable future. This book is designed as a stand-alone introduction to the story-based strategy methodology and as a resource that can accompany story-based strategy workshops.

The story-based strategy approach is relevant for anyone who is interested in understanding narrative, power and possibility. Although communication specialists are certainly one of our audiences, this book is intended for anyone engaged in any type of social change work. Understanding narrative and how to implement effective story-based strategy are crosscutting skills that every 21st-century change agent needs in order to succeed.

As the story-based strategy approach has evolved, it has generated greater specificity of concept and language. Language structures thought, and story-based strategy is first and foremost a way of thinking; thus, the text includes some specialized terminology. Our intent is not to mystify with jargon, but rather to embrace the power of naming to clarify ideas and elevate important practices. We have provided a glossary to define key terms throughout the manual. Words that are included in the glossary are marked in bold the first time they appear in each chapter. We have included endnotes where practical with background info and references to help the curious dig deeper into unfamiliar issues or follow the various threads raised in the text.

We have done our best to structure the book to facilitate quick reference and easy use by frontline change agents. The book opens with a visual overview charting the Story-based Strategy Campaign Model and then is divided into six primary sections. Chapter I addresses the deep roots of narrative in the human experience and argues for why social change efforts must address narrative in order to make systemic progress. Chapter II explores various aspects of narrative power and introduces the theoretical framework of **narrative power analysis**, including the **elements of story** as a framework for deconstructing or creating new stories. Chapter III presents the **battle of the story** framework for creating and contesting social change narratives. Chapter IV outlines the **points of intervention** model with a focus on action at the **point of assumption** as a means of shifting narratives. Chapter V presents six short case studies of story-based strategy applied in contemporary grassroots struggles. Finally, Chapter VI is a call to innovation, inviting a deeper exploration into the unique relevance and possibilities for story-based strategy in facing our present political moment.

This book is intended as an entry point to these practices. There are numerous tools and resources that have been created by CSS to support grassroots activists and organizers in applying these concepts either as individual strategists or as a participatory framework with groups and alliances. Many of these resources can be found on CSS's website at www.storybasedstrategy.org. Also, throughout the text we offer reflection questions to help readers integrate and apply these ideas.

Chances are that if you are reading this book, you are already a story-based strategist—you just may not know it yet. This book was written for you and we hope it will serve as a resource to structure and sharpen your interventions. And if you don't think of your own work in terms of narrative now, we hope by the time you reach the end of the book you will be ready to join the ranks of self-identified story-based strategists working on pressing issues around the world.

A final note of orientation: this book was written primarily for a U.S. audience. In order to anchor the ephemeral world of narrative power in some shared reference points we draw heavily on political dynamics and examples from within the U.S. context. This is certainly not because the best story-based strategy examples come exclusively from inside the U.S. or because we believe U.S. movements have nothing to learn from our international brothers and sisters. In fact, quite the opposite. The historic role of U.S. social movements—even the definition of what one is—has been mostly erased from the dominant culture with the remaining residual impressions safely tamed by sentimentalism and caricature. Meanwhile, the U.S. is an epicenter of the financial, military, diplomatic, and cultural systems that literally threaten the future of all life on the planet. This book is part of our strategy, as residents of earth who are also U.S. citizens, to strengthen transformative organizing inside the U.S. We hope international colleagues will find some relevance and ideas that can be adapted to your own political and cultural context.

As practitioners, we continue to approach this work with a curious spirit of experimentation. Even after 15 years of developing and applying these ideas, we still have far more questions than answers. It is our sincere hope that *Re:Imagining Change* will be a conversation starter with people from all walks of life who are willing to think big, dream hard, and struggle like hell for a better world. We offer *Re:Imagining Change* as an invitation to change agents from all walks of life to embrace your transformative visions and step into your power as strategists and storytellers. Please share your applications, critiques, innovations, questions, and stories with the wider community doing this work. Join the conversation at www.storybasedstrategy.org.

"Many stories matter. Stories have been used to dispossess and to malign. But stories can also be used to empower and to humanize. Stories can break the dignity of a people. But stories can also repair that broken dignity."

–Chimamanda Ngozi Adichie

"The universe is made of stories, not atoms."

–Muriel Rukeyser

I

Why Story

1.1 The Narrative Animal

There is no agony like bearing an untold story inside of you.
—Zora Neale Hurston

Story has been central to the human experience for as long as we have
been human. Evolutionary biologists increasingly believe that our capacity for **narrative** is what helped to make us human.[1] As Lisa Cron writes
in *Wired for Story*, "Opposable thumbs let us hang on; story told us what
to hang on to."[2] There is growing consensus in the scientific community
that the neurological roots of both storytelling and our enjoyment of
stories is tied to our social cognition and the way individuals connect to
form groups.[3] It is this expanded capacity for narrative that makes humans truly unique in the animal kingdom.

Humans are hardwired for narrative. Brain researchers have discovered
that hearing a powerful story about an experience will stimulate the same
neurological region as having the actual experience. A 2006 study found
that when participants read words with strong smell associations like
"coffee" and "perfume" their olfactory cortexes light up as if they were
experiencing the real scents.[4] When a story carries us into another world
(what narrative theorists call "transportation") that experience is literally
real at the level of our brain chemistry.[5]

Narrative is so deeply embedded that often we see it even when it's
not actually there. In one foundational 1944 experiment, psychologists
Fritz Heider and Marianne Simmel showed subjects an animation of a
pair of triangles and a circle moving around a square, and asked what
was happening. Overwhelmingly, the subjects did not describe the literal
events of shapes moving around on the screen, but instead their responses

REFLECTIONS: STORYTELLING

- **Name Stories:** What is your full name? Why is that your name? Tell the story.
- **Family Stories:** Are there stories, fables, or tall tales that you were told as a child? Choose one and retell the story. Where did it come from? Are there lessons you draw from this story? How does it impact your life today?

revealed how they mapped a narrative onto the shapes in order to tell a story about what they observed. People would describe the film as the social interactions of three human-like characters who possess personalities, emotions, and intentions. The big circle was a "bully" who was "chasing" the triangles, the square was a "house," the events were a "fight." Numerous subsequent studies have reiterated how humans, as social creatures, project stories and narrative qualities onto almost everything we perceive.[6]

> We remember our lived experiences by converting them to stories and integrating them into our personal and collective web of narrative.

Humans are the narrative animal constructing our social reality through our ability to create, interpret, and contest the stories around us. We remember our lived experiences by converting them to stories and integrating them into our personal and collective web of narrative. We think, dream, imagine, and believe through the filter of narrative.

This is what led narrative theorist Walter Fischer to suggest that rather than scientifically classify ourselves as *Homo sapiens*, which roughly means "knowing person," we should consider our species *Homo narrans*, "storytelling person."[7] In fact, these two concepts—knowing and storytelling—have always been deeply linked in the human experience. The word narrative itself derives from the Proto-Indo-European root *gnō-* meaning "to know" because to know something is to know the story about it.

Participants in the Center for Story-based Strategy's 2016 Advanced Training learn how to harness the power of narrative for their campaigns.

1.2 Hacking at the Roots

> *The law locks up the man or woman*
> *Who steals the goose from off the common*
> *But leaves the greater villain loose*
> *Who steals the common from off the goose.*
> —folk poem, 17th-century England, author unknown

In July 1846 the philosopher and author Henry David Thoreau was confronted with a choice: either pay his taxes to support America's expansionist war against Mexico or go to jail. He took a stand of conscience—against imperialism abroad and slavery at home—and chose imprisonment. His single night in jail inspired his essay "Resistance to Civil Government" advocating for civil disobedience in the face of unjust government.[8] His writing would inform Mahatma Gandhi, Dr. Martin Luther King Jr., and generations of people of conscience.

Thoreau famously lamented that most activists spend their efforts fighting the symptoms of contemporary problems rather than confronting the roots. Concerned that his abolitionist and antiwar values weren't reflected in the political discourse of his time, he wrote: "*There are thousands hacking at the branches of evil to one who is striking at the root.*"

Thoreau's metaphor of branches versus roots continues to frame a common question: Why isn't there more outrage about the causes of injustice? Why isn't more energy going into confronting the roots of our problems rather than just the symptoms?

One answer is that the types of injustice Thoreau decried are often invisible, even as they are hidden in plain sight. These are structural evils that have been consciously made invisible within the day-to-day work-ings of institutions, concealed by oppressive cultural norms, or the inten-tionally limited terms of political debate. Taken in total as a "system" the institutional relationships of power that constitute modern society are of-ten opaque. They become hidden by the dominant stories of the culture that justify the status quo of power relations and define "normal." These stories become so routine that most people in positions of privilege (for whom the system is working) don't think to question them. In this way unquestioned mythologies (as we'll discuss in Chapter II, mythologies are the most powerful form of narrative) emerge to bolster historic power structures while concealing the roots of systemic problems.

For social change practitioners to hack at the root, we must build the capacity to identify, analyze, and intervene not only in the institutional power structures, but also in the stories that are preventing the changes we know are needed. Through agitation, successful social movements change more than policy—we reimagine the story of what is possible in our society. Particularly now, for those of us who feel both the urgency and the opportunity of this unique historic moment, this book argues that our movements must prioritize narrative as a lens to shape our strate-gies. This is the arena of story-based strategy.

1.3 The Era of Outdated Stories

The past is never dead. It's not even past.
—William Faulkner

Five centuries of European colonial expansion and organized white su-premacy have wiped out countless cultures, devastated ecosystems, and left us with a legacy of racism, economic disparity, militarism, and global inequity. Over 200 years of resource extraction, industrialization, and fos-sil fuel–driven economic growth have pushed our planet's life-support systems to their breaking point.

Over time, the greed, racism, and violence of this history has become hardwired into many of the institutions and operating as-sumptions that define the global system: from government policies, to the influence of multinational

corporations, to international financial and trade regimes, to the collective sense of what is politically possible. Underlying these overlapping systems is the logic of the past: rationalizing, justifying, normalizing. The mythologies of the conquistador, the slave master, and the Indian-killing "pioneer" live on in the economist who sees looted ecosystems merely as entries on a corporate balance sheet; the politician who exploits fear and racism to build their own power; or the corporate CEO who maximizes profits by paying his workers poverty wages.

When we look at our current world of intersecting social and ecological crisis through this lens, we can see we are living in an era of outdated stories. This is a time when many of our dominant political and economic institutions are shaped by destructive stories rooted in the violence and exploitation that has accumulated over hundreds of years. These stories were never true but through concentrated power they were normalized and many people were forced to accept them, but now their grip on common sense is loosening.

Giant oil, coal, and gas corporations (and their allies in governments) are still telling us we need every last bit of fossil fuel, even if it means blowing up mountaintops, poisoning our kids, and destabilizing our climate. That's an outdated story.

Giant corporations like McDonald's and Walmart claim, despite profits that dwarf the GDP of many nations, they can't afford to pay their workers a living wage. That's an outdated story.

Politicians repeat old racist lies: that people murdered by the police deserved it and that Black people leading the fight for freedom, dignity, and racial justice are thugs. That's an outdated story.

And, of course, the onslaught of pervasive and ever more personalized advertising tells us that happiness and progress means consume more, more, more, regardless of the price tag to people and planet. That's an outdated story.

Powerful, ruthless interests push these outdated stories, but that doesn't mean that they are unchangeable. In fact, with their obvious hypocrisy and contradictions they often can't withstand the power of public scrutiny. The story-based strategy approach helps us see them as critical vulnerabilities (what we will later call **points of intervention**) in our current unjust system.

As the grip of outdated stories on mass consciousness weakens, space for new stories opens. The historic narratives are being challenged every day by the transformative organizing that is happening in communities around the world. These outdated stories are challenged by an inspiring new generation of civil rights leaders emerging from the Movement for Black Lives. They are challenged by workers organizing for a living wage,

- What are some examples of outdated stories you are confronting in your work?
- Who still believes in them?
- What are you doing to challenge these outdated stories?
- Are they beginning to change?

the right to form a union, and countless other efforts to make workplaces safe, dignified, and just. They are challenged by actions around the world to keep fossil fuels in the ground and redirect investments toward clean, renewable, decentralized energy solutions.

More and more people are helping our global society outgrow these stories that have been used to limit human freedom and justify the destruction of the planet. Resistance to these toxic stories of the past is sparking new alliances, and new movements are charting paths toward alternative possibilities and better futures. By drawing attention to how power operates through narrative and offering some basic approaches to contest for power in the narrative realm, this book aspires to support momentum toward a brighter future.

1.4 Movement as Narrative

A social movement tells a new "story."
—Marshall Ganz

It is easy to see the results of social change once organized constituencies have forced changes to the existing power structures: striking workers win a pay increase, a corrupt politician gets voted out of office, a community mobilization shifts police department policy. The process of winning those victories is, however, often less visible.

Social change efforts happen in many different arenas, but regardless of the type of initiative, there is a shared arena of struggle that unites them all: the fight for public understanding. This often invisible arena of struggle encompasses the intangible realm of stories, ideas, and assumptions that frame and define the situations, relationships, or institutions we are working to change.

There are lots of tools for measuring public opinion that can be important resources for any campaign. But story-based strategists don't just respond to public opinion, they shape it. To succeed, we must develop strategies to reframe the debate and then commit to the time and resources needed to **change the story** and win public support for social change efforts.

For instance, look at the shift in U.S. public opinion on LGBTQ rights, and particularly on the issue of marriage equality. Decades of organizing, pushing back against violent homophobia, and campaigning across political, economic, and cultural arenas eventually led to ongoing changes in attitudes. Along the way reactionary forces responded by amending state constitutions in 30 U.S states to explicitly deny the rights of same-sex couples. This realm of the courts, and particularly constitutional law, backed by the full authority of the state, is an entrenched, seemingly immutable form of power.

While the movement continued various legal strategies, the larger fight was already far progressed in many different arenas as a broader, multi-

This 1958 comic book produced by the Fellowship of Reconciliation told the story of the Montgomery bus boycott in an accessible format and encouraged its readers to join the movement for racial equality. It continues to be reprinted (most recently by WagingNonviolence.org) and has been translated into multiple languages.

faceted force. High-profile campaigns challenged the U.S. military's homophobic "Don't Ask, Don't Tell" policy and turned hate crimes and bullying into national issues. Continuing a decades-long trend of growing visibility, more and more people came out publically as LGBTQ, including celebrities, professional athletes, and prominent business people. Meanwhile LGBTQ characters, rights, and the issue of marriage equality itself became more visible themes in popular songs,[9] movies, and television.[10]

Finally, in June 2015 the Supreme Court ruled in *Obergefell v. Hodges* that same-sex couples have a right to marry, thereby overruling all the various state and federal laws that legalized discrimination. Although this aspect of the victory was achieved in the judicial arena, it would be a serious mistake to believe that it was only smart lawyers that won these changes. As Evan Wolfson, longtime leader in the fight for marriage equality and founder of Freedom to Marry, put it: "We persuaded the country and the courts followed."[11]

The LGBTQ movement and the marriage equality fight showed what countless social movements have demonstrated:

Movements have won public support with powerful stories like Rosa Parks' refusal to change seats, the AIDS quilt carpeting the National Mall in Washington, or courageous undocumented youth dressed in college caps and gowns marching to demand immigration reform.

making progress in shifting the narrative drives structural change in other arenas as well. When culture moves, power moves. When the story changes, new possibilities emerge.

Historically, the power of stories and storytelling has always been at the center of social change efforts. Movements have won public support with powerful stories like Rosa Parks' refusal to change seats, the AIDS quilt carpeting the National Mall in Washington, or courageous undocumented youth dressed in college caps and gowns marching to demand immigration reform. A single widely viewed image can carry a new story and shift the emotional landscape of an issue, leading to dramatic changes in public opinion and policy: an image of a Syrian refugee child traumatized by war; a polar bear stranded in a sea of melting ice; people from all walks of life holding up their hands to draw attention to police shootings of unarmed Black people.

The U.S. resistance to corporate globalization, which burst into public view with the dramatic shutdown of the 1999 World Trade Organization meeting in Seattle, united many different constituencies with a shared narrative demanding "global justice."

But alongside these large, public narratives that inspire mass support, story also is at the heart of the day-to-day, person-to-person work of making social change. Organizers and movement builders rely on storytelling to build relationships, unite constituencies, and mobilize people. As people come together and share their stories, they identify common problems and create a narrative of how things could be better. These stories motivate actions, and the stories of those actions are retold to inspire, hone strategy, and recruit people to take even more actions. Eventually, as the story spreads and more people see their own experiences and aspirations reflected within it, the movement grows.

Shared narrative is a defining feature of a social movement—connecting people across space and time in a shared sense of identity and purpose. This common understanding helps participants feel the power of a whole that is greater than the sum of all its diverse, individual parts.

But building the collective power to make changes in society takes more than just telling good stories. The other side of the equation is that movements have to change the existing stories that are limiting the popular imagination of what's possible (what we will discuss in Section 2.7 as the idea of "hegemony"). The story-based strategy approach is an invitation to view social change work through the lens of storytelling and understand how power is tied up in narrative.

1.5 From Improvement to Innovation

We can't solve problems by using the same kind of thinking we used when we created them.
—Albert Einstein

Re:Imagining Change is an introduction to the story-based strategy methodology—an approach to social change that has emerged from the experiments and innovations of a diverse community of practitioners affiliated with the Center for Story-based Strategy over the past 15 years.

This approach emerged from the pressing question of how to innovate social change strategies in response to the movement building and messaging demands of the globalized information age. The heartbeat of movement building—deep relationships; critically analyzing power; taking strategic action; and reflecting to inform future effort—remains constant, but how do these practices evolve for the shifting landscape of 21st-century struggle? What does community mobilization look like amidst the accelerating pace of changing media technologies? How can voices for justice compete in the algorithm-driven, multiplatform, click-bait media environment of 24-hour infotainment?

Storytelling is a timeless art and has always been at the core of social change work, but in contemporary society the power of narrative has become even more central to maintaining social control. The historic narratives that have legitimized inequality and exploitation for generations live on in more subtle applications with coded appeals to carefully segmented audiences. And they have been supplemented with the latest sophisticated techniques of corporate public relations, perception management, and information warfare. How can grassroots organizations and popular movements for change level this playing field of contested narratives?

This collective inquiry into the shifting terrain of narrative, movement building, and social change would eventually yield the story-based methodology outlined in this book. The initial impetus emerged from two powerful political moments in recent U.S. history that reverberated around the world. The first was the mass mobilization against the World Trade Organization's (WTO) 1999 Ministerial Conference in Seattle, which showcased the power of shared narrative to transcend single-issue silos and align diverse sectors around more visionary goals. The second moment was the double tragedy of September 11, 2001. The attacks were a tragedy of horrifying destruction and loss of life, made doubly tragic through their exploitation by the U.S. government to justify fear-mongering, wars of aggression, and domestic repression.

The organizing and mass nonviolent direct action against the WTO in Seattle created a powerful clash of worldviews. The undemocratic vision of a commodified, corporate-controlled future was pitted against tens of thousands of people uniting to demand justice and declare, "Another World Is Possible." The spectacle of the actions and the drama of state repression accelerated the wave of cross-sector organizing across the U.S. These emerging political networks—referring to themselves as the "global justice" movement—joined the global resistance (albeit a bit late) to neoliberal ideology and the corporate "free trade" agenda.

It was a political moment of new alliances, expanding political imagination, and media-ready spectacular action that earned the nascent movement its proverbial 15 minutes of fame from a curious global media establishment. Movement spokespeople (including several future CSS founders) had unique opportunities to experiment with articulating systemic critiques and transformative visions in the corporate controlled, for-profit media. But unlike blockading a corporate HQ or organizing a community, there was no activist tool kit for contesting dominant narratives, sound bite by sound bite, in a corporate-controlled media that was more interested in demonizing protest than debating worldview. Advocates of change needed better frameworks to navigate the shifting terrain of media representation, spectacle, and narrative.

This period was abruptly bookended by the tragedy of the attacks on September 11, 2001. The U.S. government response brought its own bitter lessons in weaponizing narrative to poison public opinion with fear and fragment communities along historic divisions. There were powerful alternative currents: millions pushed back against racism and state terror, challenged the assumptions of U.S. militarism, and championed reconciliation over retribution. Yet the Bush administration's propaganda machine systematically justified rollbacks of civil liberties while reasserting overt U.S. empire building and selling an illegal war based on lies.

For many who had assumed there was a connection between the factual truth of a narrative and its power to persuade or rationalize, it was a disconcerting time. It was also another unavoidable indicator of how desperately our movements needed better tools to understand narrative power. CSS emerged in 2002 as a strategy project exploring narrative's role in movement building, experimenting with culture-shifting interventions, and building the capacity of grassroots activists to "change the story." Over the course of the following decade, as CSS trained thousands of organizers and partnered with hundreds of grassroots organizations and alliances around the country, these experiments evolved into what came to be called story-based strategy.

Innovation doesn't just mean improving upon what already exists. Innovation requires us to rethink underlying assumptions and find the courage to reimagine what could be. To honor this insight, the title of this book carries a double meaning to combine two related but distinct imperatives. "Re" is the Latin for "in the matter of" and has been popularized (through bureaucratic convention and mass e-mail addiction) to mean "regarding," or more formally, "with reference to." Its two letters in the title are meant to draw our attention to the issue at hand. In the case of this book and the broader approach it documents, the issue is imagining change, a call to recognize and embrace techniques that prioritize imagination as a strategic engine for building a better tomorrow.

The title should also be taken in another sense of Re—the call to reconsider, to reexamine how we go about working for change. Given this unique time of mounting crisis and accelerating change, advocates for social and ecological justice need to innovate how we go about making change. Exploring narrative as a key arena of struggle provides new opportunities to understand what has made our existing victories successful and to experiment with more transformative interventions.

1.6 The Story-based Strategy Approach

> *Those who do not have power over the story that dominates their lives, the power to retell it, rethink it, deconstruct it, joke about it and change it as times change, truly are powerless, because they cannot think new thoughts.*
> —Salman Rushdie

Story-based strategy links social movement building with an analysis of narrative power that places storytelling at the center of social change. It means, first and foremost, looking at social change strategy through the lens of narrative.

Every issue already has a web of existing stories and cultural assumptions that frame public understanding. Story-based strategy provides a process to understand the current narrative around an issue and identify opportunities to change it through strategic intervention. The approach goes beyond traditional messaging and pushes us to analyze the role of narrative in maintaining the entrenched relationships of power and privilege that define the status quo.

Re:Imagining Change outlines some of the analytical tools and practical techniques that have been traditionally used to infuse campaigns with transformative storytelling. This book provides tools to craft more

Musicians and dancers from Son Del Centro in Santa Ana, California, lead a pageant of creative resistance at the 2005 Student/Farmworker Alliance Youth Encuentro in Immokalee, Florida.

effective and holistic social change strategies with the power to intervene and shape prevailing cultural narratives. It is a call to build our collective capacity to frame the critical debates of our times and direct the public imagination toward the solutions we need.

The frameworks outlined in the pages to follow have emerged both from contemporary experiments and from examining historic social change efforts through the lens of narrative power. While the approach specifically responds to the unique and changing dynamics of narrative power in our 21st-century context, it is also deeply rooted in the time-tested methods of organizing and movement building. In fact, it is difficult to find any movement victory that doesn't contain aspects of story-based strategy.

One of the goals of this book is to offer terminology and frameworks to understand the what, how, and why of narrative's role in social change. Documentation is the first step toward replication, collective assessment and innovation. Although some of the book's language may be new, most of the techniques explored are not, having emerged from traditional movement practice in one form or another.

As this is a book about strategy, a word with many loaded connotations, it's worth reflecting on that term: strategy derives from the Greek word for the commander of an army, *strategos*, and roughly means "the art of the generals."[12] One of the problems with the term and its origins in the traditions of militarism, war, and violence is that it suggests exclusivity, specialization, and hierarchy. The general is on the hilltop, above the battlefield looking down from a privileged position of detachment and sweeping perspective.

But in the context of social change work where the struggle is often not just in physical space but also embedded in identities, narratives, and perceptions, there is no one hilltop, no single universalized perspective.

Instead, successful movements need to cultivate a culture of strategy that can replace the lone ancient general with multiple diverse perspectives, emerging from lived experiences and adapting to changing conditions. Strategic thinking about narrative and power cannot be the exclusive realm of specialists and experts. Particularly now in the era of networked society where social media connectivity is facilitating a new generation of open source campaigning[13] and leaderful movements,[14] understanding narrative is a critical orientation for all change-makers. This book and the story-based strategy approach it describes are intended to contribute to that larger goal of making the powerful world of narrative, framing, and story accessible to organizers and activists. ■

NARRATIVE VS. STORY

Narratives and stories frequently appear to be similar, and the terms are often used interchangeably. The content and scale of stories is as varied as human experience—from sacred tales that carry wisdom revered by billions, to ephemeral celebrity gossip, to what happened at the office today—but they are all discrete and bounded accounts of events with a clear beginning, middle, and end. One helpful definition of narrative is a coherent "system of stories."[15] Narratives are stories that are bigger: often more open-ended and less bounded in a linear sequence while containing lots of smaller interrelated stories that are emblematic of the larger narrative. Individual stories that fit within the logic of the symbolic system can easily be added to the narrative while others fade away over time, but the narrative persists. For instance, the American Dream is best understood as a narrative because it connects many different stories. Stories referencing the Declaration of Independence, or buying a first house, or parents aspiring to give their children a better life could all be part of the larger American Dream narrative. The story-based strategy approach is relevant to stories and narratives of all sizes.

"We dream in narrative, daydream in narrative, remember, anticipate, hope, despair, believe, doubt, plan, revise, criticize, construct, gossip, learn, hate, and love by narrative."

–Barbara Hardy

"Language is also a place of struggle."

–bell hooks

II

Narrative Power

2.1. Truth vs. Meaning

*Politics is that dimension of social life in which things become true if
enough people believe them.*
—David Graeber

We live in a world defined by stories. They come in all shapes and sizes:
mundane anecdotes, Hollywood blockbusters, prepackaged "news" stories, cherished childhood memories, religious stories conveying ancient
lessons. . . . A story can unite or divide people(s), obscure issues or spotlight new perspectives. A story can inform or deceive, enlighten, or entertain, even do all of the above. Stories are the threads of our lives and the
fabric of human cultures. But how does narrative power actually work?

We absorb stories from many sources: family, personal experience, the
media, and religious, cultural, and educational institutions. Some stories we learn consciously while others are just part of the cultural background. These stories teach us how society functions and create a sense of
shared culture and identity. The most powerful of these stories operate as
contemporary mythologies.

Lesson one in narrative power: myth is meaning. Don't be limited by
the common pejorative use of "myth" to mean "lie" and miss the deeper
relevance of mythology as a framework for shared meaning. Myths are
often mistakenly dismissed as folktales from long ago describing fantasti-
cal realities, but even today a sea of stories tell us who we are, what to
believe, and toward what we should aspire. These stories play the same
role that myths always have: answering fundamental questions of identity, origin, and worldview. Today we may be less likely to believe that the
sun is pulled across the sky by a god in a chariot, but many people are

Humans are the narrative animal, so when we look at the night sky we naturally connect the dots to create meaning.

perfectly willing to believe a specific personal care product will make us more beautiful, or accept the claims that their country is "exceptional," superior or even specially favored by God.

As the narrative animal, we use story to structure the patterns we observe around us. Take the example of the night sky. In the illustration above you see an image that you probably recognize. Were you taught a name for this grouping of stars?[1] Different cultures have given it different names: the Plough, the Wagon, the Great Bear, the Saucepan, and frequently, different versions of the Big Dipper.

But is there really a giant saucepan in the sky?

Of course not (at least we don't think so?), but that's not the point. The stories used to map constellations helped our ancestors make sense of the night sky and pass down practical skills like finding the North Star to navigate at night. Different cultures connect the dots to see the shapes associated with their own stories, but across the world, people looked to the sky and created myths that gave them meaning.

The Big Dipper is a simple example, but it shows us a critical aspect of narrative power: the difference between truth and meaning. Meaning doesn't just exist in the world waiting to be discovered, rather meaning is produced by human interpretation as we translate it into language (what cultural theorists call "representation"[2]). The power of the story does not derive from its factual truth but rather from the story's ability to provide meaning. Narrative is one of the primary ways we humans create meaning in the world.

Understanding the complicated relationship between truth and meaning is the foundation of story-based strategy.

Too often progressives think that just because a story is factually true, it will be meaningful to our audiences, and therefore build our power. But the reality is just the opposite: If a story is meaningful to people, they will believe that it is true. *The currency of narrative is not truth but rather meaning.* In other words, there is no inherent connection between the power of a story and whether or not the content is objectively true. After all, if having the facts on your side was enough to win, we would live in a very different world.

Narrative power manifests as a fight over how to make meaning. We often believe in a story not because it is factually true but because it connects with our values or is relevant to our experiences in a way that is compelling. Having the facts on your side is only the first step toward winning, because the facts alone are not enough to transform understanding and reshape meaning in people's hearts and minds.

Thus people fighting for a better world need to take our truths—about injustice, racism, environmental destruction, or whatever issue we are working on—and make them *meaningful* to the people we are trying to reach. Story-based strategy is not an invitation to ignore or distort the facts but rather a recognition that to be persuasive you need to use the power of story to make the most important facts matter.

THE ETHICS OF STORY-BASED STRATEGY

"But wait!" Some people in our trainings have protested at this truth vs. meaning ah-ha moment, asking, "Does that mean we can just say anything we want, or just lie to make the best story? Doesn't that make us just as manipulative as 'them'?" The answer—which is essential to how we implement story-based strategy in the real world—is YES and NO.

Yes: Some of the most powerful, meaningful stories animating popular culture are in fact lies. Unscrupulous power-holders have always exploited this distinction between truth and meaning to manipulate and control through well-crafted deceit. So, yes you can fabricate your story, but NO, you shouldn't.

This book does not advocate lying. Primarily because the facts do matter when it comes to real-world impact and lying is unethical. Secondarily, because in the long-term lying isn't very effective. Lies are narrative power at its most crude and, therefore, vulnerable. People are smart and if they discover a story they trusted is actually a deliberate lie, your story-based strategy will fail: belief implodes, the story's power is negated and an audience of former supporters become adversaries. Of course, the corollary to this is that the more people believe something, the less likely are mere facts to convince them that it is not true, but we will come to that in Section 2.11. So it's a matter of both ethics and goals. If your ethics and goals are aligned for a greater good, then using strategic storytelling does not make you "as bad as them." Base your story in the facts. If the facts aren't on your side, something is wrong and you need to reexamine what you are doing. The story-based strategy approach is meant for practitioners who are deeply grounded in transparent values, accountable to specific communities, and fighting for a more just, democratic, and ecologically sane future.[3] If you want to use this book's insights on narrative power for personal gain, manipulation, or to exploit others, then please stop reading now. We'd offer you your money back but we suspect, given your ethically flexible worldview, you probably have plenty of opportunities for a lucrative career.

2.2 Narrative Thinking

There's a world of difference between truth and facts. Facts can obscure the truth.
—Maya Angelou

There are lots of different ways to apply story-based strategy but they all require looking at the world through a narrative lens. Effective story-based strategists must be narrative thinkers. As we have discussed, humans understand our world through stories and often make decisions based more on preexisting ideas and feelings than on a purely rational assessment of the facts. Narrative thinking helps us understand how political power operates through story.

Many of the unjust, destructive, and downright awful things that happen in our world—from putting toxic waste dumps next to elementary schools to invading countries—happen because someone (often a highly skilled "public relations" professional) spins a convincing story to sell the public on the proposal. Perhaps the story persuaded enough people in the community that the toxic waste dump was going to be a great thing because it would bring jobs and it was pretty harmless anyway, while also successfully marginalizing the critics. Or the story might have convinced people of the absolute necessity of invading a country because of a serious threat. (Perhaps they are even stockpiling terrifying weapons of mass destruction! Cue mental image of mushroom cloud apocalypse.)[4]

The inequality of our media and communications systems means that moneyed interests will almost always have more resources to move their story—but that doesn't mean their story will be more compelling. Effective story-based strategy can help level the playing field. But it requires stepping outside of our own analysis to assess all the conflicting perspectives and preexisting narratives surrounding an issue. An effective social change effort must offer a broader narrative that defines the situation and makes the relevant facts meaningful.

Narrative thinkers understand both that reality and the complex, conflicting representations of reality are different and that in most political struggles, representation matters more because it shapes the audiences' understanding of reality.

For instance, political issues and policy proposals often operate symbolically as stand-ins for underlying concepts or larger worldviews. When right-wing politicians promote austerity programs and tax cuts they have often used racist code words to present certain people as undeserving: "those people," Ronald Reagan's infamous "welfare queens," or even calling President Barack Obama a "food stamp president."[5] The anti-immi-

Re:Imagining Change

grant "anchor baby" concept (see Section 2.10 on control myths) or Donald Trump's promise to "build a wall" on the U.S.-Mexico border are just new proxies to invoke this same old racist, completely nonfactual story of undeserving nonwhite people getting a free ride on government services.

Meanwhile, effective social change efforts can contest the same arena of cultural symbols and signifiers. For instance, "Wall Street" serves as the surrogate for the entire unequal, corporate-controlled economic system; or demanding action to prevent an iconic fossil fuel project like the Keystone XL pipeline becomes the symbol of meaningful action to restabilize the climate.[6]

Many of the unjust, destructive, and downright awful things that happen in our world—from putting toxic waste dumps next to elementary schools to invading countries—happen because someone (often a highly skilled "public relations" professional) spins a convincing story to sell the public on the proposal.

Story-based strategy requires getting accustomed to identifying these types of political signifiers and competing on the playing field of symbol, image, and character. Section 2.12 outlines the Elements of Story: a simple but foundational framework to guide narrative thinking. These building blocks of story can help craft your strategy and interventions.

2.3. Narrative Power Analysis

> *Torturing bodies is less effective than shaping minds. . . . This is why the fundamental power struggle is the battle for the construction of meaning in the minds of the people.*
> —Manuel Castells

In order to make systemic social changes, we must understand the histories and institutions that underlie contemporary social systems, as well as how these histories and institutions shape culture and ways of collectively making meaning. For example, imagine the following flashback to grade school geography:[7]

Q: What is the definition of a continent?
A: A large landmass surrounded by water.

A geographical map also provides information about the mental maps and cultural assumptions of the people who made it.

Q: And how many continents are there?
A: Seven.

Sound familiar?

Let's take another look. With the definition "a large landmass surrounded by water," and allowing that the Americas are two separate continents, there still seems to be one continent that doesn't quite qualify: Europe doesn't really fit the definition. It is neither large nor actually surrounded by water. Apparently Europe as a geographical area has different rules than the rest? So who made the rules about continents and defined the orientation of the modern map? Maybe . . . Europeans?

A map is a representational tool to navigate the physical world, but it is also an expression of the deeper shared mental maps a culture provides to make sense of the world. The continent definition is one example of how the history of European colonization continues to influence the way we collectively understand our world. Historic power relations—the social, economic, and political forces of the past—often shape how we see the present, which in turn impacts our imagination of the future.

One way to think of **culture** is as a matrix of shared mental maps that define how we collectively create meaning and interpret the world around us. Culture is the larger context of *shared meaning*.[8] When people share a culture it means they share common reference points—the production and interchange of meanings—and can make sense of the world in "broadly similar ways."[9] Inevitably, **popular culture** is an ever-evolving contested space of struggle, where competing voices, experiences, and perspectives fight to answer the questions: Whose mental maps determine what is meaningful? Whose stories are considered "true"?

As certain ideas, practices, and worldviews become normalized over time, they form a **dominant culture** that disproportionately represents powerful institutional interests and perpetuates the stories that validate their political agendas. These stories become taken for granted as they are passed from generation to generation—carrying assumptions that become "conventional wisdom."

A **narrative power analysis** recognizes that since humans understand the world and our role in it through stories, all power relationships have a narrative dimension. Stories are imbued with power. This could be the power to legitimize an unjust status quo or justify acts of coercion and brutality. Likewise, story has the power to make change imaginable and urgent, to convince people to see a better future and believe in their own collective agency.

Many of our current social and ecological problems have their roots in the silent consensus of assumptions underlying current political discourse: *Humans can dominate and outsmart nature. Women are worth less than men. Racism and war are part of human nature (and white people are better than people of color). U.S. foreign policy benevolently spreads democracy and liberation around the world . . .*

To make real and lasting social change these latent narratives must be surfaced and challenged.

A narrative analysis of power encourages us to look at how meaning is operating and ask: Which stories define cultural norms? Where did these stories come from? Whose stories were ignored or erased? What new stories can we tell to more accurately describe the world we see? And, perhaps most urgently, what are the stories that can help move us toward the world we desire?

The role of narrative in rendering meaning in our minds is what makes story a powerful force. These power dynamics operate both in terms of our individual identities—whether or not you get to determine your own story—and on the larger cultural level: Which stories are used to make meaning and shape our world? What individuals, groups, or nations are portrayed as heroic? And whose story is presented as villainous, weak, or just irrelevant?

These questions are the narrative dimensions of the physical relationships of power and privilege, the unequal access to resources, and denials of self-determination that shape contemporary society. Asking these questions can help bring a **narrative power analysis** into social change campaigns.

When discussing culture, media theorist Marshall McLuhan often reminded his students, "We don't know who discovered water, but we can assume it wasn't a fish."

THREE EXPRESSIONS OF NARRATIVE POWER

Narrative power analysis is a framework for understanding the different ways power operates through story. Three general ways stories express power are by being descriptive, prescriptive, and constitutive:

Descriptive: Stories are the way we intuitively communicate about the world, describing events in powerful ways that help our audiences connect and understand complex information. When a story is told well it conveys meaning and impacts the audience. A narrative power analysis asks, whose stories are being told, and by whom? Which stories are left out?

Prescriptive: Stories are often more than just the recounting of events. How we narrate the story can shape the story as much as the contents. How we frame the problem begins to define the possible solutions. Stories are a powerful form of persuasion and a tool to intentionally shape or reshape a discourse. A narrative power analysis examines how the story shapes the audience's understanding and why.

Constitutive: Finally, there is a deeper, often unacknowledged realm of narrative power. Powerful narratives make up the fabric of a shared culture, and in the process, constitute (or literally embody) aspects of social relationships. These are the narratives that define worldview, identity, and the boundaries of political possibility. A narrative power analysis questions the "conventional wisdom" by surfacing unstated assumptions, explores ways to shift the discourse, change the larger story, and create new norms.

2.4 Setting the Frame

> *Power intervenes in discourse to fix meaning.*
> —Stuart Hall

One of the most important concepts when applying a narrative power analysis is to understand framing. Cognitive research tells us that our brains interpret the world by relying heavily on preexisting conceptual models known as frames. Frames are how we process and mentally organize what we encounter in the world around us. In the words of journalism professor Stephen Reese, "Frames are the organizing principles that are socially shared and persistent over time, that work symbolically to meaningfully structure the social world."[10]

The roots of the modern framing discourse are in the work of sociologist Erving Goffman and his 1974 book, *Frame Analysis: An Essay on the Organization of Experience.* Goffman called frames "schemata of interpretation."[11] Framing became a buzzword, in progressive circles, thanks in large part to the popularity of cognitive linguist George Lakoff's important work.[12] But it's important to clarify that framing is not merely about coming up with a catchy slogan or magic words. Framing is harnessing the underlying narrative power that makes certain words have seemingly magic impact: the power of shaping collective interpretation.[13]

(Left) Associated Press. "A young man walks through chest-deep floodwater after *looting* a grocery store in New Orleans on Tuesday, Aug. 30, 2005."
(Right) AFP/Getty Images/Chris Graythen. "Two residents wade through chest-deep water after *finding* bread and soda from a local grocery store after Hurricane Katrina came through the area in New Orleans, Louisiana." *Emphasis added.*

From a story-based strategy perspective, framing is one of the most fundamental applications of narrative power. Framing is critical to understanding narrative power because by defining the structure and boundaries of the story, the frame defines point of view and power. Framing a story means setting the terms for how to understand it and what it means. Like the frame around a piece of art or the edges of the television screen, the frame focuses and organizes our attention—incoming information is rendered meaningful and thereby resonates with and motivates the audience. The audience makes meaning from what is inside the frame, while what is outside the frame is ignored, thus defining what is part of the story versus what is not. As media researcher Charlotte Ryan explains, "A frame is a thought organizer, highlighting certain events and facts as important, and rendering others invisible."[14] This interplay of power and representation is the essence of framing and what makes it such a critical tool for story-based strategy.

Framing is critical to understanding narrative power because the frame defines point of view and power in the story.

The example documented in the two photos on the previous page compares two different media reports covering the aftermath of Hurricane Katrina hitting New Orleans in 2005. The context of surviving in the devastated city and the specific action of taking food from damaged stores is identical, but white people are described as "finding" resources at a local grocery store, while a Black youth is described as "looting." In this case the framing difference is only one word, but it creates a completely different narrative and therefore meaning.

The power of a frame is to invoke a whole set of preexisting stories and assumptions about the world. "Finding" suggests the type of sympathetic resourcefulness needed to survive in the midst of a disaster. The word "looting," however, invokes a long-standing racist narrative that has become painfully familiar through hundreds of years of dehumanizing and criminalizing people of color in the United States.

This example shows the life or death stakes of how people and issues are framed. If the U.S. government says that you are "finding" they send the National Guard to rescue you, but if they decide you are "looting" they send the National Guard to shoot you. But an equally important lesson in framing is provided by the pairing of these two images. This side-by-side comparison told a new story exposing racist media coverage and fueling organizing around media justice.[15]

2.5 Designer Stories and the Branded World

Advertising at its best is making people feel that without their product you're a loser.
—Nancy Shalek

One of the most obvious examples of narrative power in present-day society is the onslaught of sophisticated advertising. The vast majority of this marketing is created with the specific purpose of affecting the thinking, behavior, and purchasing habits of the target audience. These are designer stories created by some of the world's most talented creative minds in order to penetrate our most personal desires and relationships.

Contemporary U.S. culture is shaped by consumer spectacles: digital advertising stalks us across platforms; edutainment and advergames have gone from buzzwords to booming businesses; and marketers compete to weave their products into the fabric of shared experience. Current estimates are that the average person in an urban or suburban area in the U.S. is bombarded by thousands of commercial messages daily.[16]

Human hardwiring for stories connects to our deepest impulses as social creatures who want to build connection in community. What does this mean in a digital, branded, and globalized world where advertising and marketing have become central engines of the economy and political system?

With spending on global advertising reaching nearly $500 billion in 2016,[17] modern society has in effect submitted to a mass psychological experiment to promote individualism, consumerism, and commodification. Many of the best storytellers and image crafters in our culture have been deployed to sell us imagined visions of ourselves, complete with the appropriate brand of carbonated beverage, designer jeans, or political candidate. As the magazine Adbusters famously described it, "The product is YOU."

Marlboro used the cowboy image and mythology to create their brand. The "Marlboro Man" campaign began in the 1950s when filtered cigarettes were most popular with women, and succeeded in dramatically increasing Marlboro's male market share.

1931 Coca-Cola advertisement with illustration by Haddon Sundblom.

Media theorist and researcher Sut Jhally has described advertising as providing "the dream life of our culture" that sells us products by selling us dreams.[18] Author Stephen Duncombe has coined the phrase the "Age of Fantasy" to describe how image and spectacle shape contemporary society and politics.[19]

Branding is one of the most commonly experienced applications of narrative power. At this point it is difficult for anyone living in a consumer society to be unfamiliar with the term, and the concept is widely applied. But despite its ubiquity, the popular discourse around branding frequently lacks a critical power analysis.

Branding operates like a magical process that endows a thing—usually an inanimate product, but sometimes a political idea, candidate, or agenda—with specific narrative and emotional qualities. The expression invokes the image of a rancher using a cattle brand to burn initials onto a cow's hide, but the notion of branding actually comes from the Greek and Roman penal system where criminals had markings representing their crimes burned onto their flesh.[20] Modern branding metaphorically burns emotional and narrative qualities into a thing so as to create a lasting connection with the potential customer. If successful, the power of narrative instills the intended meaning into the product and dish soap becomes an explosion of Joy® or deodorant is transformed into a symbol of virility.

The brand is more than a logo, color scheme, or specific flagship product. The brand is the sum total of the stories that are told about the brand and encompasses images, impressions, gut feelings, and associations. Thus, highly visible consumer brands are vulnerable to attack and can be important points of intervention in corporate accountability campaigns. See Section 4.12 for more insights on brand-busting.

The influence of advertising is not new; it has historically played a role in shaping U.S. popular culture and political life. The contemporary image of Santa Claus, visualized as the jovial white-bearded man in the red suit, is the result of a successful advertising campaign by the Coca-Cola company that began in the 1930s. Coke's branding campaign created a dominant image of Santa clothed in Coke's red and white colors that replaced a diverse variety of other depictions coming from Northern European traditions.[21]

Another example is the decades old branding strategy of the De Beers diamond company. After uncovering vast supplies of diamonds in Southern Africa, De Beers decided it needed to create demand. In the 1930s and 1940s, De Beers sought product placement in movies with romantic engagement scenes to popularize the offering of a diamond ring as *the* engagement ritual, and to

How many of these branded letters do you recognize in Heidi Cody's "American Alphabet?"[26] American children can now recognize over a thousand corporate logos but only a handful of native plants.[27]

equate the desire for life partnership with the symbol of a large diamond. Within a few decades, diamond engagement rings became the norm and "diamonds are forever" entered the cultural vernacular. This campaign is considered by the advertising industry to be one of their most successful campaigns ever.[22] In recent decades the industry has tried to expand its sales by creating more "culturally obligatory"[23] products like the diamond anniversary band, the 25th anniversary diamond, the "mangagement ring" (engagement rings targeted to men) and non-engagement "right-hand rings" for women to express their independence ("Your left hand says 'we,' Your right hand says 'me'").[24] Meanwhile, human rights and global justice campaigners have created the "conflict diamonds" brand to pressure the industry to address its role in fueling war and violence.[25]

The "corporate alphabet" (above) by artist Heidi Cody is instructive. Let's remember these aren't even full brand logos—these are just snippets of their font treatments. But just one letter can still be enough to cue your mind to a specific product and possibly an entire narrative about it, usually conveyed by a faintly remembered advertising jingle. If you are the right age you may recognize lots of them: Y is for York Peppermint Patties (and makes you feel cold like you're in the mountains), C is for Campbell's Soup ("Mmm Mmm good!"), and M is for M&M's ("melts in your mouth, not in your hands").

How did these advertising images and stories get inside of our heads? How do some stories spread and saturate popular culture while others are ignored? This is the power of **memes**.

- What recent advertisement has stuck with you? What do you remember about it? Why do you think it was memorable?
- Select a random commercial ad in any medium. Identify some of the values reflected in the ad.
- Make a list of messages you regularly see in advertising. What do these messages tell you about yourself? What do they say about society?

2.6 Memes

A meme (rhymes with dream) is a unit of information (a catchphrase, a concept, a tune, a notion of fashion, philosophy or politics) that leaps from brain to brain. Memes compete with one another for replication, and are passed down through a population much the same way genes pass through a species. Potent memes can change minds, alter behavior, catalyze collective mindshifts and transform cultures. Which is why meme warfare has become the geopolitical battle of our information age. Whoever has the memes has the power.
—Kalle Lasn

The concept of a meme is a helpful analytical tool for exploring cultural influence and the mechanics of narrative power. Memes are "units of cultural transmission," self-replicating pieces of cultural information that spread virally from mind to mind with a life of their own. Internet culture has oversimplified the concept and reduced the definition of meme to primarily refer to humorous mash-ups of an image and text that spread virally online. But the original broader definition is still a useful reference point for how narrative power operates.

A meme is any unit of culture (not just a funny picture shared on the internet!) that has spread beyond its creator—buzzwords, catchy melodies, fashion trends, ideas, rituals, iconic images, etc. Memes are like genes of culture that evolve as they pass from person to person. Evolutionary biologist Richard Dawkins coined the term in his 1976 book *The Selfish Gene* to theorize how culture replicates and spreads.[28] Writer and memeticist Glenn Grant defines memes as "contagious information patterns."[29]

Memes are everywhere, from personal mannerisms and collective ritual to the advertising slogans and political jargon that dominate the media. Almost anything can be a meme—but how effective a meme is it? Will it be a passing fad like pet rocks, or an ongoing cultural ritual, such as putting candles on a birthday cake? Over time, most memes tend to morph, disappear, or even dramatically change in meaning, but some prove to be resilient and shape the evolution of cultures.

Although the concept of memes is an inadequate, overly reductionist model for capturing the complexity of culture, it does provide a useful way to talk about how ideas, stories, symbols, and frames replicate and move through the culture. Effective memes are essentially viral frames: a capsule that can carry a whole narrative with it. This process of encapsulating a broader story into something that others can easily spread has always been part of social movement practice. From *No taxation without representation*, to *Black is beautiful*, to *We are the 99%*, powerful memes have popularized narratives of change and liberation. Effective memes must be memorable, easy to spread, and "sticky." A meme that embodies a message and spreads rapidly can dramatically increase the impact of an action or campaign.

As **change agents** we need ways to track how information spreads and shapes political discourse. By thinking in terms of memes, we can make

MOVEMENT MEMES

The term may be new, but memes are not. Nowadays memes may spread virally via a #hashtag, but spreading **memes** is an age-old movement building practice. Movements constantly generate memes that allow people to express their shared values and act with a common vision. Whether through our slogans, symbols, images, or rituals, movements create memes that:

- **Name Our Struggles:** human rights, climate justice, Movement for Black Lives
- **Create Common Symbols:** the peace sign, the raised fist, the migration is beautiful butterfly, the rainbow flag, hands up don't shoot!
- **Frame Problems:** environmental racism, prison-industrial-complex, greenwashing, wage theft, white fragility, climate destabilization
- **Communicate Our Demands:** living wage, keep fossil fuels in the ground, media justice, fair trade, zero waste, separation of oil and state, nothing about us without us
- **Pass on Lessons:** #StayWoke, Sí se puede!, each one teach one, #PrideisPolitical, move at the speed of trust, the union makes us strong

My Memes: Are there favorite slang words, fashions, ideas, slogans, or rituals that you've "picked up?" Have you spread a new meme lately? Are there memes that you don't want to spread?

Movement Memes: List some examples of memes from social movements and campaigns that you support.

our own storytelling more powerful and viral. It can also help us analyze the stories we are working to change in the dominant culture. Advertising is full of potent designer memes—catchy little phrases that get endlessly repeated, like Nike's "Just Do It!" Likewise, unscrupulous power-holders have shown considerable skill at designing memes that spread their stories through the culture: "death panels," "weapons of mass destruction," "the War on Terror," "Union Bosses," and "tax relief" have become part of the public discussion, carrying with them the right-wing worldview and agenda of their creators.

Individual memes will never be enough to communicate the full transformative vision of many social change efforts. But the reality of the current media system is that social change narratives will get encapsulated whether through traditional journalism, bystander reporting, or the mechanics of social-media sharing. How this summarizing of a campaign's core narrative occurs has a huge effect on its political power and impact. Campaigns that don't tell their own story effectively are vulnerable to others telling stories about them that may co-opt, marginalize, or vilify them. This can be a huge strategic liability. Meme your own message or risk your opponent doing it for you.

Harnessing the power of memes is particularly important in our fragmented media environment where attention-challenged audiences are rarely able to seamlessly consume our entire campaign story. Creating effective memes that carry the core framing of the story and invite audiences to learn more is an essential way to spread our messages and build our base of support.

The story-based strategy approach is not intended to be a replacement for organizing and power building, but rather a set of complementary tools made all the more relevant by the contemporary media and culture context. A well-tested sound bite or powerful image alone will not win campaigns or trigger systemic change. But the right meme *can* help **people-powered** organizing become exponentially more effective.

2.7 Power and Mythology

Myths, which are believed in, tend to become true.
—George Orwell

Just as activists apply a power analysis to understand avenues of influence between key decision-makers and relevant institutions, we can apply a narrative power analysis to understand the narratives operating around an issue, campaign or broader social context.

It is almost impossible to miss coercive power in its physical manifestations (military invasions, mass incarceration, state surveillance, firing workers who organize, etc.), but it is much harder to see when power is operating as narrative. Certain types of narratives act like glue holding the status quo together: the power to marginalize critics; the power to normalize suffering by blaming the victimized for their own oppression; the power to legitimize structural violence and rationalize injustice. For example, when forced to acknowledge an injustice, some people will shrug it off, saying "that's just the way things are" or "life isn't fair," instead of seeing the oppressive structure of the system. Framing popular narratives is as critical to maintaining social control as fighter planes, police batons, and economic coercion.

In the 1930s, the imprisoned Italian Communist leader Antonio Gramsci developed the concept of **hegemony** (coming from the Greek word *hegemonia*, meaning leadership) to explain this idea. He described how elites don't just rule society with the force of state and economic power, but more importantly, they control society's moral and intellectual leadership. Capitalism, Gramsci argued, maintained control not just through violence and economic coercion, but also ideologically,

Antonio Gramsci (1891–1937), an Italian Communist leader imprisoned by Mussolini, contributed many important ideas to modern political thought, including the concept of "hegemony."

through a hegemonic culture in which the values of the elite became the "common sense" values of all.[30] The power of hegemony is expressed through the subtle coercion of "manufacturing consent" rather than only with armed force.[31] This multifaceted cultural process limits the terms of acceptable debate to make ideas that challenge the status quo almost *unthinkable*.

Hegemony operates in cultural stories that over time gain widespread acceptance and reinforce a dominant perspective or worldview. These webs of narratives are **control mythologies**, which shape a shared sense of political reality, normalize the status quo, and obscure alternative options or visions.

As we discussed in Section 2.1, referring to these stories as "mythologies" is not about whether they are true or false, because that's not what makes them powerful; rather it is about how much meaning they carry in the culture. Like religious mythologies (both ancient and contemporary), these stories are powerful in that they give people a lens for interpreting and understanding the world. Some control mythologies evolve over time carrying harmful assumptions of hegemonic culture, while others are specifically designed by unscrupulous power-holders for their own political purposes.

From the notion that "you can't fight city hall" to the idea that our economies must always "grow," control mythologies often operate as the boundaries of political imagination and influence the dominant culture. By identifying and analyzing control mythologies, we can develop a better understanding of how power operates and expand our own sense of what is politically possible.

2.8 People-Power and Narrative

The power of the people is much stronger than the people in power.
—Wael Ghonim

Oftentimes, when stories about history or the way society operates are shared, they are framed as if politicians, generals, police officers, and corporate executives have power but the rest of us don't. This is a common control mythology that normalizes existing power dynamics and makes them appear fixed in place and unchangeable.

Fortunately, people-powered movements around the world have shown us that power is a malleable and dynamic relationship between those who have more power and those who have less. The "social view of power," (sometimes called the "consent theory of power" as in the

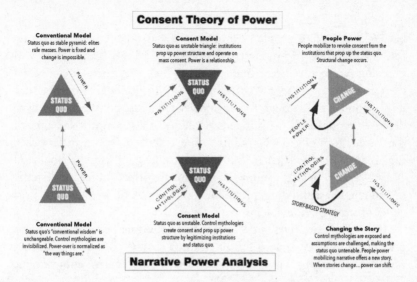

Consent Theory of Power

Conventional Model
Status quo as stable pyramid: elites rule masses. Power is fixed and change is impossible.

Consent Model
Status quo as unstable triangle: institutions prop up power structure and operate on mass consent. Power is a relationship.

People Power
People mobilize to revoke consent from the institutions that prop up the status quo. Structural change occurs.

Conventional Model
Status quo's "conventional wisdom" is unchangeable. Control mythologies are invisibilized. Power-over is normalized as "the way things are."

Consent Model
Status quo as unstable. Control mythologies create consent and prop up power structure by legitimizing institutions and status quo.

Changing the Story
Control mythologies are exposed and assumptions are challenged, making the status quo untenable. People-power mobilizing narrative offers a new story. When stories change... power can shift.

Narrative Power Analysis

This diagram overlays Gene Sharp's Consent Model of Power with the parallel role Narrative Power Analysis plays in supporting people-powered strategies. The status quo triangle can represent a specific issue, political context, or an entire political system.

diagram above) popularized by Gene Sharp,[32] posits that power structures are inherently unstable and propped up by societal institutions that rely on the tacit consent of the ruled. In other words, power does not only come from above with laws and riot police, but it also can be built from below by withdrawing cooperation on a massive scale. When the governed choose disobedience and remove their consent from the power-holders, dramatic changes can happen quickly.

The term "people-power" comes from the Philippines, where years of mass protest and civil resistance overthrew the authoritarian President Ferdinand Marcos in 1986. It communicates the same core insights as countless organizing campaigns and nonviolent revolutions around the world—from ending legalized segregation in the United States, to overthrowing dictatorships in Serbia and the former Soviet Republics, to the uprisings of the Arab Spring.

Social change efforts are often a struggle between the collaborative power ("power-with" or "power-together") that a grassroots campaign or movement builds by uniting people and the coercive power ("power-over") of power-holders maintaining their illegitimate authority.[33]

As Sharp and subsequent researchers have shown,[34] change requires a narrative that challenges the seeming intransigence of the status quo. Wael Ghonim, one of the leaders of the 2011 Egyptian democracy movement, describes that the movement's success relied on "breaking the fear barrier" by making people believe change was possible.[35] This was the role of their **framing narrative** (see Section 3.11) which started with exposing rampant police brutality and, as their organizing grew, helped their audiences see the government itself as illegitimate. A framing narrative alone is not enough to shift power relations, but when effectively deployed to unite all the different elements of a strategy, it can unleash the momentum of growing public support. Indeed, "momentum driven organizing," as discussed in Mark Engler and Paul Engler's book *This Is an Uprising*, blends seemingly spontaneous street protest and steady, incremental base building, providing a framework for applying the principles of strategic nonviolence with a narrative lens.[36]

This use of narrative, as the rocket fuel of people-powered campaigns provides important lessons for all types of change efforts. The diagram on the previous page outlines how narrative power analysis complements Gene Sharp's Consent Theory of Power.

2.9 Creation Myths of the United States

> *Thanksgiving is the holiday of peace, the celebration of work and the simple life . . . a true folk-festival that speaks the poetry of the turn of the seasons, the beauty of seedtime and harvest, the ripe product of the year—and the deep, deep connection of all these things with God.*
> —Ray Stannard Baker, 1919

> *We gave them forest-clad mountains and valleys full of game, and in return what did they give our warriors and our women? Rum, trinkets, and a grave. Where today are the Pequot? Where are the Narragansett, the Mohican, the Pokanoket, and many other once powerful tribes of our people? They have vanished before the avarice and the oppression of the White Man, as snow before a summer sun.*
> —Tecumseh, Shawnee Nation leader, 1810

Let's explore how narrative power operates by taking a closer look at an example from the United States creation mythology: the story of Thanksgiving.

The official Thanksgiving story is a snapshot of rosy relations between European colonizers and the Native peoples of the Americas that emphasizes cooperation, peace, and the Native communities welcoming the Pilgrims. Basically, some new folks, the Pilgrims, arrived in town and they didn't know how to survive in this new land so the longtime residents,

Thanksgiving is one of the most recognizable origin myths and cultural rituals of the United States. It operates as a powerful control mythology in the dominant culture.

various Native American tribes, gave them some tips, they had a giant feast to celebrate, and everyone lived happily ever after.

As most of us know, however, that was not the reality. In fact, the first historical record of the Pilgrims celebrating a "thanksgiving" is not related to a harvest festival or cross-cultural cooperation, but to a celebration of a massacre of over 700 Pequot women and children in 1637. Some historians now believe the late November date (which is six to eight weeks after harvest in New England) appears to commemorate the anniversary of the massacre, which was seen as a great military victory.[37]

This well-known example reveals key aspects of a narrative power analysis. First, that dominant stories in the culture—ones that are widely accepted as true—are often worth examining to understand what they really say and what they leave out, as well as the underlying assumptions that allow them to operate. In this case, one underlying assumption is that Europeans were a peaceful and welcome presence in the Americas.

Second, this example shows that power shapes point of view. Clearly, the story of Thanksgiving that has been passed on in the dominant culture is from the perspective of the Pilgrims, and not the Native peoples. As the famous saying goes, "History is written by the winners."[38]

Third, the Thanksgiving story has universalized the Pilgrims' perspective as the only truth and has normalized their experience. This universalization masks the realities of the genocide of Native peoples, and the mythology continues to uphold white privilege and obscure ongoing violations of Native sovereignty today.

And finally, the control mythology of Thanksgiving is both challengeable and changeable. Native peoples have always challenged the settler myth. Since 1970 Native American activists and allies have marked Thanksgiving as the "National Day of Mourning" to draw attention to the genocide of Native peoples and their ongoing struggles against racism and colonization. A group called the United American Indians of

This action, carried out in solidarity with protests against the 2014 police killing of Michael Brown, tells a larger story about the history of structural racism in the United States by connecting slavery, lynching, and mass incarceration.

New England organizes an annual demonstration at Plymouth Rock in Massachusetts. In recent years, through grassroots and legal pressure, the group has won several commemorative plaques acknowledging the Day of Mourning and Native historical figures.[39]

Thanksgiving is one widely shared origin story of the United States, but there are many others: from "Columbus *discovered* America," (notice how differently we understand the story if we say "Columbus *invaded* America") to "the land of the free," "40 acres and a mule," and "Give me your tired, your poor, your huddled masses." These origin myths distort historical reality, but that doesn't prevent them from informing the worldview and collective identity of those that believe them. These mythologies shape the terrain of our contemporary narratives. Understanding how these deep-seated narratives continue to impact social change efforts today can help campaigns win tangible victories.

2.10 Control Myths & Memes

> *Smash the control images. Smash the control machine.*
> —William S. Burroughs

We've highlighted how historic power dynamics can generate powerful mythologies of control and we've explored how memes can help spread and normalize narratives. So what happens when a control mythology becomes a meme? You get a stand-alone myth that carries the entire narrative: a **control myth** that marginalizes, co-opts, and limits the appeal of social change ideas.

44

For instance, in the 1940s when state governments in the South began criminalizing the right of workers to organize unions, they didn't call the policies anti-union laws—they called them "right to work" laws. This deliberately misleading framing continues to promote anti-worker legislation across the country today.[40]

A narrative power analysis helps us identify these dangerous stories and challenge them when they show up in the public debate. Here are just a few examples that CSS has had to confront in our work:

The War on . . ." whatever fills in the blank—Communism, drugs, terror—is inevitably going to be a debate-limiting shorthand for excessive militarization at home and abroad. Usually, the war is conducted with "surgical strikes" that magically kill the bad guys but nobody else, except of course, for the odd "collateral damage" (aka civilian casualties).

The Invisible Hand of the Market: This potent myth tells us government regulations are unnecessary; just let the market forces work their magic and everything will be great. It's often used as the underlying logic to attack environmental or workers' safety regulation as "job killers" or "red tape" that smothers business.

Trickle-Down Economics: One of the most ingenious control myths ever created, it presents a world where policies that help the wealthy accumulate more wealth are good for everyone because the rich are "job creators" and the prosperity will eventually make it down to those at the bottom of the economic pyramid.

The Bootstrap Myth: Related to trickle down, the idea that if everyone works hard they can pull themselves up by their bootstraps to make a good living. It becomes an insidious form of control because it masks structural forces and provides the excuse to blame poverty on poor people by implying they are lazy or just haven't worked hard enough.

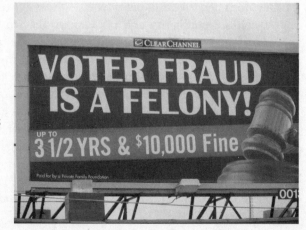

Despite the fact that statistically it is an almost nonexistent problem, "voter fraud" is a potent control myth used to suppress voter turnout and justify restricting voting rights for African Americans and other politically marginalized communities.[41]

- Is there a control mythology you once believed, but now question, challenge, or refute?
- When did you start to challenge the conventional story? What led you to question your existing beliefs?
- List some of the control myths that are influencing the debate around an issue you care about? What could you do to directly challenge them?

Jobs versus the Environment: This control myth tells us that we have to choose: Do we want people to have jobs and a way to make a living or do we want to protect the environment? We can't have both. (To which we reply in the words of radical ecologist and labor organizer Judi Bari: "There are no jobs on a dead planet.")[42]

Anchor Babies: A pejorative meme for a nonexistent trend of undocumented pregnant women deliberately entering the U.S. so their children can get citizenship. This control myth continues to be exploited by antimigrant forces to dehumanize immigrant families and attack the constitutional guarantees of birthright citizenship.

And there are many more control myths, from calling the rewriting of global laws to benefit corporate investors "free trade," to the accusation that the U.S. media has a "liberal" bias, to the fantasy of pollution-free "clean coal." Once you are attuned to apply a narrative power analysis lens you will see control myths moving throughout political discourse: Too Big to Fail, Tax Relief, All Lives Matter, Make America Great Again . . .

But don't let this dishearten you. A story-based strategist should never confuse familiarity and popularity. The worst mistake change agents can make is to accept a control myth as the terms of the debate because this only reinforces its power. Control myths are by definition well known, so often appear very powerful, but often their power comes from their uncontested ubiquity. When control myths are directly challenged with compelling, alternative narratives, their hold on popular imagination begins to fade. The history of social change from Suffragists to #BlackLivesMatter shows that no mythology holds when it is artfully and fearlessly challenged. Even if the need to make short-term incremental progress on an issue makes it unrealistic to directly challenge an entrenched control myth, it is important to at least avoid reaffirming it.

2.11 Narrative Filters

Sometimes people hold a core belief that is very strong. When they are presented with evidence that works against that belief, the new evidence cannot be accepted . . . because it is so important to protect the core belief, they will rationalize, ignore and even deny anything that doesn't fit with the core belief.
—Frantz Fanon

Have you ever tried to convince people (who didn't already agree with you) about a social issue by telling them "the facts"? Did you tell them all the statistics and data about your cause—maybe even point them toward a comprehensive report your organization has done on the issue—and they still didn't change their mind? You're not alone.[43] Applying a narrative power analysis can help us understand these common dynamics and inform our strategy to reach people with a specific message.

Around most issues, it is easy to define the problem as "the general public doesn't know the facts." Oftentimes, activists assume that if we could just inform people about the issue and give them the information they are lacking, then they will join our campaigns for change. But, in most cases, "the facts" alone are not enough to persuade; assumptions, emotions, internal narratives, and preexisting attitudes can get in the way of the facts making sense. In the words of infamous Republican pollster Frank Luntz, "It's not what you say, it's what people hear."

A narrative power analysis helps us see the larger problem is not necessarily what people *don't* know. Rather, the problem may be what they *do* know. In other words, people have existing stories about their world that act as **narrative filters** to prevent them from hearing social change messages. As years of psychological study have shown us, people are conditioned to ignore information that doesn't fit into their existing framework for understanding the world (often called "confirmation bias").[44] These biases are deep enough that we can even track our neurological pathways of denial. As Drew Weston explains in his book, *The Political Brain*:

> When confronted with potentially troubling political information, a network of neurons becomes active that produces distress. . . . The brain registers the conflict between data and desire and begins to search for ways to turn off the spigot of unpleasant emotion.[45]

Information that contradicts existing beliefs is rarely able to reach through people's preexisting filters. One way to surface an audience's potential filters is to analyze a story they believe, and particularly to surface

- Have you heard a piece of information (on the news, from a friend, etc.) that you did not believe? What made you not believe it?
- What are some other factors that make you believe or disbelieve information?
- Take a moment to write down some of the narrative filters that may prevent someone from believing the story around an issue you care about.

the assumptions underlying the story. The next section outlines one of the most simple but helpful narrative power analysis methods, which is to deconstruct a story we want to change using the Elements of Story.

2.12 The Elements of Story

Truth and power belong to those who tell the better story.
—Stephen Duncombe

In order to apply a narrative power analysis and create effective story-based strategies, it is helpful to understand the key narrative elements that allow stories to operate. Although there are many different aspects of what makes a story successful, CSS has found five elements that are particularly relevant for understanding how power operates in the story. These five elements are: Conflict, Characters, Imagery, Foreshadowing, and Assumptions. Identifying these elements helps us deconstruct the stories we want to challenge and to construct the stories we want to tell. Chapter III outlines how successfully using these elements can help win the **battle of the story**. The Elements of Story provide a versatile framework to examine any level of narrative—from examining an opponent's story, to mapping the media landscape around an issue, to analyzing deep-seated cultural narratives.

> The institutional biases of the media often present politically marginalized people as at fault for their own problems, as helpless victims, or do not let them speak at all.

THE ELEMENTS OF STORY

- Conflict
- Characters
- Imagery (Show, Don't Tell)
- Foreshadowing
- Assumptions

This simple framework can be used to apply a narrative power analysis to any story–either for deconstructing a story you want to challenge or generating your own social change narrative.

Conflict

Conflict is the backbone of narrative. No conflict = no plot = no story. Conflict is what creates the drama that makes for an interesting story and communicates what is at stake to the audience so they care about the outcome of the story. How the conflict is framed defines the story's point of view, which, as we have explored, is central to how power operates in the story. The conflict determines the moral calculus of the story and casts some characters as good guys and others as villains. Identifying the conflicts means asking: What does the story present as the problem, and how does this create conflict? Who is the conflict between? Is it a familiar "David versus Goliath" struggle or perhaps a clash of values, such as a choice between greed and dignity?

Characters

In an effective story the audience can relate to the characters. This helps people see themselves reflected in the story and choose sides. Sometimes these characters are the subjects of the story and sometimes they are the protagonists, or even narrators who act as messengers to deliver the story. Messengers are just as important as the message itself, because they put human faces on the conflict and embody the story. The institutional biases of the media often present politically marginalized people as at fault for their own problems, as helpless victims, or do not let them speak at all. The dynamics of who gets to speak, how the "sympathetic" roles are cast, and who is represented as the heroes, victims, and villains, are key to how power operates in the story.

Imagery: Show, Don't Tell

"A picture is worth a thousand words" may be a cliché but it is more true than ever. Today's mass media culture is image-driven and many stories are illustrated with carefully produced visuals. Regardless of medium, effective stories use language that offers powerful imagery. "Show, don't tell" is a classic writer's tip reminding us to avoid excessive description or exposition and communicate through action, emotion, and metaphor. A powerful story captures the audience's imagination with descriptions that speak to our senses. This can also mean not hitting your audience over the head with your moral but rather ensuring the story naturally shows its meaning. When a story is showing, instead of telling, it offers the audience the opportunity to draw their own conclusions.

Foreshadowing

Every story has a beginning, a middle, and an end—the resolution of the conflict. The literary term "foreshadowing" refers to the ways that a story provides hints to its outcome. Think of the movie that in an early scene slowly pans across the gun over the fireplace. We are trained by narrative conventions to perceive that image as relevant information and we know it means the gun will return in later scenes. Real-world narratives that shape culture and politics also foreshadow. When analyzing a story, look for how it suggests a specific future or makes promises (explicit or otherwise) about the resolution of the conflict.

Assumptions

Assumptions are the glue that holds the story together; they are the unstated parts of the story that you have to accept in order to believe the story is true. Assumptions can take the form of shared values (a belief in democracy) or distorted information (all Muslims are violent extremists). Oftentimes control myths shape stories at the level of their unstated assumptions. Identifying and challenging underlying assumptions is probably the most important element to change a story. Likewise, when we unearth the underlying assumptions of a social change narrative, we can benefit from a shared understanding—usually the worldview and values—that glue it together.

These five elements can be found in almost any story. As a story-based strategist, you must learn to see them in the stories all around you and use them as the foundation for generating your own stories. ■

Analyzing a Story: Pick a story you recently heard from someone. Retell the story to yourself, then see if you can identify the elements of story. What is the conflict? Who are the characters? What imagery was used and how was the ending foreshadowed? Are there underlying assumptions that make the story believable?

Moving Stories: Think of a story that you found personally moving. It could be something you heard secondhand, a movie, a poem, a family story, something from a book, etc. Why is the story powerful to you? How does it use the elements of story? What are some of the underlying assumptions that resonate with you?

NARRATIVE POWER ANALYSIS SUMMARY

Different methods for conducting a Narrative Power Analysis:

- Examine dominant culture stories.
- Explore how a story normalizes the status quo by universalizing certain experiences and invisibilizing oppression.
- Identify filters: not what your audience *doesn't* know, but what they *do* know, that might shape how they take in new information.
- Use the Elements of Story to analyze how power operates in the story.

"The problem is not changing people's consciousness but the political, economic, institutional regime of the production of truth."

–Michel Foucault

"Every tool is a weapon, if you hold it right."

–Ani DiFranco

III

Winning the Battle of the Story

3.1 Building on the Cornerstones

Whenever you want to achieve something, keep your eyes open, concentrate and make sure you know exactly what it is you want. No one can hit their target with their eyes closed.
—Paulo Coelho

Now that we have explored narrative power analysis we can move on to using story-based strategy to develop our own social change narratives. The starting point for a successful story-based strategy is to ground the narrative development in real word conditions and your political organizing strategy.

When you are building a house or other structure you must build the foundation first. That begins with laying the cornerstones that will hold your house together. The same is true with narrative; the first step in creating a story-based strategy is defining the **narrative cornerstones**: goals, targets, audiences, and constituency. These cornerstones offer a foundational framework on which to build the strategy. Identifying these cornerstones requires clarity and agreement among all the relevant stakeholders because the cornerstones provide the parameters that will guide strategic choices regarding the emerging story-based strategy.

If the story-based strategy is being developed around an established campaign the cornerstones are usually quite easy to identify. But it is still important to affirm them and make sure all stakeholders are aligned, so the cornerstones can serve as a reference point for future strategic decisions about the narrative. Clarity focuses creativity and with story-based strategy the point is not just to be creative, it is to be strategically creative, so that you can win.

In CSS's work we have found these four narrative cornerstones are essential starting points, along with identifying additional strategic considerations and hooks that will define the parameters of the strategy:

1. Goals:

What are we trying to achieve? It's helpful to be as specific as possible about short-term objectives, medium-term benchmarks, and the desired long-term change. To create a successful story-based strategy it is critical for the group or alliance to be unified around clear goals.

2. Target(s):

Who has the power to give us what we want? Who is the decision-maker that can make this desired change happen? What are the institutions we need to move and who are the decision-makers within those institutions? It's helpful to be as specific as possible about the various relevant relationships of influence and power.

3. Audiences:

Who do we need to reach? A clear understanding of audience is critical for successful story-based strategy. Generally, audiences are prioritized based on their ability to influence the target: the specific groups that can be persuaded and mobilized to pressure the target. "Specific" and "pressure" are the key concepts to help focus. Being precise about audiences allows you to map some of the audience's **narrative filters** (see Section 2.11) and ensure the narrative is framed in a way that speaks to their concerns. It is important to remember there is no such thing as "the general public" or "The Internet." Although seeking mass engagement is always a worthy goal, in our contemporary media-saturated environment, setting out to reach a mythic "everyone" often results in reaching no one. Audiences must be built strategically. A more reliable way to achieve scale is to design a narrative with mass relevance and target specific audiences to help popularize it beyond your current base of support.

4. Constituency:

Who is our base of support? The organized groups of people or communities with whom we already work, represent, or who share our common interests. (The constituency of existing support should also always be considered an audience.) To reach new audiences your narrative will have to be designed to move people with different assumptions and worldviews than your base. But it also has to authentically express the values and aspirations of your current constituencies. A narrative that doesn't work for your base, doesn't work.

Cornerstones

GOAL
What are we trying to achieve? What is the specific change we are trying to make?

AUDIENCE
Who are the specific groups of people that we most need to reach and persuade?

TARGET
Who is the decision-maker that can make this desired change happen?

CONSTITUENCY
Who is our base? The organized groups of people or communities who we already work with, represent or share common interests with.

STRATEGIC CONSIDERATIONS & HOOKS
What other factors or opportunities might be relevant to our efforts?

This worksheet and other tools available at storybasedstrategy.org

Strategic Considerations and Hooks:

What else will influence our strategy? In addition to the four cornerstones it's helpful to have a catchall category for the range of other factors that could affect the parameters of story-based strategy. Key issues that could be relevant strategic considerations might include resources, capacity, strength of the opposition, or overlaps with other organizational goals. Are there specific events, cultural moments, or decision-making milestones that might be opportunities to reach your audiences and spread your narrative? Some of these might not only be relevant intervals in the political process but also serve as preexisting "hooks" which you can hang your narrative on. "Hook" is a media term that refers to traditional newsworthy elements that help a story attract greater attention. Some classic hooks are: public events or holidays (Mother's Day, Earth Day), anniversaries (two years after X bill passed), superlatives (the first, the biggest, the newest), or the involvement of prominent individuals (politicians, celebrities).[1]

> **Thus the role of your story-based strategy is not to change the mind of the target, but rather to mobilize public engagement on the issue in a manner that forces the target to respond.**

In order for your cornerstones to provide a strong foundation for your story-based strategy there must be an underlying strategic relationship connecting them—that is, how all these strategic elements intersect, interact, and reinforce each other. For instance, many social change efforts address a common root cause problem: power imbalances that allow a lack of accountability between the targeted **power-holder** and the impacted constituency. In other words, the target can't be persuaded just because "it's the right thing." (If they can, great! Lobby them, achieve the goal, and move on to your next campaign.) Thus the role of your story-based strategy is not to change the mind of the target, but rather to mobilize public engagement on the issue in a manner that forces the target to respond. This is why audiences are often prioritized based on their ability to influence the target, because this can help shift the larger power relationships and provoke the social conflict in ways that are advantageous for your organizing.

Ideally your story-based strategy isn't just achieving one specific goal— it is also building connections between the constituency implementing the strategy and the audiences they are reaching, and thereby building lasting power.

3.2 Beyond the Story of the Battle

Action is the antidote to despair.
—Joan Baez

If you've ever watched the news coverage of a social justice action (maybe one you participated in), you've probably seen the **story of the battle**: "Demonstrators marched in the street today. Ten protesters were arrested and charged with disorderly conduct. Now over to sports."

These are some facts about an event, but they aren't the whole story. This story doesn't tell the audience what the protest was about, who was there, or why it matters. The story of the battle is a narrative that is heavy on facts, events and play-by-play, but light on context, characters, and big ideas. Emphasis is on *what* is happening, not on *why*. Particularly when we are operating in a media environment that is heavily biased toward the story of the battle—be it around a protest, election, legislative cycle, or news event—we must be ever mindful to proactively shape coverage with our narrative.

Without a story-based strategy, we can easily fall into the trap of telling the story of the battle. When we put the focus of our story on our tactics, or too many of the details, we are not speaking to our broader audiences about the larger significance of our actions, and in so doing cede important narrative territory to our opponents. As change agents we sometimes make the mistake of operating as if all of our audiences already understand our issues and share all of our assumptions. Telling a tactical story without attention to framing a larger, persuasive narrative is not strategic.

Created by John Beske (johnbeske.com) in 2003 to mobilize antiwar activists by promoting the launch of www.unitedforpeace.org.

But here is an important caveat: the story of the battle can, in some situations, be used strategically. When the story of the battle is crafted intentionally to reach people who already are on your side and need to be activated for a specific purpose, the **elements of story** can be used to create a message of mobilization. Action alerts, funding appeals, and progressive independent media coverage that tells an exciting insider story are examples of effective uses of the story of the battle.

One example of a strategic use of tactical messaging is the advertisement on the previous page, created in the lead-up to the invasion of Iraq to promote the newly launched United for Peace and Justice, a national clearinghouse of resources and organizing against the war. If you saw this image out of context, you may dismiss the message as self-marginalizing, but this advertisement was not designed for a mass audience. It ran exclusively in progressive and radical publications to target people who were already antiwar to get active in United for Peace and Justice. Everything about the ad is an appeal to a niche activist audience: the values-based message that war itself is wrong, the confrontational tone, and the declaration that the present political moment is "a time of madness." The ad's message isn't designed to persuade, or challenge the pro-war narrative, but rather to mobilize the existing antiwar base to take action. The narrative plays to the existing assumptions of that audience, rather than aiming to challenge underlying assumptions and shift opinions.

The story of the battle can be an effective mobilizing narrative for your base that is ready to act, but it shouldn't be confused with communicating strategically to a larger public who still needs to be persuaded to act. To use the old organizing metaphor, the story of the battle is effective for mobilizing the choir, but it doesn't necessarily reach the congregation.

REFLECTIONS: STORY OF THE BATTLE

- **Movement Stories**: Share a juicy story about a social change event, leader, setback, or victory. Passing on these stories keeps our movements reflective and connected to our histories. The stories of these battles should not be lost!
- **The Story of the Battle:** Have you been in a situation where you slipped into telling the story of the battle, when you should have been telling the battle of the story?

3.3 The Battle of the Story

The destiny of the world is determined less by the battles that are lost and won than by the stories it loves and believes in.
—Harold Goddard

Every social change effort is inherently a conflict between the status quo and the change agents to control the **framing** of an issue. This contest is the **battle of the story**—the struggle to define meaning and thereby build power and momentum for change.[2] To win the battle of the story requires a narrative designed to connect with your audiences' values, challenge underlying assumptions, and outcompete opposing narratives.

In order to reach a larger audience beyond our existing base of support we need narratives that are rooted in persuasion. This doesn't mean telling our truth louder or more stridently; it means challenging the dominant narrative in a way that changes hearts and minds. Crafting a successful story-based strategy means harnessing the power of storytelling to structure information in a way that reaches and convinces people who are not already active supporters.

In the macro sense, the battle of the story is the larger struggle to determine whose stories are told, how they are framed, how widely these stories are heard, and how deeply they impact the dominant **discourse**. The battle of the story is the effort to communicate the *why*—the interpretation and larger meaning of actions and issues—that helps a social change message reach a broader section of the public and achieve a cultural shift. To succeed in changing the dominant culture's framing of an issue, our movements must win the battle of the story.

CSS has created the battle of the story framework to help social change groups examine the multiple sides (at least two) of the story they are trying to change. The battle of the story utilizes the five elements of story—Conflict, Characters, Imagery, Foreshadowing, and Assumptions (see Section 2.12)—to apply a narrative power analysis to the competing narratives. The worksheet on the next page helps identify these elements so that you can *deconstruct* existing narratives and begin to *construct* a new narrative.

When deconstructing the power-holder or status quo story, the purpose of the exercise is not to explain what is true, but to tell the dominant story *as it is told* in the discourse you are trying to shift. Usually this story is distorted and may even include lies, but the goal is to understand how the story operates—how it makes meaning—in order to contest it strategically. Sometimes it helps to role-play a specific person such as the targeted power-holder or an opponent's public relations team.

Battle of the Story

ELEMENTS OF STORY	OPPOSITION OR STATUS QUO DECONSTRUCTIVE	ADVOCATES/ CHANGE AGENTS CONSTRUCTIVE
Conflict How is the problem being framed? Who or what is the conflict between (X vs. Y)? What's at stake?		
Characters Who are the victims? Villains? Heroes? Who are the messengers that tell the story? Do they get to speak for themselves or is someone speaking on their behalf?		
Imagery (Show, Don't Tell) What powerful images show us (rather than tell us) the story? Are there relevant metaphors, symbols, or specific examples that embody the larger story?		
Foreshadowing How does each story show us the future? What is the vision the story offers of how the conflict will be resolved?		
Assumptions What are the underlying assumptions: what does someone have to believe to accept the story as true? What values are reflected in the story?		
Intervention What are the other story's vulnerabilities? Limits? Are there contradictions or lies? How can underlying assumptions or values be exposed? (See Point of Intervention Worksheet on page 119.)		

Note that this exercise can be triggering for some participants because as you dive into the ugly underbelly of oppressive narratives it may be necessary to repeat harmful stereotypes and rhetoric. This isn't fun, but it is an essential part of the process of narrative power analysis and developing story-based strategy.

When constructing the change agent narrative in the battle of the story process, the purpose is to both identify elements currently being used and explore some new ways to tell the story. Often a group will generate new ideas, such as uncovering different framing options, identifying new characters their organizing should amplify, and gathering insights about contradictions in the opposition story.

Powerful interests wage the battle of the story relentlessly, often with the assistance of sophisticated public relations professionals and vastly greater resources than community advocates and social movements. It is painfully common for power-holders to present themselves as speaking on behalf of communities they marginalize or ignore. This "power-over" corporate model of public relations focuses on crafting the most effective story, regardless of the truth and without any accountability to the affected communities.[3]

To win the battle of the story doesn't mean just emulating our opponent's manipulative techniques. The deepest potential of story-based strategy emerges when people collectively strategize and decide how to tell their story together. In contrast to the corporate PR model, this roots narrative development in "power-with" relationships that emphasize both process and content. The most transformative story-based strategies are developed collectively with constituent leadership—and implemented through ongoing accountable relationships with the people and communities who are impacted and involved. (See "The Ethics of Story-based Strategy" in Section 2.1.)

The battle of the story framework can help surface a number of strategic issues. One of the core skills of narrative thinking is to be able to identify, synergize, and challenge different elements within a story. This chapter will explore each of these elements in depth to highlight how they can be used in a story-based strategy.

3.4 Framing the Conflict

In politics, whoever frames the debate tends to win the debate.
—George Lakoff

Conflict drives compelling stories. A lack of conflict makes for a boring story. Fortunately for us, social change is full of conflict. But this makes it even more important to carefully frame our conflict since that decision will shape the rest of our story, and our strategy. Let's examine an infamous historic example of what it means to frame the conflict in a narrative from the propaganda pros at the Pentagon.

In 2003 the U.S. government disregarded international law and invaded Iraq despite massive global opposition. Around the world tens of millions of people took to the streets in one of the largest peaceful protests in world history.[4] The antiwar movement mobilized so many people that some commentators began to refer to global public opinion as a "second superpower" that could rival the uncontested military and economic dominance of the United States.[5] In this context, the Bush administration was particularly focused on ensuring their narrative framed the conflict for the U.S. audience, including manipulating media coverage with embedded journalists and information warfare techniques. (See sidebar on page 79.)

When U.S. troops arrived in central Baghdad, people in the United States saw the footage of what appeared to be throngs of Iraqis cheering as the statue of Saddam Hussein was toppled in Baghdad's central plaza. This image spread throughout the mainstream U.S. media as a symbol of the quick and decisive success of the U.S.-led invasion. You can see it below as a screenshot from CNN. The story was about liberation—a grateful civilian

(Right) Screenshot of CNN covering the arrival of U.S. troops in Baghdad's Firdos Square on April 9, 2003. (Left) Wider-angle-photo of the same events taken by unembedded journalists from the vantage of the Palestine Hotel. Picture from the Reuters International News Wire. The two different framings convey very different stories.

Re:Imagining Change

population rising up to overthrow a symbol of the dictatorship of Saddam Hussein. The image gives the impression of widespread support for the U.S. invasion. It also invokes the iconic images from the end of the Cold War, as Soviet-era statues were pulled down across Russia and Eastern Europe.

> **Q:** So who has the power in this story?
> **A:** The Iraqi people, of course!

The second image is a picture of the same event, taken at almost the same time—shortly before the statue is toppled. It was taken by a photographer from the one place where the U.S. military had allowed unembedded journalists to be: The Palestine Hotel (although they did "accidentally" bomb it anyway). Unlike the image framed by the U.S. military, this long shot image shows that the vast crowd is really a small group gathered near the statue, and that the dominant force in the square are the U.S. tanks surrounding the plaza. So, who has the power in this story? Expanding the frame of the picture reframes the entire story and changes our understanding of who has the power and legitimacy.

While this is an extreme example, these two images provide a simple and effective visual definition of framing—you see what is inside the frame and you don't see what's outside it. When we expand the frame or reframe, we get a very different understanding of the conflict. In the first

---

INFORMATION WARFARE

"If you don't have goose bumps now, you will never have them in your life," gushed Fox News anchor David Asman as he described the toppling of the Saddam statue.[6] But the coverage from the international media presented a very different picture. British journalist and Middle East correspondent Robert Fisk reporting for the UK *Independent* newspaper described the toppled statue as "the most staged photo opportunity since Iwo Jima."[7] The toppling of the Saddam statue was a Pentagon orchestrated information warfare operation intended to reinforce the Bush administration's narrative that the invasion would be quick and easy, and U.S. troops would be greeted as liberators. In subsequent years a fuller picture of the military's use of information warfare to shape U.S. public opinion of the invasion of Iraq emerged. These operations included the targeting of unembedded media, such as the deliberate bombing of Arabic-language satellite news stations *Al Jazeera* and *Al-Arabiya*, and a Pentagon coordinated program to shape the message provided by retired military personnel serving as analysts for U.S. media outlets.[8] The chilling implication is that U.S. public opinion is a priority military target.[9]

---

framing, when the conflict is defined as between the Iraqi people and a dictator, the story is one of liberation. In the second, the conflict is framed as the U.S. military against unknown antagonists and it becomes the story of occupation. This has become a famous example of a U.S. information warfare operation: a fabricated media event targeting U.S. public opinion.

3.5 Creating Narrative Frames

> *Dreams and reality are opposites. Actions synthesize them.*
> —Assata Shakur

How do movements create frames to shift the popular understanding of important stories and issues? Social change efforts can help shape the interpretation of important events not by manipulating the physical frame on information (as the U.S. military did in Iraq), but rather by creating a **narrative frame** for our audiences to see an issue in a way that is meaningful and builds the power of our side of the story.

A narrative frame operates in the same way as a physical frame: it structures our impressions, highlighting some aspects of the situation and de-emphasizing others. The various elements of story within the frame all connect to provide the narrative the audience will receive.

This banner was hung by the Ruckus Society and the Rainforest Action Network as a framing action the day before mass protests shut down the Seattle meeting of the World Trade Organization in November 1999. Photo courtesy of Rainforest Action Network.

Re:Imagining Change

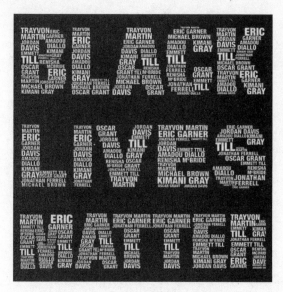

#BlackLivesMatter has provided a unifying narrative frame connecting the ongoing history of anti-Black racism and the police murder of Black people.

Defining the conflict is often the most influential aspect of crafting the frame. For example, the "WTO vs. Democracy" banner on the previous page was an intervention on the day before massive protests shut down the World Trade Organization meeting in Seattle on November 30, 1999. The action was intended to shape media coverage in the lead-up to the mass nonviolent direct action. The larger frame of democracy connected many of the issues that had brought people into the streets such as labor standards, environmental protection, and human rights. By providing an overarching narrative that the WTO is a threat to democracy, the action offered a frame to understand why people were protesting, the importance of the issue, and how it could affect them.

Part of why this action was so effective as a narrative framing device was that the WTO was largely unknown to the U.S. public, so activists could define many people's first impressions without having to overcome preconceptions about the WTO. By defining the WTO as undemocratic from the beginning it created a narrative frame through which audiences processed all additional information about the WTO. This type of a high-profile intervention timed to shape public understanding of an unfolding narrative or upcoming confrontation is often called a *framing action*.

The right narrative frame can connect and galvanize a social movement and even dramatically shift global discourse, as Black-led organizing has shown by elevating the Black Lives Matter frame into a household term and rallying cry for a powerful global movement.

#BlackLivesMatter began as the final line in a "love letter" posted online, then as a hashtag co-created by three Black women—Alicia Garza, Patrisse Cullors, and Opal Tometi (all longtime organizers)—in response to the 2013 acquittal of George Zimmerman, the vigilante who murdered Black teenager Trayvon Martin. The frame powerfully connected that specific moment of outrage to the long history of white supremacist violence, racist cultural norms, and the control mythologies that justify anti-Black racism and the murder of Black people.

Black Lives Matter spread as a potent **meme** (see Section 2.6) through the grassroots protests against the Zimmerman verdict.[10] Then, in the summer of 2014, after the police killings of Eric Garner in New York and Michael Brown in Ferguson, Missouri, Black Lives Matter erupted as a shared frame connecting local police accountability and antiracist organizing around the country and even internationally.

A well-designed narrative frame can't magically shift power relations on its own, but when that frame embodies and aggregates effective organizing, the impact can be historic.

The three words "Black Lives Matter" have become a frame that operates as a powerful mobilizing narrative. BLM provides a clear, overarching meaning—affirming values, naming the problem, and articulating a demand as a de facto vision: a society where Black Lives do Matter. As Alicia Garza writes in her official movement herstory: "Black Lives Matter is an ideological and political intervention in a world where Black lives are systematically and intentionally targeted for demise."[11]

Black Lives Matter shows how a narrative frame can link a fluid web of stories that are mutually reinforcing examples highlighting the ongoing epidemic of anti-Black racism and police violence. The core of the stories are the tragic accounts of Black people killed by the police in the U.S, but the frame is expansive enough to include the full range of systemic issues affecting Black people, as well as solutions for racial justice articulated by the visionary Movement for Black Lives policy platform.[12]

Effective frames like Black Lives Matter are by their nature open-ended: articulating a vision and inviting participation to collectively move the narrative forward. Within the broader narrative, different stories have been encapsulated into memes that allow them to easily spread and become plot points in the evolving Black Lives Matter narrative. In the case of Eric Garner, his final words, "I can't breathe" became a movement slogan; and after Michael Brown's killing, "Hands up, don't shoot" went viral. The gesture of raised hands that began in street protests soon appeared across the culture: from professional football players to television pundits to elected representatives in the U.S. Congress. Related social-media driven meme campaigns emerged, such as #IfIDieinPolice Custody[13] and #SayHerName,[14] amplifying the movement's intersectional analysis and the need to highlight the unique experiences of Black women and members of the Black trans community.

A well-designed narrative frame can't magically shift power relations on its own, but when that frame embodies and aggregates effective organizing, the impact can be historic. Through their on-the-ground leadership, creative actions, digital strategy, and media magic, Black Lives Matter organizers continue to shift the discourse around racism in America. Black Lives Matter has ended the convenient illusion of the U.S. as a "postracial" society and forced an otherwise unwilling media to acknowledge anti-Blackness and the ongoing brutality of policing in communities of color. Their tireless organizing has earned BLM a place in the Smithsonian's African American History Museum, alongside the Little Rock Nine, the Montgomery Bus Boycott, and relics of the Underground Railroad.

3.6 Amplifying Compelling Characters

> *If you will practice being fictional for a while, you will understand that fictional characters are sometimes more real than people with bodies and heartbeats.*
> —Richard Bach

If conflict is the engine of a story, then the characters are its heart. In order for stories to resonate, the audience must identify and empathize with the characters. Believable storytelling relies on compelling characters that help audiences see themselves reflected in the story and choose sides.

Audiences naturally look for characters with whom to identify. This is one of the ways narrative power operates. Which characters do we sympathize with or relate to? The right characters personalize the story and deepen the audience's connection by putting a human face on the conflict, (or sometimes personifying animals or other nonhuman characters).

Every social change story has lots of characters; deciding which characters should be the focus is a significant organizing and strategy question. For example, when grappling with how to tell the story of climate destabilization, should the narratives emphasize polar bears, residents of threatened low-lying regions, those who could benefit from clean energy jobs, or all of the above? The answer depends on your overall strategy determined by your narrative cornerstones (as discussed in Section 3.1).

Who is impacted? Who are the victims? Are there villains or heroes? Casting characters in the roles that communicate the core conflict is one of the most important aspects of framing a narrative, as will be discussed in the next section on the **drama triangle.** The messengers who tell the story are also a critical part of the story. Particularly in our current media environment where we are bombarded with messages, the messenger is often *more* important than the message because it is how audiences assess credibility.

The battle of the story is often the battle over who gets to speak for the sympathetic characters. Do impacted people get to speak for themselves or are they merely cast as extras in the power-holder's story? For example, efforts to defund welfare are presented as benefiting working mothers. The timber industry uses fears about forest fires as an excuse to "protect" public forest lands by clear-cutting them. Corporate tax cuts are sold as job creation tools to help the unemployed. Time and time again, unscrupulous power-holders employ Orwellian logic to hide their agenda behind the stories of real people who are more sympathetic characters than the actual beneficiaries of the scheme.

Farmers have been used as symbols of wholesomeness and an idealized American way of life for generations. When it comes to food and agriculture they are the most trusted spokespeople—just look at the images in food marketing. CSS has supported family farmers challenging corporate control of agriculture and the unregulated genetic engineering of food crops. But as with many issues, the battle of the story over "who are the real farmers?" takes center stage.

(Left) This biotech industry group advertisement uses a "farmer" (actually an actor) as a sympathetic character to make their agenda appear to be pro-farmer. (Right) Real Vermont family farmers marching against agricultural biotechnology.

The biotech industry is constantly trying to associate itself with family farmers, despite the fact that family farming and peasant farmer organizations around the world are united in their opposition to genetically modified organisms (GMOs). Advertisements like the one on the previous page produced by the biotechnology industry often feature a "farmer," but he's not a real farmer—he's an actor dressed up to look like a farmer. The real farmers are protesting with homemade banners, as in the picture of family farmers leading a march with the organization Rural Vermont. But, to the average person disconnected from farming communities, which image looks more like a farmer, the iconic image from the ad, or the real farmer attending a protest?

Representation in the media operates symbolically, not mathematically. Oftentimes a specific individual will be perceived as speaking on behalf of a whole constituency, regardless of whether or not they are actually an authentic representative. Herein lies one of the conundrums of waging the battle of the story against media-savvy power-holders and their slick PR machines. When the impacted people are cast as characters in the power-holder story, the fight often becomes a contest to assert who the real impacted people are, and which side they are on.

Characters can be a powerful way to reframe a story, often by centering a character that has been invisibilized in the story. In 2014 an international collective of artists installed the giant image below in a region of northwestern Pakistan where U.S. drone strikes as part of the so-called War on Terror have killed numerous civilians. This image (provided to

In 2014 an international collective of artists installed this giant image called #NotABug-Splat in northwestern Pakistan so that U.S. military drone operators would be able to see the face of a drone victim.

the artists by human rights attorneys) is of an anonymous little girl whose family was killed in a drone strike. The piece was called #NotABugSplat[15] in reference to U.S. military slang referring to people killed by drones as "bugsplats." The artists' intention was to directly challenge the dehumanization of the dominant U.S. government narrative that drones kill "terrorists" by putting a face on civilian casualties.

Grassroots organizing can win the battle of the story against multi-million-dollar propaganda efforts. But it requires an effective story-based strategy to amplify the voices of the characters and communicate the reality of the issue. At times, this can play out in the crude but important dynamics of representation. For instance, a single religious leader, healthcare worker, or veteran wearing the recognizable signifiers of their role (such as a priest's collar, nurse's scrubs, or a military uniform) can have a bigger impact than 20 members of the constituency wearing jeans and T-shirts.

The Best Weapon in the War on Poverty Is a Job

This advertisement ran in the *New York Times* and other major newspapers in January 2014 during the height of the campaign to raise the federal minimum wage. The ad, created by infamous right-wing PR hatchet man Richard Berman (known as "Dr. Evil," a title he has embraced), is an example of hijacking a character to move a manipulative narrative. The ad pretends to speak for all unemployed people in claiming that increasing wages doesn't help address poverty but will increase unemployment. The narrative is an orchestrated lie but because of the effective character-driven framing, it is much more believable to bystanders, and therefore dangerous.[16]

70   *Re:Imagining Change*

Although this is one of the ways narrative power operates, it is not an excuse to take organizing shortcuts or exploit the same manipulative techniques that are often used against our communities. Effective story-based strategies should leverage the roles of your characters, but this doesn't mean speaking on behalf of others without mandate. The story will build more lasting power and have greater transformative potential when the characters are speaking about their real-world circumstances. (See "The Ethics of Story-based Strategy" in Section 2.1.)

3.7 The Drama Triangle

Nobody is a villain in their own story. We're all the heroes of our own stories.
—George R.R. Martin

Narratives are often defined by the relationships between their characters. A basic narrative equation (that has been around since at least the time of ancient Greece) is the "drama triangle," which describes the interlocking relationships between a Hero, Villain, and Victim. We are all familiar with this basic script: the villain threatens the victim with some horrible fate, and the hero acts to save the victim and defeat the villain.

A narrative power analysis helps us understand that how these roles are cast is one of the ways power operates in the story. Attaching a label that "flattens" individuals or whole communities into being defined solely as

Actions by courageous undocumented youth leading the national movement to pass the D.R.E.A.M. Act immigration reform bill presented migrants as heroes rather than either villains or victims.

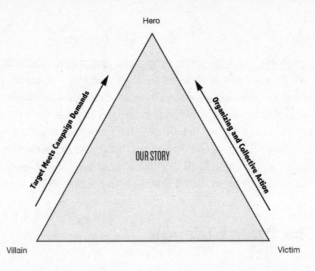

The drama triangle is a narrative power analysis tool for casting the different roles in the story. Story-based strategy can help a campaign shift the roles and change the story.

villain ("thugs") or victim ("helpless women") is not an accurate depiction of the complexity of the world and is often a form of systemic oppression.[17] The purpose of understanding and using the drama triangle is not to legitimize this narrative structure as inherently "real," but rather to acknowledge it is a common narrative equation that can be used to understand how a conflict is being framed. Identifying a narrative's drama triangle can provide powerful insights about how power operates in the story and offer a microcosm of the larger battle of the story between competing narratives. The ability to define the labels in the story—and to change them—is a very clear expression of narrative power and therefore a critical dimension to think about when creating a story-based strategy.

How the different roles on the drama triangle are assigned influences perceptions of different characters' integrity and agency and inevitably reflect broader social relationships or power and privilege. Dominant culture narratives often present oppressed people as powerless victims, blame them for structural problems, or simply leave them out of the story altogether. Navigating these dynamics skillfully in order to authentically amplify the voices of marginalized constituencies is an important aspect of an effective and principled story-based strategy.

Since an effective narrative not only defines the conflict but also foreshadows (see Section 3.9) the solution we want to see, it is important to remember that the roles on the drama triangle are not static. As the narrative progresses it should provide opportunities to recast the characters and shift the power dynamics. Effective campaign narratives should always be built around choices that highlight a path toward resolving the conflict.

An organizing narrative may emerge in a situation where a community is being victimized. For example, the community is suffering because the current city manager has systematically defunded their local school and other services. As community activists start to plan a campaign, they decide the story should emphasize their collective agency. Although the families are all being individually victimized, they choose to be more than just victims. Instead they cast themselves and the families who join the organizing campaign as heroes who are building the power to make change. Likewise, when they cast their campaign target—the city manager and his austerity policies—as the villain, they structure the narrative to offer them a way out: the city manager can choose to abandon their destructive policies and join the community in solving the problem. The extent to which the target adopts the campaign's demands is how far they move from the villain label toward the hero label. Of course, as future accountability efforts are needed and new campaigns are launched, the city manager's role in the narrative will be in question again.

Another common model is to build a campaign narrative in which the campaign's target and the villain are different. In this case the goal is to force the target to distance themselves from the villain. For instance, in campaigns targeting the political influence of the fossil fuel industry, the drama triangle may cast Big Oil (personified by their lobbyists or as a composite character itself) as the villain and demand that politicians refuse their contributions and denounce their undue influence.

3.8 Imagery: Show, Don't Tell

> *Numbers numb, jargon jars, and nobody ever marched on Washington because of a pie chart.*
> —Andy Goodman

Anyone who has dabbled in creative writing has probably heard the expression, "show, don't tell." This adage encourages us to use images, metaphor, visualization, and the five senses to illustrate what is important in the story, as if we were painting a picture with our words.

The saying that "a picture is worth a thousand words" is even truer in today's image-driven media environment. Effective story-based strategy requires powerful images that communicate the core framing. For instance, many communities fighting the expansion of natural gas extraction (aka fracking) had long complained that gas companies were contaminating their drinking water. The industry denied the claims; then the documentary *Gasland* showed people lighting their tap water on fire,

The "life vest graveyard" outside the UK Parliament, used the "show, don't tell" principle to draw attention to the scale and impact of the European refugee crisis.

creating a memorable image of industrial pollution and discrediting the industry lies.[18] The cognitive dissonance of burning tap water continues to be a powerful image communicating the dangers of fracking and gas development.

Images can be a powerful way to make numbers and data come to life. In September 2016 activists filled Parliament Square in London with over 2,500 life vests worn by refugees who had made the treacherous journey across the Mediterranean. The action, created by Snappin' Turtle Productions in conjunction with the London Mayor's office and refugee organizations, was timed as the United Nations convened its first-ever Summit for Refugees and Migrants. At a time when anti-migrant and xenophobic sentiments were gaining traction in the discourse, the powerful imagery helped humanize refugees and show the scale of the crisis. The graveyard drew attention to the nearly 7,000 people who had drowned in the previous 18 months trying to cross the Mediterranean to reach the European Union.[19]

This basic approach of translating unseen impacts into clear visuals is a common template: from placing crosses to mark unacknowledged deaths to using visual metaphors to capture scale. For instance: "The U.S. military budget is so large that if you lined it up as $1 bills end to end around the equator it would encircle the planet nearly one and a half times."[20]

Another important aspect of "show, don't tell" is to present your story in such a way as to allow the audience to reach their own conclusion, rather than "telling" your audience what to believe. Preachy is not persuasive. For example, there are over 10,000 different chemicals in cosmetics and personal care products; less than 11 percent of them have ever been tested for the effects on human health and the environment.[21] There is mounting evidence that many of these chemicals could be linked to birth defects, miscarriages, and cancer. The Campaign for Safe Cosmetics is a coalition of women's, environmental justice, and health organizations working to remove known toxins from everyday personal care products and to create a cancer-free economy.[22]

The information about cancer-causing cosmetics could be presented with long lists of chemical formulas and graphs of data from toxicity studies, but the Safe Cosmetics Campaign knew that it would not communicate the message effectively. They needed a good story. CSS (then known as *smart*Meme) worked with the campaign to develop a story-based strategy around a powerful metaphor that *shows* what the issue really means. The strategy was launched with an ad (below) highlighting the sympathetic character of a little girl to invoke the values of parental responsibility as a challenge to irresponsible corporate behavior. Most importantly, instead of trying to *tell* people about the issue of toxic chemicals, the ad shows people the issue through the use of a well-known metaphor for recklessness: "playing with matches." By connecting your issue to ideas your audience already understands, the right metaphor can effectively *show* your message and avoid lots of ineffective *telling*. When working to make new information accessible, look for things people already know (beliefs, values, metaphors) that you can use to connect them to the issue.

Advertisement created by *smart*Meme (designed by J. Cookson) for the Safe Cosmetics Campaign in 2004.

The ad was used as part of a **narrowcasting** strategy to leverage the campaign's limited resources to have maximum impact by targeting a specific audience of industry leaders. This is sometimes called "fishbowling your target" because you place your campaign all around the target—as if the target where a fish placed in its proverbial bowl—so since they see the message everywhere they go, they assume the message is everywhere. The ad ran in *USA Today* but only in the New York City edition, which made it much less expensive than a national ad buy. The ad was timed to run when 20,000 cosmetics industry leaders from around the world were gathered in New York for a conference. *Smart*Meme chose *USA Today*, even though few New Yorkers read it, because the newspaper is delivered free to every hotel room throughout the conference area and thus every out-of-town cosmetics executive got it slipped under their hotel door.

The same day the ad ran in the newspaper, activists infiltrated the conference and stealthily distributed copies of the ad around the premises. Soon the campaign was the talk of the conference, particularly since the ad named three specific companies and demanded that they reformulate their products to remove toxic chemicals. By the final day of the conference an industry lobbyist had even included the ad in their presentation in order to alert their fellow executives to a powerful new public opinion campaign demanding reform from the industry. Within several weeks of the conference, all three of the targeted companies had started to respond to the campaign's demands.

3.9 Foreshadowing

What we call the beginning is often the end. And to make an end is to make a beginning. The end is where we start from.
—T.S. Elliot

An underlying premise of modern advertising is that people can only go somewhere that they have already been in their minds. This rings true for social change narratives too! Our stories must offer a compelling vision of the changes we want.

Foreshadowing is a literary device in which an author drops subtle hints about plot developments to come later in the story. Incorporating foreshadowing into social change narratives means offering vision, posing solutions to the problem we're highlighting, and including the future in our narrative frame. How will the conflict come to resolution? What is our vision for a solution to this problem? What does a better world look, feel, and taste like? When we forecast the future we desire, we invite people to imagine and embrace a visionary solution.

Foreshadowing is essential for taking on one of the most common control mythologies: "There Is No Alternative" or TINA. The term was coined by Margaret Thatcher—the leader of Britain's Conservative Party throughout the 1980s—but it is undoubtedly an ancient strategy of manipulation. The TINA narrative acknowledges that the controversial proposal in question is not ideal, but it is the only realistic option, and so it must move forward. The subtler version that often crops up sounds like: "Don't let the perfect be the enemy of the good." This control myth, in whatever form it's used, shuts down political imagination and attempts to derail more transformative solutions before they can even be generated. When viewed through a narrative lens, however, TINA is vulnerable to a foreshadowing strategy that offers viable prefigurative suggestions for other ways of doing things.

The Klamath River begins in a series of wetlands and lakes in Southeastern Oregon and winds through the mountains of Northern California to drain into the Pacific Ocean. For thousands of years the river's abundant salmon runs anchored the regional ecosystem and provided the foundation for local indigenous cultures, including the Yurok, Karuk, Hoopa, and Klamath peoples. When white settlers arrived and displaced many of the Native peoples, the U.S. government allowed a private utility to build six dams on the river, blocking 350 miles of salmon habitat and driving the catastrophic decline of the river and its fish population. In addition to generating electricity, the dams also became part of the irrigation system for the white farmers in the Upper basin.

Incorporating foreshadowing into social change narratives means offering vision, posing solutions to the problem we're highlighting, and including the future in our narrative frame.

For years, the local tribes, environmentalists, and commercial fishers had feuded over how to address the dwindling stock of salmon. As conditions worsened the historic adversaries realized that their only chance of restoring the basin was to work together. Starting in 2004 CSS (then known as *smart*Meme) began working with a coalition of the four tribes, environmentalists, and commercial fishermen to explore a possible campaign to remove the outdated dams. The dams had been in place for generations, and given the historic marginalization of many of the local communities, it was hard to imagine the dams would ever be removed. The campaign needed to foreshadow a future of the river and salmon running free, and the abundance that it would create for all of the region's communities. CSS facilitated the various stakeholders through a story-based strategy process and the shared narrative that emerged focused on the demand to "Bring the Salmon Home." This vision, which encapsulated the coalition's call to restore the

Average height of a Klamath River dam: 84 feet

Average height a salmon can jump: 6 feet

A direct-mail piece created by *smart*Meme (designed by J. Cookson) for a coalition of Native American tribes and their allies in Northern California as part of the campaign to "Bring the Salmon Home" by removing dams on the Klamath River.

salmon's natural habitat, communicated the interdependence between all the cultures in the basin and a healthy salmon run.

The campaign launched by sending out the mail piece (above) to local communities. The piece uses the "show, don't tell" principle to effectively frame the conflict as dams versus salmon. The mailer doesn't say, "Dams are bad!" Rather it explains the impact of the dams on the salmon and lets the reader draw their own conclusions. When combined with foreshadowing the return of the salmon, the mailer offers a hopeful narrative that invites the audience to expand their sense of what's possible. The alliance's story-based strategy helped reframe people's understanding of the conflict from "farmers versus fish" to the "power company versus rural communities." Eventually, as this new story gained momentum, it shifted the debate enough that even the farmers, a historic adversary, joined the alliance to find solutions that would work for everyone.

Over the next decade Klamath residents lead a multipronged campaign that overcame powerful corporations, one of the world's richest men (Warren Buffett), the federal government and state governments of California and Oregon, and, most significantly, the ingrained belief that real change was impossible. The campaign is on track for a historic victory by 2020: one of the largest dam removals in world history and a new era of cultural and ecological restoration in one of California's most important remaining salmon rivers.

While presenting a compelling solution is important, this doesn't mean foreshadowing has to only be positive. Foreshadowing a scary future can also draw attention to the consequences and urgency of an issue. For instance, when internet freedom advocates wanted to rally opposition to two bills in the U.S. Congress that threatened online freedom of speech, they called for a coordinated shut down of websites to foreshadow a potential future of internet censorship. January 18, 2012, became known as "The Day the Internet Went Dark" after over 100,000 websites, including high-profile sites like Wikipedia, Google, and Craigslist, blacked out their homepages.[23] Many of the websites provided mechanisms to comment on the proposals, and over 14 million people contacted their elected representatives on that one day alone.[24] Due to the outpouring of public opposition, the bills were withdrawn.

People often ask: Should our narrative focus more on the problem, or more on the solution? Foreshadowing solutions is critical to making change seem attractive and possible. As advertising shows, positive sells: marketers don't bombard us with visions of broken, decrepit products. But social change isn't a product, and audiences that don't feel impacted by the problem are unlikely to care much about a campaign's proposed solutions. As many political campaigns show, fear is also a powerful mobilizer. Going negative can be risky, but sometimes it is strategic. Ultimately, it all goes back to understanding the cornerstones of the strategy (Section 3.1). There is no one-size-fits-all answer; communities, political circumstances, and campaigns vary. But an effective story-based strategy must find the right balance of visionary and dystopian possibilities that will inspire the target audiences to engage.

3.10 Challenging Assumptions

Why is it, when you see a black kid in a hoodie you think thug, but when you see a white kid in a hoodie you think Mark Zuckerberg?
—Van Jones

A narrative power analysis helps us understand that underlying assumptions are one of the most important aspects of any narrative. This is because assumptions are what we have to believe, in order to believe the story is true. Please reread that sentence. It is very important.

Oftentimes the assumptions are not stated in the story but they are the embedded ideas that make the story function. The underlying assumptions are what are "between the lines" of the story—the unstated, implicit ideas which provide the narrative's coherence and meaning. This is often

**McPoverty Wages
No Thank You**

The #ChangeTheMcStory viral video used story-based strategy to challenge the assumption that fast-food workers are temporary workers who don't need a living wage.

how historic systems of oppression like racism, sexism, or homophobia play out in a narrative. So, if you are trying to change a story, the best place to start is by identifying the underlying assumptions that allow it to operate as truth, and devising a strategy to challenge and reframe those assumptions. Challenging the assumptions of your opponent's story is often one of the most effective ways to reframe an issue.

In 2015 CSS produced the #ChangeTheMcStory video supporting the McDonald's workers organizing with the Fight for $15 campaign for better wages and unionization. The short video parodies McDonald's advertising and repurposes their signature Mc prefix to describe the problem of McPoverty wages. (See Section 4.12 for more insights on **brand-busting**.) The story is told from the perspective of a struggling worker named Angie and was designed to challenge some of the underlying assumptions of the anti-wage-increase narrative, specifically the central assumption propagated by the industry: that most fast-food workers are teenagers and not long-term workers with families to support.

The reality, of course, is that the vast majority of workers (88 percent by some counts) who would benefit from a federal minimum wage increase are adults. Naturally, many of them are supporting families, as the video shows when Angie kisses her sleeping child and heads off to her early morning shift. By challenging assumptions about the identities and lives of fast-food and other low-wage workers, the campaign is communicating that all workers require and deserve a living wage. The video was widely distributed through the Fight for $15 movement and was viewed by over 3 million people, helping to promote cultural acceptance of a $15 minimum wage.[25]

Homosexuality is found in over 1,500 species. Homophobia is found in only one. Which one seems UNNATURAL now?

Another common way to expose an assumption is to expand the frame. A traditional justification (either stated or unstated) for homophobic and anti-LGBTQ policies is that homosexuality is "unnatural." The slogan to the left is an example of challenging this hateful narrative by

Re:Imagining Change

dramatically expanding the frame with new information. The reframing uses the latest scientific research to show that homosexuality is actually very common in nature, found in over 1,500 species,[26] whereas humans are the only species that has been observed being homophobic. By putting "natural" in the larger, logical context beyond just the human species, it shows that the concept isn't something bigots can arbitrarily wield to justify discrimination. This expansion of the frame challenges the assumption of what is normal and changes the story to show the real problem is homophobia.

Another common way to expose an assumption is to expand the frame.

There is a long tradition of using humor to challenge underlying assumptions, even around the most serious life and death issues. Indeed, comedy and satire are some of the most potent forces for critique and resistance under oppressive regimes. Late-night comics can often get more support for their takedowns of the powerful than the average straight news journalist. Our colleagues at Intelligent Mischief—a creative action design lab—used parody and satire to expose the racist assumptions underlying police violence and anti-Black racism. In the wake of the 2012 murder of African-American teenager Trayvon Martin and similar shootings of unarmed Black people, Intelligent Mischief produced the *Black Body Survival Guide*, a multimedia compilation of satirical tips for "surviving in the U.S. as the owner of a Black body." With insights like "Tip #7 Keep your hands up at all times," and "Tip #48 Have every possible form of ID with you at all times," the guide uses humor to challenge the dominant narrative of a "post-racial" America. In the words of the project tagline: "When the problems of race become absurd it's time to get (Sur)real!"

Assumptions are the glue that holds narrative together and, thus, learning to identify and articulate unstated assumptions in narratives is a critical skill for story-

Tip 1: Wear a customized "I am not a threat" t-shirt.

This example from Intelligent Mischief's *Black Body Survival Guide* uses humor to expose racist assumptions in the dominant narrative. See more at theblackbodysurvivalguide.com.

- **Identifying the Elements of Your Issue:** Use the Battle of the Story framework to workshop an issue you care about. Identify the elements for each side. What is the conflict? Who are the characters and what roles do they play on the drama triangle? Identify images, foreshadowing, and the underlying assumptions that inform the story. Who has the better story?
- **Making Headlines:** A news story's headline can capture (or distort!) the essence of a story. A good headline tells us what's important (usually who, what, and why) and makes us want to read more. Check out a popular news publication for inspiration. Which headlines make you want to read more? What makes them good? Now brainstorm some headlines that communicate your story.

based strategists to cultivate. Chapter IV will return to the issue to explore intervening and changing the story. The flip side of challenging unstated assumptions in oppressive narratives is to understand the assumptions underlying our own stories, which we will discuss in the next section.

3.11 Designing a Framing Narrative

> *It is in speaking their world that people, by naming the world, transform it.*
> —Paulo Freire

The previous sections have provided examples of how the different elements of story play out in campaigns and actions. Hopefully, these examples will inform and inspire readers who are developing their own story-based strategies.

Once your group has identified the overt elements of your story (conflict, characters, images, foreshadowing) the next step is to identify your own underlying assumptions. These assumptions are often the shared values and core beliefs of your organization, coalition, or alliance. For instance: "all people should be guaranteed basic human rights" or "nature has intrinsic value and should be protected for future generations."

Just as the work of identifying the underlying assumptions of the story you seek to change can surface the unstated (and at times unspeakable) values of your opponent, the work of identifying your own underlying assumptions may surface some tensions in your own group. Ultimately though, identifying shared assumptions will deepen group alignment and help clarify the battle of the story the group will wage together.

With your core values articulated and the elements of your story in place, your next step is to synthesize these elements into a **framing narrative**. This is the part of the story-based strategy process where creativity, strategy, imagination, and political savvy all have to converge to create a compelling and effective narrative.

First, review the cornerstones to ensure the goals, audience, target, and constituency are anchoring your process. Next, examine your narrative power analysis and specifically the work that has been done on the battle of the story. What is the central conflict of their story? Why are your opponents choosing to emphasize some facts and not others? Who are their heroes, victims, and villains? Where are they getting traction, and where does their framing fall short or reveal potential weaknesses that could be exploited to reframe their narrative to our advantage?

Striking the right tone for a story-based strategy can be one of the most critical and dynamic parts of crafting a framing narrative. How do you want the story to feel? Hopeful? Heartbreaking? Enlivening? Motivational?

When you compare the battle of the story elements side by side you may see similar characters or images being used by both sides. In these cases it's important to reconsider how to reframe and differentiate your frame from your opponent's. Remember, just saying that their story is a lie is not enough, you must tell your own story in powerful and compelling terms. Arguing with your opponent's narrative while not offering a better one is a recipe for failure.

The process of synthesizing the framing narrative often requires multiple iterations and collective commitment to experimentation. Designing your framing narrative is both a creative and a political process: what facts are inside the frame? Who is not part of this story? What must be emphasized to offer a new angle on our issue? What can't be left out or compromised? For many grassroots groups, this process of prioritization leads to difficult but essential decisions that can ripple out beyond the narrative to influence broader aspects of your campaign or organization.

The most important thing to remember is that all of the elements of the story should reinforce each other to connect seamlessly into a coherent story. As you brainstorm images, develop slogans, and hone your messaging, these elements must adhere to a common **narrative logic**: a coherent, cumulative narrative arc that produces cognitive *consonance* (as opposed to cognitive dissonance) in the minds of your audience. In other words, the story has got to make sense! Don't mix metaphors. Your narrative has to be consistent across all of your platforms, even if it is expressed with different framing for different audiences. Keep the story focused by emphasizing the important details and letting the other ones fade to the background.

Maintaining a common narrative logic takes discipline, especially when you have a diverse group with many creative ideas. You must be vigilant about choosing your framing of the conflict and keeping this frame at the forefront, choosing the right **meta-verb(s)** (see Section 3.12) and developing the appropriate spokespeople as the leading characters in the narrative.

After the appropriate amount of group strategizing it's often helpful to delegate a person or smaller subgroup to synthesize the framing narrative. Usually this takes the form of an internal, living document that builds on the cornerstones and important aspects of the narrative power analysis to articulate the campaign's core framing and all the elements of story that populate the frame. Ideally, it is a compelling narrative that engages the target audience by defining a problem and inviting them to be part of the solution. This articulation of your story-based strategy provides the overall messaging for all campaign activities as well as the fodder for talking points, slogans, and other materials. An effective framing narrative can help unify many areas of an initiative: campaign strategy, organizing, alliance building, communications, fundraising, as well as group cohesion and morale. Chapter V provides examples of story-based strategies in action and Section 5.6 provides an example of a framing narrative.

Sometimes the framing narrative doesn't jell on the first or even the tenth try. While getting your story right is important, creative synthesis is a process and integrating new elements that emerge is part of the process. Don't be afraid to test multiple ideas and see what sticks or what new angles appear.

The battle of the story tool is not a one-time exercise—it is a framework for ongoing strategic thinking. As your campaign's framing narrative spreads in the real world you should carefully evaluate the impacts, adapt to new conditions, and iterate as needed.

Remember: as story-based strategists, we aren't just telling stories—we are *changing* stories. More often than not, this means challenging stereotypes and dominant cultural assumptions. There are strategic considerations and values-based choices about how to meet short-term campaign objectives, while also achieving longer-term, transformational goals of shifting the dominant culture. These are political calculations you must make within your own circumstance and principles.

Re:Imagining Change

F.R.A.M.E.S. NARRATIVE CHECKLIST

How do you know if you've created a good framing narrative? Compare it to this handy checklist,[27] because an effective narrative F.R.A.M.E.S. the issue.

F = Frame the Issue
Does your narrative set the terms for understanding the issue? Does it reinforce the vision and values that you are promoting? Framing means defining the problem: explaining what's at stake and defining the solution. Don't communicate your tactics–what you are doing–but rather *why* you are doing it.

R = Reframe Opponent's Story and Reinforce Your Frame
Make sure your narrative is not just reiterating your opponent's frame. Reframing means changing the terms of the debate on the issue: Does your narrative elevate new characters, redefine the issue with different values, or expose a faulty assumption of your opponent?

A = Accessible to the Audience
Will your narrative work for the audience(s) you are trying to persuade? Is it presented with language, context and values that will be appealing to them? Your narrative should always be factual, but it may need to be tailored. Finding the right messengers to deliver the message can help make it credible.

M = Meme
Can you encapsulate your narrative's core messages into effective memes? They need be memorable, easy to spread, and sticky. Is there a powerful metaphor that captures the essence of the issue? Is there an existing meme that you can reference or remix, such as a popular catchphrase or well-known idea? Paragraphs don't spread, but phrases do. If you aren't distilling your narrative into core memes you risk letting your opposition's memes define you.

E = Emotional
People don't swing into action because of a pie chart. An effective narrative should connect to real-world impacts and speak in the language of values. Engage your audience's emotions with themes like hope, anger, tragedy, and determination. Humor (as long as it strikes the right tone) can be a powerful way to make your narrative memorable.

S = Simple and Short
This doesn't mean dumb down your narrative, it means, get to the core essence of the issue. Why does it matter to your audience? As journalists say, "Don't bury the lead!" Or less famously, "Simplify, then exaggerate."[28]

3.12 Action Logic and Meta-Verbs

Change will come. As always, it is just a matter of who determines what that change will be.
—Winona LaDuke

Social change narratives, almost by definition, involve action: articulating the actions needed to address a problem (Rebuild, Save, Stop), inviting our audiences to take action (Divest, March, Share), and the action that will drive the plot of our unfolding campaign (Resist, Defend, Elect).

Two concepts that can help keep the focus on action while designing a framing narrative are the related ideas of **action logic** and **meta-verbs.** Action logic means that the campaign's actions—both physical and metaphorical—have an overarching clarity of purpose that is self-evident enough to communicate the narrative. Verbs are the action words, so inevitably a framing narrative will rely on a few core verbs. These are called meta-verbs, because they should help explain everything else that is happening and convey the essence of the demands of the campaign.

The action logic is how an action makes sense politically to an outside observer. Having clear action logic means that people who witness the action will be able to understand the significance of what is happening, even if they don't have any background information. Honing your action logic can ensure the narrative is accessible to the widest possible audience and create the kind of powerful stories that move hearts and change minds.

The Occupy Wall Street movement was built around the meta-verb of "occupying" to communicate the action logic that Wall Street's unchecked power needed to be directly confronted.

Although a narrative may have several meta-verbs that anchor the action logic, a specific campaign moment is frequently summarized with shorthand of a single action-oriented meta-verb that is part of how the action or campaign is publicized. The meta-verb you choose—Protest! Rally! Shut down! Mobilize! Stop! Transform!—will likely become the benchmark for success, not only to the participants, but also to media observers and the general public. If you are planning a "march on" something, it better be big and loud and colorful, whereas a "vigil" can be small and intimate. If you said "shut down" many people will want to know: Did you actually succeed in shutting your target down?

History is full of famous examples of action logic with clear meta-verbs: The Montgomery Bus *Boycott* of 1955, the WTO Protests in 1999 ("*Shut down* the WTO!"), and "*Levitate* the Pentagon" of 1967 (well, sometimes the action logic takes some imagination).

A potent example of effective action logic and meta-verbs was the rise of Occupy Wall Street (OWS) in the aftermath of the 2009 economic recession. OWS began in 2011 as a call, inspired by the dramatic uprisings of the Arab Spring and Spain's anti-austerity Indignados Movement, to physically occupy Wall Street. The action birthed an ongoing encampment near the actual Wall Street in Lower Manhattan's Zuccotti Park, which served as a continuous protest highlighting extreme economic inequality. OWS galvanized mass outrage about the financial sector's role in triggering the economic recession and the corrupt political system that had failed to hold banks accountable. As the occupy meme spread, encampments sprung up in nearly a thousand cities in over 80 countries and protest chants of "Banks got bailed out! We got sold out!" echoed around the world.[29]

OWS's clear action logic named Wall Street as a systemic villain and highlighted the urgent need to transform the failing neoliberal economy. Occupy was a powerful intervention that touched millions of people and dramatically influenced the entire economic discourse. The wave of occupations popularized useful new memes, including the distinction between "the 99%" of the population suffering through the economic recession and the wealthiest "1%" who reap the benefits of the economic system.

But just as Occupy's action logic and meta-verb anchored a powerful mobilizing narrative, it also created challenges for growing the scope of the movement. OWS started in New York City, where Wall Street provided what our colleagues at the Design Studio for Social Intervention call "the symbol and the thing."[30] The physical address of Wall Street as the universally recognized epicenter of finance and banking provided the perfect proxy for the entire economic system. But with the hundreds of physical encampments that were "occupying," but not occupying the actual Wall Street, the logic of holding big banks accountable was less self-evident. Encampments at federal buildings and town squares carried the message of outrage and opposition to the status quo, but the tactic of "occupation" often failed to communicate the specific critique.

> **Having clear action logic means that people who witness the action will be able to understand the significance of what is happening, even if they don't have any background information.**

Additionally, maintaining radically democratic physical occupations in the face of government harassment, cold weather, and social divisions is an incredibly challenging task. In many areas, local organizing became fixated on merely sustaining the encampments as a yardstick for success. The occupy meta-verb devolved into a focus on maintaining the tactic that often overshadowed the purpose of the occupations as an intervention in the broader system.

Although local authorities used the police to forcibly remove almost all the remaining encampments by early 2012, the Occupy Movement had powerful long-term impacts. From shifting discourse, to politicizing tens of thousands of new activists, to bolstering numerous local initiatives for economic and racial justice, the spirit of Occupy Wall Street lives on and will no doubt resurface in some new form.[31]

The moral of this telling of the story is: chose your meta-verbs wisely! Your meta-verbs should communicate a clear action logic that anchors all your actions in a broader narrative. If you are successful, your framing narrative will spread and inspire others. Plan for success. The action logic should communicate as much as possible about the problem, your vision and the tone of the story you want to tell. As Occupy Wall Street shows, the right action logic can help spread a narrative far and wide, but as conditions change it is important to find ways to evolve your action logic and ensure your meta-verbs aren't limiting the next phase of your story. In the next chapter we will further explore how to use interventions of all types to win the battle of the story. ■

"If there is no struggle, there is no progress. Those who profess to favor freedom and yet deprecate agitation, are men who want crops without plowing up the ground, they want rain without thunder and lightning. They want the ocean without the awful roar of its many waters. This struggle may be a moral one, or it may be a physical one, and it may be both moral and physical, but it must be a struggle. Power concedes nothing without a demand. It never did and it never will."

—Frederick Douglass

"Nothing happens in the 'real' world unless it first happens in the images in our heads."

—Gloria E. Anzaldúa

IV

Points of Intervention

4.1 Social Change as Intervention

Imagination is intervention, an act of defiance.
It alters belief.
—David Mura

You want to take action to change a story that is hurting your community . . . but how? Whether you're targeting a specific brand narrative put forward by a powerful corporation or resisting racist policies rooted in generations of oppressive assumptions, it can be a daunting task to take your story off the flipchart and into the streets.

After using the **battle of the story** tool to deconstruct the story you want to change and to construct the narrative you want to spread, the next dimension of the **story-based strategy** model is taking action at **points of intervention (POI)**.

Intervention is an action meant to change the course of events. It can take many forms, but generally means interacting or interfering with a situation, physical space, institution, audience, social structure, system, or narrative, with the intent of shifting popular understanding. Often this is called taking "direct action." Direct action is an age-old method to make positive changes in the world by acting directly as an individual, group, or a community rather than waiting for some intermediary to do something. From a community putting up their own radio transmitter to give voice to local residents, to mass civil disobedience to physically shut down a corporate war profiteer, to reclaiming public land to grow food, direct action is an established, common-sense remedy for social problems.

Intervention is a useful general term for this direct action spirit to capture any effort where people step out of their traditional, scripted roles (passive consumers, spectators, disempowered nobodies, etc.) and challenge the dominant expectation of obedience. Intervention is often a tactic within a broader strategy, but it also represents a political ethic of creating fundamental change at the deepest levels of power relations. When a creative intervention is effective, it can shift power relationships and leave an imprint of new possibilities on the collective imagination.

Intervention is one of the easiest and most effective ways to change a story. Social change forces don't have equal access to the privately owned infrastructure of mass media and communication, thus we often need to creatively tell our stories through our actions. In the classic words of the progressive radio news commentator Wes "Scoop" Nisker: "If you don't like the news, go out and make some of your own."[1]

Points of intervention are specific places in a system where a targeted action can effectively interrupt the functioning of the system and open up opportunities for change.

By understanding these different points, organizers can develop a strategy that identifies the best places to intervene in order to have the greatest impact.

Narrative Power Analysis reminds us that interventions at physical points can go beyond disrupting a system to pose a deeper challenge to underlying assumptions and legitimacy.

Social movements have traditionally intervened at physical points in the systems that shape our lives: the **point of production** where goods are produced (such as a factory or farm), the **point of destruction** where resources are extracted or an injustice is most visible (such as a coal mine or a site of police brutality), the **point of consumption** where products are purchased (such as a store or ticket counter) and the **point of decision** where the **power-holders** are located (such as a corporate headquarters or a politician's office).

Well-designed interventions at physical points can go beyond simply disrupting a system to pose a deeper challenge to its underlying assumptions and perceived legitimacy. This holds true whether it is a physical system, such as fossil fuel extraction, or an ideological system like racism, sexism, or market fundamentalism. Through the lens of story-based strategy, we can see points of intervention that operate not only in physical space, but also within dominant narratives. Chapter IV will provide some more tangible examples of each of these interventions in the following sections.

Points of Intervention are the places in a system where taking action can make change. Social movements have a long history of taking action where production, consumption, destruction, or decision-making is happening. Story-based strategy helps us expand these efforts to envision interventions into the narratives that shape popular understanding by taking action at the point of assumption.

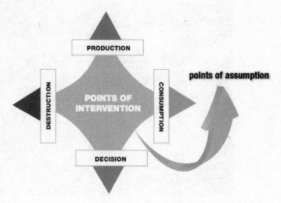

4.2 Point of Production

> *If the workers took a notion they could stop all speeding trains;*
> *Every ship upon the ocean they can tie with mighty chains.*
> *Every wheel in the creation, every mine and every mill;*
> *Fleets and armies of the nation, will at their command stand still.*
> —Joe Hill, labor organizer executed by the state of Utah in 1915

Action at the point of production is the foundational insight of the labor movement. Workers organize to target the economic system where it directly affects them, and where that system is most vulnerable—at the site of production. Strikes, picket lines, work slowdowns, and factory takeovers are all common point-of-production actions. Other points of production are factory farms or facilities where new products or technologies are created. Strikes like the famous 1937 sit-down strike in Flint, Michigan, have been instrumental to expanding worker organizing and building unions. This spirit lives on today as in 2008 when over 200 workers at the Republic Windows and Doors factory in Chicago responded to their bankrupt company's plan to not pay them their wages (a violation of federal labor law) by occupying their shuttered factory. It was at the beginning of the so-called Great Recession and the dramatic intervention immediately won widespread public support, including from then President-elect Barack Obama! After six days, the action won new concessions from the company's creditors and the workers received their just compensation. The workers continued organizing and eventually launched their own cooperatively owned, worker-run factory, New Era Windows, in 2013.[2]

The 1937 Flint sit-down strike is an iconic moment in U.S. labor history. By occupying and stopping production at three General Motors factories for over six weeks, workers won recognition of their union, the United Auto Workers.

4.3 Point of Destruction

Find something that you love that they're f*cking with and then fight for it.
—David Gessner

A point of destruction is where harm or an injustice is actually occurring in its most blatant form. It could be the place where industrial resource extraction like mining, drilling, or logging is happening, or the site of obvious oppression like the location of a police shooting. The point of destruction can also be the place where the waste from the point of pro-

Starting in 1987, members of the Penan indigenous resistance in the Malaysian state of Sarawak blockaded illegal logging roads built in their traditional homelands. The Penan's movement to protect the rainforests helped inspire North American direct action techniques of tree sitting and road blockades to stop industrial logging.

Re:Imagining Change

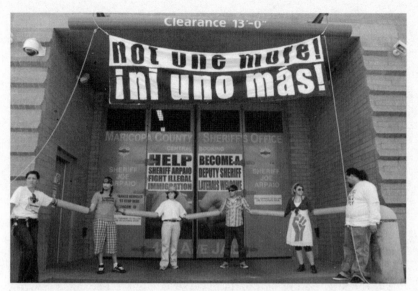

A community-led blockade in Phoenix, Arizona, targets a point of destruction: shutting down notorious racist Sheriff Arpaio's jail to prevent harassment of undocumented residents.

duction is dumped—an effluent pipe in a river, diesel emissions along a trucking route, or a leaky toxic waste dump.

Intervening at a specific point of destruction can be an effective strategy for exposing a broader systemic problem. For instance in 2010 Arizona passed SB 1070, a draconian, anti-immigrant law allowing police to racially profile and demand people show proof-of-citizenship or risk immediate arrest pending possible deportation. On the first day that it was to be implemented, community members and allies in Phoenix blockaded the jail of infamous racist Sheriff Joe Arpaio to prevent him making any arrests. The action showed the world that Arizonians would not allow racist attacks on undocumented community members to go unchallenged.[3]

It is critical to bring public attention to the point of destruction because it is almost always (by design) out of the public eye. In many cases, the point of destruction is made invisible by distance, oppressive assumptions, or ignorance. Power-holders have a long track record of locating extractive operations and polluting facilities in communities with less political power. From remote rural and wilderness areas, to polluted inner cities, impacted communities frequently mobilize to take action at the point of destruction.

Intervention at this point can halt the practice in the moment, as well as dramatize the larger battle of the story around the issue.

4.4 Point of Consumption

Consumerism turns us all into junk-ies.
—Earon Davis

The point of consumption is the place where we interact with a product or service that is linked to injustice. Point of consumption actions are the traditional arena of consumer boycotts and storefront demonstrations. Examples include: the civil rights movement's sit-ins at the Woolworth's lunch counters to confront legalized racial segregation, protesting fossil fuel dependency at gas stations, or efforts to change purchasing habits with **memes** like "sweatshop free," "dolphin-safe tuna," and "fair trade." The point of consumption is often the most accessible point of intervention in our consumerist society. Point of consumption actions can also be an effective way to influence public opinion around an issue or get the attention of corporate power-holders when lawmakers aren't listening.

Over the past two decades, "markets campaigns" have emerged as a model that aims to shift the dynamics of an industry by shutting down the market for destructive products:[5] This strategy goes beyond **brand-busting** (see Section 4.12) and operates with a comprehensive analysis of an industry and its key institutional players. Campaigners have effectively pressured retailers, investors, shareholders, wholesale suppliers, subcontractors, and other links in the chain of production, destruc-

Workers and community allies affiliated with the OURWalmart (Organization United for Respect at Walmart) protested at over 1,000 Walmart stores on Black Friday 2012 (the biggest shopping day of the year). By targeting the point of consumption they leveraged their campaign for higher wages and more dignified working conditions.[4]

tion, and consumption, to meet their demands. Human rights activists have confronted retailers selling sweatshop products. Labor unions have organized workers in the supply chain of their target companies. Forest defenders have pressured companies to stop purchasing wood and paper from old growth forests. Public health crusaders have targeted cosmetics and chemical companies with actions aimed at impacting brand profiles and eroding market share. Intervention at the point of consumption is often useful for creating economic pressure on a campaign target.

4.5 Point of Decision

Change means movement. Movement means friction. Only in the frictionless vacuum of a nonexistent abstract world can movement or change occur without that abrasive friction of conflict.
—Saul Alinsky

The point of decision is the location of the power-holders who possess the ability to meet the campaign's demand. Whether taking over a slumlord's office, bursting into a corporate boardroom, or protesting at the state capitol, many successful campaigns have used some form of action at the point of decision to put pressure on the key decision-makers.

The point of decision can seem very self-evident, but power structures aren't always transparent in how they operate. Sometimes a campaign needs to target a decision-maker whose role has not been part of the public discussion. Point-of-decision actions that unmask hidden interests or challenge assumptions about who is responsible for a problem can help reframe an issue. For instance, when community activists fighting an unjust policy don't target the political decision-makers (who perhaps have ignored them) but instead go after their financial backers. Or when a well-known company is held responsible for the actions of a distant subsidiary they own. In these cases action at the point of decision can help tell an important story about how power is operating and what is needed to make change.

In 2011 the proposed Keystone XL pipeline, which was intended to transport Canadian Tar Sands oil into the U.S., was a little-known issue. Indigenous rights and climate activists decided to make it a public flashpoint by exposing President Obama as having ultimate decision-making power over the project. They mobilized over 1,200 people to engage in civil disobedience at the White House and helped galvanize a national movement around the issue. The strategy of making the pipeline a litmus test for the Obama administration's action on climate and targeting

Representatives from Native communities impacted by the Tar Sands and their allies in the Indigenous Environmental Network led mass point-of-decision actions against the Keystone XL Tar Sands pipeline at the White House.[6] © 2011 Shadia Fayne Wood/Survival Media Agency

a specific point of decision helped amplify frontline community voices and build the climate movement. Ultimately the multifaceted campaign forced the U.S. government to reject the project in 2015.

4.6 Point of Assumption

> *People do not change with the times, they change the times.*
> —PK Shaw

The four points of intervention outlined above are interventions in physical space. These points focus on the tangible mechanisms that drive injustice, oppression, and destruction. Historically, social movements have succeeded in winning changes when these physical actions have also changed popular understanding of the issue. This means reframing the problem, building a base of committed people, and winning a critical mass of support for solutions. The end result is a repatterning of popular consciousness to a new story. But how do we make sure our interventions shift the story around the issue in a way that builds the broader momentum for change?

This is where assumptions come back in. Points of intervention within a narrative are called points of assumption because, as we explored in Sections 2.12 and 3.10, the underlying assumptions are what an audience has to be-

INTERVENTION AT THE POINT OF ASSUMPTION

- Reframe Debates
- Offer New Futures
- Create/Subvert Spectacles
- Repurpose Existing Narratives
- Make the Invisible Visible

lieve to interpret the story as true. In order to change stories, we need to shift assumptions because they are the glue that holds the meaning of a narrative together. Assumptions are the building blocks of ideology, the DNA of political beliefs. Many assumptions operate best when they remain unexamined. If the underlying assumptions of a dominant story can be exposed as contrary to people's values or lived experience, belief in the story can be shifted.

Actions at a point of assumption are actions with the explicit goal of changing the story. They focus on intervening in the narratives that obscure, rationalize, or justify the injustices occurring at all the other points. If a point of assumption strategy succeeds it can shift the discourse around an issue and open up new political space. For this reason, the point of assumption is probably the most important of all the points of intervention.

Challenging an assumption is more difficult than merely informing people of something they didn't previously know. People don't easily let go of existing beliefs. Shifting an assumption means altering current understanding and requires getting past the target audience's **narrative filters** (see Section 2.11). To succeed, we must apply a **narrative power analysis** to map out the elements of the story and identify which assumptions we need to target. Since points of assumption within a narrative are often quite ethereal, it can be helpful to combine them with an action at a physical point to make the intervention more tangible.

> **If the underlying assumptions of a dominant story can be exposed as contrary to people's values or lived experience, belief in the story can be shifted.**

The point of assumption plays out in how the specific intervention challenges the dominant story. There are many ways to intervene at the point of assumption. Depending on the situation, it may mean exposing hypocrisy, reframing the issue, offering an alternative vision, or amplifying the voices of previously silenced characters in the story. We will now explore five general strategies for targeting the point of assumption, but these are by no means exhaustive.

4.7 Reframing Debates

The fight is never about grapes or lettuce. It is always about people.
—César Chávez

Winning the battle of the story often requires reframing, which is the process of altering the meaning of the old story to tell a different story. Successful reframing shifts the perspective and changes the terms of the debate. This can happen by widening the frame, narrowing the frame, or moving the frame to another scene entirely. Redefining the debate is the best way to win an argument.

How do you do this? The first step is a thorough narrative power analysis to study how the issue is currently framed, and in particular, to identify the underlying assumptions that are shaping the dominant narrative. For example, you might surface unstated assumptions like: "corporate tax cuts will benefit everyone by growing the economy," or "undocumented migrants should be treated as criminals with no rights," or "U.S. foreign policy benevolently spreads democracy."

From this analysis, you can begin to develop another story that exposes the flawed assumptions of the status quo framing. There are many ways to do this and the elements of story offer different avenues for reframing. For instance, interventions that successfully reframe might amplify new characters who previously haven't been heard, redefine the problem with a different set of values, or pose a new, more compelling solution.

A successful reframe can launch new memes and a whole new narrative around an issue. For instance, successful reframing by workers'

2015 New York protest by restaurant, nail salon, and other workers from New York's Securing Wages Earned Against Theft (SWEAT) Coalition.[7]

Re:Imagining Change

In 1981, visionary environmental activists "cracked" Glen Canyon Dam to challenge the assumption that mega development projects were permanent. This intervention helped reframe the debate around dams and wilderness preservation.

rights advocates has created the "wage theft" meme. Too often workers get cheated by their bosses and get underpaid—or denied pay altogether—for work they have done, such as not getting paid for overtime or getting paid less than the legal minimum wage. This mistreatment of workers used to be referred to as "nonpayment of wages," which was the official terminology used by the U.S. Department of Labor and echoed by the mainstream media. This framing assumes that the wages belong to the employers and it is their prerogative to decide when their workers actually deserve to be paid.

Workers' rights organizations reframed the issue and began calling it "wage theft." This makes it clear that the wages belong to the worker and have been stolen by the boss. This reframing makes the conflict much clearer and encourages us to sympathize with the wronged workers. Through organizing public campaigns, exploited workers and their allies have been successful at turning wage theft into a meme that has entered the broader economic discourse. The term is now routinely used in the media and has even been used in the name of legislation. As with any effective reframing, wage theft is shifting the public understanding of the issue and providing momentum to campaigns to win stronger worker protections.

Sometimes an issue can be reframed with a well-designed intervention in an unexpected and previously uncontested place. In 1981, environmentalists in the western United States were fighting to defend wilderness areas from the assault of industrial extraction and megaprojects like giant dams. The newly formed radical ecology network Earth First! was thinking bigger than the usual protest at the point of destruction. They wanted to challenge the deep-seated narrative of technological progress "conquering" nature. So they decided to confront the assumption that industrial megaprojects like giant dams were permanent, immovable structures and foreshadow a future of undoing damage to the planet.

Their intervention was staged at Arizona's Glen Canyon Dam, the second highest concrete arch dam in the United States. On the anniversary of the dam's opening, the activists unfurled a huge black plastic banner down the face of the dam, visually creating a giant crack, and foreshadowing a day when dams would be removed and rivers restored.

Until their iconic action, the industrial paradigm of humanity dominating nature had rendered the question of removing a mega-dam off limits in the public debate. The "cracking" action challenged that assumption and expanded political space. Decades later, struggles against mega-dams continue around the world. But today, dam removal is increasingly embraced as a solution to restore damaged watersheds and the communities that call them home.

The yellow ribbon has symbolized hoping loved ones return safely from military service since the U.S. Civil War. During the 1979 Iran hostage crisis it became a ubiquitous symbol of public support for the safe return of the U.S. hostages. But over time pro-war forces associated the ribbon and the related "Support our Troops" slogan with overt support for war. The narrative was used to frame critics of both the 1991 and 2003 invasions of Iraq as not supporting the troops. Meme campaigner Andrew Boyd helped launch an alternative narrative combining what had previously been opposing symbols–the antiwar peace symbol and the pro-war yellow ribbon. This new symbol reframes the conflict to show that being antiwar is being pro-troops by adding "bring them home now." It was widely used by the antiwar movement and eventually adopted as the logo of an organization of military families challenging U.S. war policies.

- Read or watch a piece of media relating to an issue you care about and apply a narrative power analysis. How are the elements of story being used to frame the issue? Pay particular attention to the assumptions underlying the current frame.
- Identify shifts you could make to different elements of the story that could reframe the issue.

4.8 Offering New Futures

For all of our ability to analyze and critique, the left has become rooted in what is. We often forget to envision what could be. . . . All organizing is science fiction.
—Walidah Imarisha

One place to find points of assumption is at the point in the story where the endings become contestable—where effective action can forecast a different future. Such vision-driven actions have always been a staple of successful social change. But by understanding them as interventions at a

Reclaiming public space to grow food, sometimes called guerilla gardening, is an example of literally creating a different future. Even if the garden is only temporary it still prefigures a different possibility.

point of assumption we can focus on what has made them successful and work to replicate those aspects. Sometimes, this specific type of intervention is called the Point of Potential to highlight alternatives.

One of the most common assumptions in power-holders' narratives is some version of the "There Is No Alternative" (TINA) **control myth**.[8] (See Section 3.9.) In these instances, the effective articulation of a plausible story about a different future can be a powerful challenge to the status quo narrative, particularly when the alternatives promoted are both "visionary and oppositional."[9]

Actions that contest a seemingly predetermined future are one type of action at the point of assumption. A few examples of this type of intervention include:

- Activists confront agricultural biotechnology and the corporate takeover of the food system by transforming an empty lot into a garden where neighbors can grow healthy, organic food.
- Homes Not Jails activists challenge city officials to provide more housing for low-income families by occupying an abandoned building to create a place for people to live.
- Public housing residents who have been pushing for a better childcare space take action at the local government office, and instead of just protesting, they transform the office into the day care center the community needs.[10]

There are many ways to offer new futures and to reflect choices between the different paths. One of CSS's collaborative, long-term strategy projects explored three competing visions of the future of the San Francisco Bay Area by producing different "newsfeeds" from the year 2030.[11] Each newsfeed portrayed a very different world based on the way social and political forces had responded to the ecological crisis. The newsfeed from the "Grey" scenario—where denial and fossil fuel addiction continue to shape policy—has stories about criminalizing "water poachers," salmon extinction, and increasing militarization. Meanwhile a "Pale Green" scenario revealed a world where efforts to address the ecological crisis fail to confront the social and economic roots of the problem. This newsfeed has stories about dangerous techno-fixes like geoengineering, "gene spill" quarantines, and economic apartheid alongside ads for personalized genetics and luxury eco-homes. Finally the "Gaia" scenario newsfeed shows (on the next page) a 2030 in which social movements lead a just transition away from fossil fuels and features stories about creating a new regional food system, defining the rights of eco-refugees, and struggles to implement an International People's Protocol on climate resilience.

What future are we working toward? CSS created multiple newsfeeds from the year 2030 to spark long-term movement strategy conversations. Design by Micah Bazant

The fundamental question for these types of interventions, in whatever form they occur, is: "What if . . . ?" Even if the action is a symbolic foreshadowing rather than a concrete plan, it can still challenge the status quo narrative by offering glimpses of alternatives. This type of intervention can reframe a problem and open up collective imagination to new ideas, new possibilities, new solutions, and new ways of being.

4.9. Subverting and Creating Spectacles

Disneyland is presented as imaginary in order to make us believe that the rest is real.
—Jean Baudrillard

We live in an age of media saturation where political battles are often waged with clickbait headlines across social media and 24-hour news cycles. In this context, shaping media coverage has become even more important and decision-makers and power-holders often supplement their usual diet of sound bite politics with sophisticated media events. These events range from routine press conferences and rituals like ribbon cuttings to action-

Iraq veterans were among the over 5,000 people who participated in the "Turn Your Back on Bush" mobilization to challenge George W. Bush's 2005 presidential inauguration.

oriented political stunts. Particularly, politicians are now well schooled in how to create effective media spectacle—by choosing powerful locations, appearing with the right supporting characters or engaging in symbolic actions. Spectacles are everywhere in the **popular culture**, and they can provide unique opportunities for creative interventions to change the story.

In the wake of President George W. Bush's 2004 re-election, some creative organizers saw the opportunity to mobilize the disillusioned into the longer-term progressive movement. "Turn Your Back on Bush" was born: a point of assumption action organized by Action Mill, with some support from CSS.[12]

It was clear that the Bush administration's draconian security measures would limit protest along the 2005 inaugural parade route, and that it would be difficult for traditional protest tactics to break out of the media's existing frame. So their action mobilized over 5,000 people to covertly enter the security zone, line the parade route, and then turn their backs on the presidential motorcade as it passed. This form of symbolic protest may seem trivial (given the scale of Bush's crimes against humanity), but it was an action that was targeting a specific point of assumption: the Bush narrative that the election had provided him a "mandate."

The **action logic** of turning your back was clear. It was carried out by thousands of people representing constituencies that Bush was claiming to speak for: veterans, military families, farmers, firefighters and people of faith. The action communicated a mass symbolic withdrawal of consent from Bush's presidency.

Re:Imagining Change

The action effectively subverted the spectacle of Bush's grand triumph and launched a counter story about the broad base of resistance to his policies. The action received major media coverage around the world, and was even the subject of a skit on the popular television program *Saturday Night Live*.

"Turn Your Back on Bush's" simple and unique action logic allowed the protest to go viral as a meme, and reports of Bush being greeted with backs turned in protest emerged from around the country and the world. This action provides an easy, replicable template to subvert any pompous power-holder's spectacle.

Disrupting a presidential spectacle can be as easy as one person bravely acting at the right time. Jennicet Gutiérrez, an undocumented transgender Latina, hijacked the spectacle of President Obama's June 2015 LGBT Pride Month White House reception by interrupting Obama's speech to declare in front of all the gathered guests and media, "Stop the torture and abuse of trans women in detention centers!" Gutiérrez's action was unpopular with many of the primarily white, gay male attendees (described by one journalist as "elite members of the LGBT community") and she was removed by the Secret Service. But the action drew national attention to the abuse of a community that had been largely invisibilized. Particularly since the intervention occurred just days before the highly anticipated Supreme Court ruling in favor of same-sex couples' marriage rights, it was successful in helping to expand the debate about what full human and civil rights for all people should mean.[13]

Story-based strategies don't need to just subvert our opponent's spectacles, creating our own spectacles can be a powerful component of a

Activist Jennicet Gutiérrez intervening in the spectacle of President Obama's LGBT Pride reception in order to highlight abuses of undocumented trans women.

Plastic Jesus's 2016 guerrilla art action used then-candidate Donald Trump's Hollywood star to mock his openly racist campaign to build a giant border wall.

successful intervention. Whether it's a dancing flash mob or a pageant of political theater, a well-designed spectacle can project a clear message and change the story. For example, in 2016 reality TV star, notorious authoritarian demagogue, and future president Donald Trump campaigned on an openly racist and anti-immigrant platform focused on building a wall on the Mexican border. Trump's candidacy was met with many powerful protests and numerous creative actions, including when Los Angeles street artist Plastic Jesus installed a miniature replica wall complete with barbed wire and American flag around Trump's star on the Hollywood Walk of Fame. The wall was only six inches tall but it made a big statement with its own media spectacle mocking both Trump's celebrity and xenophobia.[14] The action shows that creating a spectacle doesn't require large numbers of people or high production values, just a smart story and the right point of intervention.

U.S. athletes Tommie Smith and Juan Carlos (right) captured global headlines by making a Black Power raised fist salute on the medal stand at the 1968 Olympics in Mexico City. This famous action subverted the spectacle of the medal ceremony to make a statement rejecting racism and oppression.[15] Nearly 50 years later in 2016, professional football player Colin Kaepernick (left) drew mass attention to similar issues by refusing to stand for the national anthem, saying, "I am not going to stand up to show pride in a flag for a country that oppresses black people and people of color." Inspired by his example athletes across the country, from students to professionals, began taking similar action and politicizing the common spectacle of sporting events.

ETHICAL SPECTACLE

We live in a world of consumer and political spectacle and much of it is exploitative, manipulative, and deadening. So, when creating your own spectacle, how can you ensure it's not replicating some of the very dynamics you are challenging? Our colleague Stephen Duncombe, cofounder of the Center for Artistic Activism, provides a useful framework in his wonderful book *Dream: Re-Imagining Progressive Politics in an Age of Fantasy*.[16] As he describes it, an ethical spectacle should strive to be:

- Participatory: Seeking to empower participants and spectators alike, with organizers acting as facilitators.
- Open: Responsive and adaptive to shifting contexts and participants' ideas.
- Transparent: Engaging the imagination of spectators without seeking to trick or deceive.
- Realistic: Using fantasy to illuminate and dramatize real-world power dynamics and social relations that otherwise are hidden in plain sight.
- Utopian: Celebrating the impossible—and therefore helping to make the impossible possible.

SELLING THE WORLD BANK ON EBAY

In 2004 activists at the World Bank Bonds Boycott teamed up with CSS (then known as *smart-Meme*) to expose the World Bank's role in perpetuating poverty and injustice. Protest outside the Bank's annual meetings had peaked several years earlier so it was time for a new way to hijack the spectacle of media attention around the Bank's annual fall meeting. CSS decided on a creative intervention and posted the World Bank  for sale on the online auction website eBay. The **action logic** of "Selling 'The World Bank' on eBay" was a humorous way to point out that, contrary to its stated mission, the Bank is actually for sale to the highest bidder. The posting on eBay described the World Bank as "Antiquated: does not work" and generated headlines like: "'World Bank' for sale on eBay—Activists say the bank 'will do a lot less harm to the world gathering dust in your attic'" (CNN) and "'World Bank' Bidding Starts at 30 Cents on eBay" (Reuters). The media stunt used carefully crafted language on the eBay post to embed the substance of the issues into the action, such as explaining the asking price of $0.30 was the average hourly wage of a sweatshop worker in Haiti. This action used a very clear and humorous action logic to engage a serious topic and garner high-profile global press coverage for the campaign.

4.10 Making the Invisible Visible

When you change the way you look at things, the things you look at change.
—Max Planck

Oftentimes, to reframe a story it is necessary to expose aspects of the story that have been hidden; to make what has been invisible to your target audience visible so it will change their understanding of the issue. In 2007, CSS helped Iraq Veterans Against the War (IVAW) design a powerful action at the point of assumption.[17] Their goal was to change the story from the "U.S. is at *war* in Iraq" and therefore must stay until we "win," to the "U.S. is *occupying* Iraq," and the presence of America troops was making the situation worse. They wanted the U.S. public to understand that occupations inevitably create violence and can never be "won."

IVAW knew that simply telling people that the occupation was undemocratic and oppressive wasn't enough. They decided to make the realities of occupation, which were largely *invisible* to the U.S. public, *visible* by showing how occupation actually looks and feels. IVAW's intervention was a series of street theater actions (sometimes called "invisible theater") where their members re-enacted their typical activities on patrol in Iraq. Veterans in uniform, miming their weapons, went on patrol in

Iraq Veterans Against the War made the invisible impacts of the US occupation visible, with their "Operation First Casualty" actions.

Above are two pictures, taken at the same time, of the same innocuous-seeming oil and gas infrastructure. The top image is from a regular camera, while the bottom image is from a FLIR camera that makes invisible pollution visible. Photos courtesy of Earthworks.

U.S. cities, including simulating crowd control actions and civilian arrest operations. IVAW invited the public to consider how they might respond to foreign troops acting in that manner in the U.S. and how it would inevitably lead to violent resistance. To attract more attention and create memorable images they deployed the action in iconic settings like Times Square in New York City and the National Mall in Washington, D.C. They called these actions "Operation First Casualty," after the old adage "the first casualty of war is truth," in order to help the media and the public make the connection. Through these actions IVAW successfully contrasted the first-hand experiences of IVAW members with the propaganda of the Bush administration.

Sometimes making the invisible visible is even more literal, such as when countless community groups expose pollution and its impact with data collection or new technologies. The two images above are of the exact same rural landscape in a region of North Dakota with extensive oil and gas extraction. The image on top is taken with a normal camera while the other is taken with a special FLIR (Forward Looking Infrared) camera which shows otherwise invisible pollution. The FLIR reveals the dark black plume of pollution, invisible to the naked eye, which positively identifies at least one of the approximately 20 pollutants the camera detects. These very expensive types of cameras are used by industry to identify pollution, including potent climate pollutants like methane and known carcinogens like benzene. But in this case the FLIR is being used by thermographers from Earthworks, a nonprofit organization dedicated to protecting communities and the environment from the adverse impacts of energy development. Once they've made the problem visible Earthworks and their community partners can use the images to confront polluters and regulators to demand sustainable solutions.[18]

In 2014 Columbia University student Emma Sulkowicz drew world attention to the frequently invisibilized issue of rape with her act of carrying a 50 lb. dorm mattress everywhere she went for 9 months. The action, which was her senior arts thesis entitled "Mattress Performance (Carry that Weight)," made visible that she was raped by a fellow student and the university's failure to take any action. Her action inspired ongoing solidarity as fellow students helped her carry the mattress as well as national days of action with protests against campus sexual assault at hundreds of universities.[19]

4.11 Repurposing Popular Culture Narratives

*If there's any hope for revolution in America, it lies in getting Elvis
Presley to become Che Guevara.*
—Phil Ochs

The mass familiarity of popular culture can provide unique opportunities
for social change messages to "hitch a ride" on specific memes, metaphors, and cultural narratives. For instance, proposals to tax speculative
financial transactions have been around since the 1930s but they started
getting popular traction after campaigners renamed the proposal the
Robin Hood Tax. The familiar Robin Hood story of taking from the rich
in order to give to the poor is both attention grabbing and provides the
elements of the story to frame the issue. As in the picture below, campaigners could even dress the part to strengthen the connection.[20] When
thinking about an intervention it can be helpful to consider what stories
are universally known among your audience that might offer relevant
metaphors. Maybe your campaign is a David versus Goliath, or a policy
proposal is a Trojan horse situation, or perhaps there is a local legend or
community story that will resonate?

Contemporary pop culture products, such as movies, television programs, commercials, popular music, and viral videos are often promoted
with huge marketing budgets that create familiarity with their characters,
images, and plots. These pop culture narratives are like rivers running
through mainstream culture, splashing across people's consciousness,
shaping workplace small talk, and often creating dedicated communi-

Campaigners for an international financial transaction tax borrow the Robin Hood story
to personify their issue.

Natural Gas

METHane cartels are cooking our planet.
#BreaktheAddiction #FrackingBad

CSS repurposed the imagery of the popular TV show *Breaking Bad* to challenge the natural gas industry narrative and promote an anti-fracking message.

ties of fans. If a campaign can craft a message that floats on the river—without the message being trivialized or submerged—then the campaign might be able to repurpose that existing narrative.

The imagery, characters, and narratives of popular Hollywood franchises like Star Wars, Lord of the Rings, and Harry Potter have all been borrowed and repurposed for social change ends. Likewise social movement imagery and messages often ripple through pop culture and expand our opportunities to include social justice themes in everyday conversations.[21]

The mass familiarity of popular culture can provide unique opportunities for social change messages to "hitch a ride" on specific memes, metaphors, and cultural narratives.

The danger in appropriating popular culture narratives is that the references are ever-changing and ephemeral. Some iconic images and narratives become cultural touchstones that can stand the test of time, while others are fleeting and are quickly replaced by a flurry of media promoting the next Hollywood blockbuster or consumer product. Pop culture may create a common meme for millions of people, but it could soon be yesterday's joke if you don't move fast. In this age of niche marketing and **narrowcasting**, it's important to understand who exactly knows the specific pop culture code you're using and who doesn't.

Timing can be critical. CSS saw an opportunity in the fall of 2013 to harness the cultural moment around the finale of the popular television

Re:Imagining Change

drama *Breaking Bad* to reframe people's understanding of natural gas with an attention-grabbing addiction metaphor. The show itself was about a drug kingpin selling "meth" (as in methamphetamine) so it provided an opportunity to borrow the show's logo and imagery to talk about a different type of dangerous meth: methane, the main component of so-called natural gas. The intervention challenged the gas industry's narrative that gas is cleaner and safer despite the fact that methane is actually 86 times more heat-trapping than carbon dioxide, making it incredibly destructive to the climate.[22]

As CSS's former Senior Associate Danielle Coates-Connor wrote at the time: "Natural gas? Why not call it what it is . . . METHane Gas. These cartels are cooking our planet, contaminating our air and water, destroying rural landscapes and livelihoods, and leaving behind nasty, toxic pollution . . . sound like a meth lab or what?" CSS released the image to a target audience within the youth climate and anti-fracking movements and within days it had been shared by over 100,000 people across the country and became part of the broader cultural conversation around the television show's finale.

In March 2010 Palestinian activists in the West Bank community of Bel'in dressed as the Na'vi, the oppressed, blue Indigenous people who are the protagonists of the global blockbuster movie *Avatar*. (As of 2017 *Avatar* was still the highest grossing film in world history.) The action was part of an ongoing weekly protest against the construction of the Israeli Separation Barrier (called by many an "Apartheid Wall") which had been largely ignored by the world media. But by repurposing a high-profile Hollywood narrative that echoed themes similar to their own struggle, and timing their action to the week the movie was being featured in the Academy Awards, their intervention drew global attention. Does a pop culture link trivialize a life-or-death situation? Is it worth risking minimizing your issue to help it break through a media blackout? These are important strategy questions to carefully explore when considering using a pop culture hook.

- **Surfacing Assumptions:** Make a list of some assumptions in the dominant culture you think need to be changed. You can carry this assumption list with you and keep a running tab of times when they show up, and track new destructive assumptions that surface in your work.
- **Intervention:** Chose one particularly toxic assumption and think about actions you could take to challenge it. When and where do you encounter the assumption? Are there physical points of intervention that could be used to expose this assumption? Are there institutions that perpetuate it or vehicles that replicate it in popular culture? What is invisible that must be made visible? Let your imagination help you think big.

4.12 Brand-Busting

Buyer-driven brands have reputations at risk.
—Rebecca DeWinter

As discussed in Section 2.5, a brand is an ongoing and evolving relationship that is shaped by the perceptions of its audience. A brand is not what a company or organization says it is—it's what everyone else says it is. A corporation may own their brand, but they do not have the power to dictate their brand. The vulnerability of the brand to attack in the media can be an Achilles heel for corporations that rely on their public image to sell products. Brand-busting is any effort that associates the brand of a specific company with injustices they are perpetrating. It is an effective way to target brand-dependent corporations and also reveals aspects of contesting narrative power that are relevant in many different instances.

For example, when Pepsi's familiar logo is superimposed over images of a rainforest clearcut into a wasteland by industrial logging[24] or LEGO's Shell Oil branded toys are slowly drowned in a rising tide of oil,[25] the power of the corporate images are turned against themselves. *Adbusters* magazine founder Kalle Lasn has dubbed this practice of co-opting advertising's images and slogans as "**culture jamming**" or "subvertising."[26]

In recent years, brand-busting tactics have been artfully used by corporate accountability campaigns in many sectors. Targeting a brand can be a powerful form of narrative aikido since it uses a corporation's own

The dairy Industry's iconic *Got Milk?* ads featuring celebrities with milk mustaches were one of the longest-running (1993–2014) and widely seen advertising campaigns in recent history. This 2002 repurposing using then Vice President Dick Cheney was created by Chicago-based StreetRec to highlight the connections between the oil industry and the Bush administration's push to invade Iraq.[23] The image became a meme that spread from antiwar demonstrations to media and through popular culture around the world. The Bush administration denounced the image as "hate speech."

advertising budget against it by hijacking the imagery already familiar to their customers to present a social change message. Since the long-term damage of attacks on the brand can't be easily measured (and therefore can't be easily dismissed), brand-busting can help a campaign get the attention of top corporate decision-makers.

The right brand-bust at the right time can help win a campaign or even amplify a historic alliance. In 2012, with the political climate still shaped by the Occupy Wall Street narrative, there was a historic groundswell to hold big banks accountable. CSS supported a cross-sector mobilization at the Bank of America's (BofA) annual shareholders meeting in Charlotte, North Carolina.[27] The action united economic and racial justice groups with immigrant rights, financial reformers, and environmentalists because lots of groups had good reason to join the action. BofA had the highest number of home foreclosures in the country, was the top funder of mountaintop removal coal mining, and the largest ben-

This brand-bust of Bank of America created an umbrella narrative to unite a diverse coalition mobilizing at the 2012 shareholders meeting.

eficiary of corporate tax loopholes. They were also involved in predatory lending, redlining, workers' rights violations, private prisons, and immigrant detention centers. Reciting the bank's litany of abuses might create a relevant policy platform but it doesn't create a narrative. CSS worked with the coalition to translate this shared analysis into a brand-busting umbrella narrative by simply shifting Bank of America to Bank *versus* America! See image on previous page.

The brand-bust was effective because it reframed the core conflict and told a different story. BofA presented itself as a caring neighbor, helping communities rebuild in the wake of the economic recession. Yet the diverse mobilization exposed the Bank's role in creating and profiting from so much suffering. The larger Bank versus America narrative provided the context to connect and amplify mobilization spokespeople sharing their profound stories—Appalachian families resisting the coal industry's destruction of their homes, victims of BofA's predatory lending, survivors of immigrant detention centers. One former homeowner whose house had been illegally foreclosed even went inside the meeting and in an act of civil disobedience directly confronted the CEO. These firsthand testimonies all helped reinforce the mobilization's framing narrative that BofA's almost exclusively white, male, wealthy board of directors does not represent America. Rather, America is the diverse alliance of people from all walks of life, uniting across race, class and gender lines to demand justice and a better future by holding big banks accountable. The mobilization generated extensive global media coverage and added momentum to several campaigns demanding bank reforms. ∎

(Left) The "Mac & Genes box" created by *smart*Meme (designed by J. Cookson) targeted the Kraft Corporation's flagship brand as part of a national campaign pressuring Kraft to stop using genetically engineered ingredients in their products; (Right) Activists from Chicago's Genewise used Halloween as an opportunity to take the box Trick-or-Treating in the gated community where the Kraft Foods CEO lived. All the CEO's neighbors got to experience the brand-bust and the public health issues it raised firsthand.

Re:Imagining Change

THE POINTS OF INTERVENTION	IDENTIFY THE POINT	INTERVENTION IDEAS
Point of Production Factory, croplands. The realm of strikes, picket lines, crop-sits etc.		
Point of Destruction Visible oppression or destruction: sites of resource extraction, toxic discharge, police shooting, etc. Realm of direct interference: protest, occupations, blockades, etc.		
Point of Consumption Chain stores, supermarkets, etc. Places where customers can be reached. The realm of consumer boycotts and markets campaigns.		
Point of Decision Government or corporate HQ. Slumlord's office, etc. Location of targeted decision-maker.		
Point of Assumption Challenging underlying assumptions and control mythologies, subverting spectacles, actualizing alternatives, foreshadowing different futures, intervening in popular culture, and . . . ?		

> **"** *Our strategy should be not only to confront empire, but to lay siege to it. To deprive it of oxygen. To shame it. To mock it. With our art, our music, our literature, our stubbornness, our joy, our brilliance, our sheer relentlessness—and our ability to tell our own stories. Stories that are different from the ones we're being brainwashed to believe."*

—Arundhati Roy

> *"I'm no longer accepting the things I cannot change . . . I'm changing the things I cannot accept."*

—Angela Davis

Re:Imagining Change

V

Changing the Story

5.1 Strategic Improvisation

It is necessary to develop a strategy that utilizes all the physical conditions and elements that are directly at hand. The best strategy relies upon an unlimited set of responses.
—Morihei Ueshiba

Thus far this manual has examined various aspects of the **story-based strategy** approach. The foundational framework is **narrative power analysis**: understanding the critical difference between truth and meaning and viewing power relationships through the lens of story. We explored concepts, such as framing, **control mythologies**, and how stories can encapsulate and spread as **memes**. We showed how the **elements of story** are a tool to deconstruct the narratives we want to change and construct the stories of our own campaigns. In Chapter III we distinguished between mobilizing and persuasion narratives and offered techniques for applying the element of story to waging the **battle of the story**. Chapter IV examined the **points of intervention** and presented ideas for action at the **point of assumption** to reframe narratives and shift popular understanding of an issue.

The methodologies in this manual are most effective when used together, but different campaigns and situations will require different applications. Which is why experimentation is an important aspect of any effort to change the story. After all, successful strategy is not just a premeditated plan or rigid set of instructions—it also must evolve in the context of changing conditions. Effective strategic practice requires reflective, thoughtful leadership, and navigating choices in the face of rapidly changing situations. There is always an improvisational element.

The same is true when setting out to change a dominant narrative. This book provides various frameworks to simplify the complexities of narrative into specific strategic choices and creative challenges that grassroots campaigns can address. But stories are not math. These frameworks are not formal equations that if you follow the appropriate sequence will guarantee victory. There is no one surefire prescription to design and implement a story-based strategy. There is no one magic **frame** or supercharged meme that offers a universal blueprint for success.

Narrative has an alchemical aspect that allows the different elements to blend into a synergistic whole. A single potent metaphor or well-crafted image can communicate an entire narrative to the audience; or not. There is an inherent unpredictability to how a story might be received.

> **Successful strategy is not just a premeditated plan or rigid set of instructions—it also must evolve in the context of changing conditions.**

Which is why once a campaign narrative is distilled, it's important to test it. Many grassroots campaigns make the mistake of thinking that since they can't afford focus groups or polling they must forgo assessment. But regardless of scale there are always ways to test your strategy. It's important to consult allies and other stakeholders to ensure buy-in. It is even more important to informally poll members of your audience, particularly ones unfamiliar with the issue or the campaign and who ideally don't share the same political **assumptions**.

One of the primary obstacles to effective communication is expertise. The expert's specialized knowledge base always creates a risk of overshooting an audience's reference points. The same is true for an organized constituency that is deeply immersed in a campaign. It's hard to see our own assumptions that may be rooted in the everyday experiences of a constituency but which might be obstacles for the narrative reaching wider audiences. Even if it's just bouncing the narrative past some cantankerous in-laws or an apolitical neighbor, it's always valuable to get feedback from a more removed source.

Once a story-based strategy has moved off the flip charts and into fast moving media ecosystems it is important to be prepared to track how the story is evolving. The power of a new story is often emergent. A story might be spread by unexpected messengers or be translated to new constituencies in unanticipated forms. Then it is time to improvise! To be successful at improvisation—be it in cooking, hip-hop, or social change—requires resourcefulness, creativity, and a stash of good ideas. Improvisational forays are often the edges of yet unseen innovations.

In this chapter we will turn our attention to more in-depth examples of how story-based strategy comes to life in the real world. The chapter presents six case studies of applied story-based strategy that exemplify some of the methods outlined in the previous chapters. The first is a widely known historic example from the 1970s: Greenpeace's "Save the Whales" campaign. Three other case studies come from CSS's (then known as *smart*Meme) earlier work in the first decade of the 21st century applying story-based strategy on the ground with constituency-led organizing campaigns. The three campaigns range from the local, to the state, to the national level, but all involve frontline communities defending their rights against the unchecked power of giant corporations. In Vermont the fight is led by farmers protecting their seeds and livelihoods against genetic engineering; in California a community fights to protect everyone's water; and in Florida farmworkers lead a national campaign for dignity, rights, and fair wages.

The final two case studies share some of CSS's more recent work implementing story-based strategy with coalitions and alliances. Section 5.6 provides a behind-the-scenes view of CSS's story-based strategy partnership with the California Environmental Justice Alliance. It includes excerpts from the internal strategy documents, including examples of cornerstones, drama triangle, and a framing narrative. Finally, Section 5.7 presents an ongoing big-picture story-based strategy rooted in alliance building and transformational responses to the climate crisis.

Each of these examples offers some lessons and inspiration about how to apply story-based strategy concepts in real-world struggles. We hope these case studies inspire you to experiment with narrative in your own efforts to change the world.

5.2 Case Study
Greenpeace: Save the Whales

Greenpeace's "Save the Whales" campaign is a great example of changing the story, and is credited with shifting public perceptions of whales around the world.[1] When Greenpeace began the campaign in the mid-1970s, industrial whaling was driving many species of whale to the brink of extinction, and there was little public awareness about the issue. Greenpeace was a new organization, and they had successfully mixed media-savvy, non-

violent direct action, and the Quaker tradition of "bearing witness" into a grassroots campaign against nuclear testing. When they set out to challenge the whaling industry, they knew they would need to push their new campaign tactics even further. Greenpeace understood they could never intervene at every **point of destruction** and save every whale. So they set out to change the way the dominant culture thought of whaling—to change the story of whaling.

Greenpeace campaigners asked themselves: What is the popular understanding of whaling, and where did it come from? They realized that people knew relatively little about whales, and that much of what they thought they knew came from a book that was commonly read in high schools: Herman Melville's 19th-century novel *Moby Dick*. The vision of whaling presented in *Moby Dick* depicts heroic whalers taking to the sea in tiny boats and risking their lives to battle giant evil whales.

But by the late 20th century, whaling was an industrial enterprise. Giant factory whaling ships dwarfed the endangered mammals, slaughtering them en masse in a manner that was neither risky nor heroic. Greenpeace knew they had to expose the invisible reality of industrial whaling. They set out to create a series of "image events"[2]—**spectacles** that told a dramatic story—which could replace the popular culture's concept of whaling.

The iconic images they created were of Greenpeace activists in small Zodiac boats placing themselves directly between the giant factory whaling ships and the whales. The drama was real. Not only was it life-or-death for the whales, the interventions were dangerous and activists did get hurt. Greenpeace used the recently invented first generation of hand-held video cameras to record their attempts to get between the harpoons and the whales and succeeded in getting the images broadcast around the world.

Greenpeace activists are shot with water cannons as they fight to save a captured whale. Images such as this helped replace the *Moby Dick* mythology and shift the hero, victim, and villain roles in the story's drama triangle.

Re:Imagining Change

Greenpeace activists in Zodiac boats place themselves between the factory whaling ships and the whales.

This intervention at the point of destruction created an effective direct action at the point of assumption. Publicized through the larger global campaign, these interventions **reframed** the story by shifting the **drama triangle**. The actions showed it was the activists, not the whalers, who were the courageous people on small boats risking their lives—not to kill whales, but to save them. In this new narrative, whales were not big and evil; rather it was the giant whaling ships that were the dangerous monsters, the villains of the new story. The whales, now recast as helpless victims, became sympathetic and worthy of protection. The Greenpeace activists (and the burgeoning environmental movement they represented) became the heroes. The roles of hero, victim, and villain were all shifted by the campaign and the story changed.

The campaign won the **battle of the story** of whaling, and ultimately succeeded in securing international treaties to protect endangered whales. Unfortunately, in recent years, whaling interests have exploited loopholes in these treaties. Activists are once again campaigning to protect whales and, because of this successful story-based strategy, these new campaigns have the power of public support on their side.[3]

5.3 Case Study
Rural Vermont:
One Contaminated Farm Is One Too Many

Starting in 2004, CSS partnered with the grassroots economic justice organization Rural Vermont, a membership organization led by family farmers. Rural Vermont's mission to support "regenerative agriculture and wise use of all resources in meeting the needs of people and our environment" had made them leaders in the fight against unregulated genetically engineered (GE) agriculture. This rapidly spreading and untested technology poses threats to family farmers, human health, and the

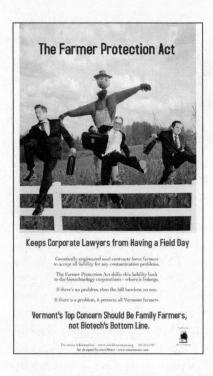

Elmer the scarecrow driving corporate lawyers off the family farm. The face of the middle lawyer has an uncanny similarity to Monsanto's chief lobbyist in the state. Just a coincidence, of course . . .
Ad created by *smart*Meme (designed by J. Cookson).

environment.[4] CSS supported Rural Vermont as a key constituent-led, membership organization that was tackling a critical global issue at the local and state level.

In 2004, Rural Vermont successfully passed the Farmers' Right-to-Know GE Seed Labeling and Registration Act. This law put the USDA organic standards' definition of "genetically modified" into Vermont statute and required that GE seeds be clearly labeled. This was a tremendous victory. With GE defined in the law books, Rural Vermont had the ability to move the issue further.

There was a serious danger that pollen from genetically engineered (GE) crops planted on one farm could drift and contaminate neighboring farms that had not chosen to plant GE crops. The giant biotech companies like Monsanto, who own the patents to the GE seeds, were covering up the contamination issue. Their Orwellian tactic was to claim the farmers whose crops had been contaminated were not victims, but actually thieves, and sue them for "patent infringement" and "unauthorized pirating" of Monsanto's copyrighted seed technology. Monsanto would use the lawsuits to threaten farmers with bankruptcy and force them to sign gag orders that ensured they couldn't tell the public about this spreading crisis.[5]

The farmers of Vermont decided to stand up to this corporate bullying and demand that the state legislature pass a law to hold the manu-

Re:Imagining Change

(Top) As the meme spread, farmers and their allies gathered across the state to show their support for the Farmer Protection Act by making and displaying scarecrows. (Middle) Elmer the scarecrow featured in the ads began to show up in real life at the Statehouse. (Bottom) Inexpensive ads ran in local papers to coincide with appearances by Elmer and his growing scarecrow army at the Statehouse. Ads created by smartMeme (designed by J. Cookson).

FARMER PROTEST

GOOD POLICY makes GOOD neighbors

facturers of genetically engineered seeds accountable for contaminating "drift." This would mean that if a farmer's field was contaminated, instead of suing his neighbor he could hold the real culprit accountable—the patent-holding corporations like Monsanto.

When GE crop contamination was uncovered on an organic farm in the state, the campaign rallied around the slogan "One contaminated farm is one too many." Rural Vermont organized farmers and local-food advocates to pressure state lawmakers to adopt policies to protect farmers' interests. They called their proposed legislation the Farmer Protection Act, a framing that stuck throughout the campaign connecting corporate liability with protecting farmers.

The Farmer Protection Act

Leaves Corporate Lawyers with No Place to Hide

Rural Vermont's story-based strategy used many tactics: letter writing, rallies, media, print advertisements, and nonviolent direct actions. The campaign's narrative kept the focus on the farmers—the impacted sympathetic characters—and based the campaign in Vermont's rural culture of family farming. An aggressive media strategy and emphasis on popular education made "genetic engineering" a household term across the state.

Based on input from Rural Vermont, CSS developed the scarecrow as the icon and central character of the narrative. The scarecrow was a powerful symbol because it embodied the idea of protecting the farmers and the crops from predators. It personified the story that Rural Vermont was protecting the seeds against the latest threat from Monsanto. Now the challenge was to get the scarecrow imagery to spread as a meme.

The scarecrow meme was launched with a series of inexpensive newspaper advertisements featuring "Elmer" the scarecrow. Elmer was depicted confronting corporate lawyers, and these images framed the conflict as local farmers vs. out-of-state corporate interests.

The farmers were explicit that they did not want to be cast as the victims, and so the campaign imagery depicted the scarecrow as powerful. The images show the scarecrow chasing corporate lawyers out of the pasture, using a light-saber-like flashlight to catch them in the hen house, and standing proud against the backdrop of an iconic Vermont landscape. In this way, the story-based strategy was **reframing** who had the power in the story, and foreshadowing victory.

As the campaign gained ground, scarecrows showed up in real life in front yards across the countryside, and at the Statehouse for Rural Vermont rallies. The meme spread, carrying Rural Vermont's story of protecting local agriculture and the rural way of life. Farmers and their allies gathered across the state to make and display scarecrows as a show of public support for the campaign.

All of Rural Vermont's hard work and organizing paid off and the Vermont state legislature passed the Farmer Protection Act in 2005. It was a major victory for the coalition of concerned Vermonters who rallied behind the scarecrow. Despite thousands of calls to the Republican governor's office in support of the bill, however, he vetoed it in 2006.

Fortunately, Vermont farmers and their allies did not stop their organizing. Over the next decade Vermont continued to be on the forefront of efforts to assert democratic control over corporate-driven genetic engineering. This work led in 2016 to the historic adoption of the country's first law requiring food manufactures to clearly label whether their products were produced with genetic engineering.[6]

5.4 Case Study
Protect Our Waters: Our Most Precious Resource

Around the world, transnational companies are moving to aggressively privatize water and turn what has historically been a life-sustaining shared resource into a lucrative commodity. Bottled water is projected to be a $195 billion global market by 2018.[7] Perversely, much of this market is in affluent countries like the U.S. that generally have safe tap water available for free.

In 2007, community residents of the Mt. Shasta area of Northern California invited CSS to support their efforts to prevent the construction of the largest water bottling plant in the United States. Nestlé Corporation—the Swiss food and beverage conglomerate is the world's largest water company, owner of over 60 different bottled water brands—was going to build the plant in the small town of McCloud. The company had been preparing the plans for several years and had convinced the five-person local Community Services District to sign a 100-year contract to pump unlimited ground water before there was any public debate. In response, local residents formed the Protect Our Waters Coalition (POW) to protect the ecological, cultural, and economic integrity of Mt. Shasta's unique headwaters area for future generations. The coalition brought together the McCloud Watershed Council and two locally active sporting and conservation organizations—California Trout and Trout Unlimited.

CSS worked with the residents and their allies to provide training, facilitate group strategy sessions, and apply a narrative power analysis to the campaign. It was clear that Nestlé had targeted McCloud because

Siskiyou County, California, residents mobilize to protect their water and way of life.

This image created by *smart*Meme (designed by J. Cookson) shows that clean, cold water is a precious resource and a symbol of the region's cherished rural way of life and independence.

OUR MOST PRECIOUS RESOURCE...

IF WE CAN KEEP IT.

Mt. Shasta's clean, cold water is our most precious resource. It supports our rich agricultural production, ranching, healthy forests and rivers, industry, and our communities. Our water is our future. Our water is our pride.

The increasing demand from multi-national corporations to bottle our most precious resource is a wake-up call. Siskiyou County has no legal controls over how much water a bottler can export from our communities. Nestlé Corporation wants to build an Arrowhead water bottling plant six times the size of the Coca Cola water bottling plant in Mt. Shasta, and has locked-in a 100 year contract. Is there enough? Without scientific studies, nobody knows.

Take pride in our waters. After all, it's our waters not Nestlé's waters. Together, we can decide how best to keep control of our water, and the future of our county. Please visit our "Take Pride in Our Waters" fair entries: Homebrew with famous McCloud spring water, Decorated Cake in the Home Arts Building, and Mailbox in the Ag/Hort Building.

PROTECT OUR WATERS IN SISKIYOU COUNTY!

www.ProtectOurWaters.org

of its history as a former company town. It was once home to "Mother McCloud," a timber company whose mill was the heart of the town until it closed some 25 years ago. POW realized that Nestlé was tapping into a nostalgic narrative of the "good old days." The company presented themselves as Father Nestlé who would save the town by providing jobs and tax revenue. One local resident described how Nestlé's representative even tried to build rapport with locals by mimicking McCloud fashion, exchanging his business suits for jeans and cowboy boots.

As the campaign heated up, Nestlé used many of the common divide-and-conquer tactics that big corporations often use to derail local opposition. Nestlé framed the issue around the **control myth** of *jobs versus the environment*. They cast opponents of the plant as "out-of-towners"

Re:Imagining Change

and "second-home owners" who were obstructing the "economic progress and development" the town desperately needed. They dismissed local concerns about large-scale water extraction as coming from "unreasonable environmentalists" who were more concerned about fish than jobs.

Nestlé had a signed contract with the town and had already secured seemingly unmovable support from the pro-development County Board of Supervisors. But the concerned local residents did not give up. The coalition continued organizing and building alliances, and with help from CSS, effectively waged the battle of the story. They framed their campaign around water as a precious resource, both economically and as a symbol of the local way of life. They challenged Nestlé's There-Is-No-Alternative framing by releasing their own economic report which revealed that the plant would offer only low-wage jobs while dramatically increasing local truck traffic on the area's only two-lane highway. They showed how Nestlé's contract was a bad deal for the town. They foreshadowed a more hopeful vision of the town uniting around a fair development project that would protect the local ecosystem.

CSS worked to find a meme that could communicate the potential threat that Nestlé's bottling plant represented to the ranchers and the entire county.

A key strategy was to expand the frame beyond the impacted people of McCloud to tell a story about the region-wide threats of unchecked water development. In particular, Protect Our Waters knew they had to reach the ranching community who were among the most influential groups in the county.

Nestlé's *jobs versus the environment* framing was designed to tap into the ranchers' history of contentious battles with environmentalists and it successfully kept the issue off the ranching communities' radar. But the threat to ranchers was real, and since the area is the headwaters of Northern California's largest river, the unrestricted groundwater extraction could have devastating consequences for the entire state. At the time there was no regulation of groundwater pumping in California (the first rules were adopted in 2014) so the company could suck up as much water as they wanted. Additionally, the proposed plant was so large that it could easily serve as a bottling plant for expanded future operations across the region.

In supporting the campaign, CSS worked to find a meme that could communicate the potential threat that Nestlé's bottling plant repre-

This ad created by *smart*Meme (designed by J. Cookson) launched the Nestlé spurge meme and helped alert the broader community to the potential threat of Nestlé's proposed water bottling plant.

sented to the ranchers and the entire county. We experimented with **brand-busting** and combined a humorous appropriation of Nestlé's signature striped straw from their flagship Nestlé Quik chocolate drink, with a threat that was already familiar to the ranchers: "the spurge." The spurge is a well-known and dreaded invasive plant species that degrades ranch land by absorbing too much water.

A double entendre was born—the Nestlé Spurge—a new type of invasive plant that also degraded the land and threatened the local way of life by sucking up too much water. The campaign printed up materials modeled on preexisting invasive plant alerts (mimicking familiar local signage). POW launched the meme at the biggest community event of the year: the County Fair.

Nestlé had also set up an informational table at the event. The spurge meme experiment proved successful! By all accounts, Nestlé's representatives heard from numerous county residents who were starting to see Nestlé as a bad neighbor and the proposed plant as the first step in a full-scale corporate water grab.

The Protect Our Waters coalition won a major victory in 2008 when Nestlé agreed to renegotiate the contract it had signed with the town. For the next year the community explored options that would minimize environmental damage and ensure real economic benefits to the town. In September 2009, nearly six years after Nestlé's intentions became public, the company announced that it was abandoning its plans and leaving McCloud for good. This was a victory not just for the people of McCloud and their local ecosystem but also for people everywhere who are standing up to corporate water privatizers and changing the story around water.

FINDING THE RIGHT META-VERB

Given the depressed economic conditions in McCloud and the power of Nestlé's propaganda campaign, the town was very divided on the issue of the proposed water bottling plant. The local resistance combined two different positions, people who were against the plant under any circumstances, alongside people who would support the plant but only if the town got a better deal. The tension between these two constituencies bubbled up in a CSS-led strategy session when the group began to discuss what meta-verb to use regarding the central issue of the town's signed contract with Nestlé. One participant suggested the narrative should revolve around "renegotiate the contract." Immediately another member interrupted, protesting that the group should be against all industrial water extraction and should therefore "reject the contract." The room erupted into opposing comments, tempers flared and the group's fragile unity seemed on the brink of collapse, taking any hope of winning the campaign with it. Fortunately, a quick-thinking CSS facilitator jumped in to suggest a third choice: "reconsider the contract" since that metaverb was broad enough to encompass both political positions. After a little thoughtful discussion everyone agreed and the campaign moved forward. Sometimes the right meta-verb can make all the difference.

5.5 Case Study
The Coalition of Immokalee Workers:
Consciousness + Commitment = Change

For over two decades, the Coalition of Immokalee Workers (CIW) has led inspiring organizing efforts to build power and improve conditions for tomato pickers in southwestern Florida.[8] Immokalee is the state's largest farmworker community with mostly immigrants from Mexico, Guatemala, Haiti, and other countries.[9] Poverty wages, abuse of workers, and even literal enslavement were common problems. Over the past two decades CIW has united their community, built national alliances, and won industry-changing concessions from over a dozen major corporations. CSS was honored to support CIW and their allies, the Student Farmworker Alliance, in their first major campaign targeting a national corporation: the landmark Taco Bell boycott campaign.[10]

CIW began organizing in 1993 as a small group of workers meeting in an Immokalee church. In the 1990s they took action at the **point of production,** including three general strikes, and built public pressure on

The Coalition of Immokalee Workers have brought the struggle of tomato pickers–some of the poorest and most marginalized workers in the country–to the point of consumption in the fast-food industry.

tomato growers with marches, hunger strikes, and other tactics. From 1997–2001, CIW helped expose three modern-day slavery operations and freed 500 workers from indentured servitude. These efforts won better conditions in the tomato industry and built more power for CIW.

But with their power analysis, they knew that in order to change the tomato industry, they had to go further up the corporate food chain. So they set their sights on changing the purchasing practices of the fast food companies that buy the tomatoes they pick.

In 2001, CIW launched the national boycott of Taco Bell—calling on the fast-food giant to take responsibility for human rights abuses in the fields. They demanded that Taco Bell pay one penny more per pound of tomatoes in order to give farmworkers a fairer wage for their labor. CIW also proposed an enforceable human rights code of conduct that includes farmworkers in monitoring working conditions and holding companies accountable for sourcing tomatoes from sweatshop operations.

The Taco Bell boycott gained broad student, religious, labor, and community support in the nearly four years of its campaign. Boycott committees operated in nearly all 50 states. One of the most vibrant aspects of the campaign was the Student/Farmworker Alliance (SFA), which led a fast-growing movement to "Boot the Bell" from college and high school campuses across the country.

SFA operates as an ally to CIW, organizing students and youth across the country. This was a critical constituency on the campaign power map since Taco Bell's marketing targeted young people. Working with CIW, SFA creatively engaged in brand-busting tactics like appropriat-

CIW's inspiring campaigns have won wage increases for farmworkers and enforceable human rights agreements with tomato purchasers like Taco Bell, McDonald's, Burger King, Whole Foods, and Walmart.

ing the company's Chihuahua dog mascot and advertising slogans and subverting the company's omnipresent "Think Outside the Bun" tagline to become "Think Outside the Bell!" They supported the boycott with actions at the point of consumption, protesting at restaurants on and off campuses and campaigning for the repeal of Taco Bell's concession agreements with universities.

Large-scale national actions at **the point of decision** included a 10-day hunger strike outside of Taco Bell headquarters in Irvine, California. This was one of the largest hunger strikes in U.S. labor history, with over 75 farmworkers and students fasting during the 10-day period in 2003. In 2004 and 2005, the Taco Bell Truth Tours went cross-country and culminated with marches and actions at the corporate headquarters of Taco Bell's parent company Yum! Brands, in Louisville, Kentucky.

All the while, the CIW was telling their story with dramatic imagery: pyramids of the tomato harvesting buckets representing the amount of tomatoes picked in a day's work, photo galleries of workers' calloused hands, colorful giant puppets of tomatoes, and the Taco Bell Chihuahua recast as a corporate exploiter. The campaign amplified the voices of workers telling their stories about life in Immokalee. The campaign's core meme was their demand "One more penny per pound!" The framing of the boycott around slavery targeted assumptions and made the invisible visible by exposing that human enslavement was still happening in the 21st-century United States.

In March of 2005, on the eve of a major national mobilization at their headquarters, Taco Bell's parent company, Yum! Brands, signed an agreement to meet the CIW's demands. The CIW's successful alliance building within Immokalee, and with student and faith communities nationally, has created a powerful movement for justice. In 2006 they launched the Alliance for Fair Food network to build power for human rights throughout the U.S. food system.[11] Since that time, the Coalition of Immokalee Workers has successfully expanded the model of the Taco Bell campaign to win historic concessions from numerous giant corporations including McDonald's, Burger King, Whole Foods, and Walmart.

The CIW's core philosophy is "consciousness + commitment = change" and they have proved it to be true! The Coalition is an inspirational challenge to corporate power and an innovative model for combining community-led movement building with sophisticated corporate campaigning.[12] Their local efforts in Immokalee include a radio station, community center, ongoing popular education, and exposing slavery and human rights violations. They also support cultural work in the community and help build cooperatives of growers who pay fair wages. As CIW says about their community's incredible success, it shows that "nothing is impossible."

5.6 Case Study
#Healthy Hoods: Environmental Justice for All

The California Environmental Justice Alliance (CEJA) is a statewide coalition of grassroots, community-based organizations that have worked together since 2001 to challenge systematic environmental racism and injustice.[13] The Alliance members[14] are local and regional organizations rooted in predominantly low-income communities of color that continue to bear the brunt of both environmental pollution and social injustice. As CEJA articulates in their mission statement: "We build the power of communities across California to create policies that will alleviate poverty and pollution."

CEJA partnered with CSS in early 2013 to develop a messaging framework and communications plan to strengthen CEJA's campaign work and organizational narrative. Over the next six months, CSS facilitated a series of story-based strategy sessions with coalition staff and representatives of all the different member organizations.

Below is some of the content of this internal process in order to provide a deeper look at how story-based strategy can be applied in a real-world organizational and campaign context.

The first step was to identify the **narrative cornerstones** (see Section 3.1) for their strategy. For CEJA's campaign at that time these included:

NARRATIVE CORNERSTONES

1. Goals
- *Shift Discourse:* Project a powerful vision of environmental justice that amplifies the voices of low-income communities of color who are most impacted by pollution and injustice
- *Claim Political Space:* advocate for policies that support clean, healthy, and safe communities
- *Win Campaigns:* Persuade key audiences to join CEJA campaigns and pressure the necessary targets to achieve CEJA's programmatic goals

2. Targets (generally)
- Elected officials who are key votes on important EJ bills
- Relevant state agencies

3. Constituency
- Base of current CEJA member groups
- Other allied EJ groups organizing in low-income communities of color across California

4. Priority Audiences
- Organized labor
- The base and allies in the faith-based and civil rights sectors
- Progressive and small business community
- Health advocates

Next, CSS led the alliance through a narrative power analysis and identified some specific assumptions in the dominant culture that CEJA would need to challenge. These included some common control myths, such as "regulations are killing the economy" and "people are poor because they are lazy," as well as misconceptions that the EJ movement was "blocking economic development" or "just about saying No rather than presenting solutions."

CEJA knew they needed to publicize the negative health impacts on their communities but also put out a positive vision communicating their policies for transforming toxic hot spots. As their cornerstones identified, they wanted the narrative to mobilize their constituents and help strengthen their alliances with organized labor and small businesses. Together, using tools like the battle of the story, we explored ways to articulate CEJA's holistic vision and bring health and economic frames together.

CSS staff followed up on the group session by generating different possible framing options for CEJA's narrative and helping assess them.

CEJA decided to develop a framing narrative around Healthy Hoods. The healthy hoods frame was designed to communicate the core idea that *Healthy Communities are the Foundation of a Healthy Economy.*

Below are the **drama triangle** (see Section 3.7) and the **framing narrative** (see Section 3.11) that CSS and CEJA created for healthy hoods. The framing narrative is more than just specific language, it is fundamentally the idea—the meaning—that is being convened. Here, that is represented as the bulleted key points. This framing narrative has an arc through six main parts that could be easily customized to include local demands or specific campaign asks. The underlined text represents key language that was developed into messages and sound bites.

CEJA rolled out the frame by bringing over 200 EJ leaders from around the state to a "Stand Together for Healthy Hoods Rally" at the capitol. Together they rallied to transform toxic hot spots around the state into Healthy Hoods through CEJA's innovative Green Zones policy agenda.

DRAMA TRIANGLE

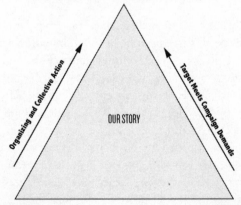

HERO
Organized communities (families, kids, people from all walks of life) creating Healthy Hoods by uniting with labor, green business, and other allies to build a healthy economy from the ground up. Legislators, when they support justice.

Organizing and Collective Action

OUR STORY

Target Meets Campaign Demands

VICTIMS
All Californians are impacted by environmental degradation and the lack of economic innovation, but particularly low-income communities that currently suffer the highest levels of pollution and lowest levels of opportunity.

VILLAINS
1. Shortsighted corporate polluters who are putting profits ahead of the community's well-being and preventing the creation of sustainable, clean, just economies.
2. Legislators (and other campaign targets) who side with polluters.

#HealthyHoods:
Healthy Communities are the Foundation of a Healthy Economy

Key Points
- Frame the conflict with a clear moral anchor rooted in justice values.
- Offer a big positive vision linking Health and Economy. Healthy Families = Healthy Workers = Healthy Economy.
- Offer a Jobs message that resonates with labor, progressive business, and decision-makers.
- Name Big Polluters, such as Big Oil companies or other local targets, as the villain.

Narrative Arc
1. *Frame Conflict with Values:*
   Everyone cares about the health of their families and neighbors so <u>why are *our* communities still sacrifice zones</u>? In this day and age, no neighborhood, not yours or mine, should have to live with toxic industries polluting their air and water.
2. *Define Problem/Name the Villain:*
   Big polluters, such as [INSERT: local target] are reaping the benefits of operating in our communities while getting away with literally poisoning our families. We have too many <u>parents who can't go to work</u> because they are too sick or their <u>kids suffer from asthma attacks</u>. And we have even more residents who don't have <u>quality jobs</u> because our neighborhoods lack economic opportunity.
3. *Offer Vision:*
   It's time for a change. <u>A healthy economy starts with healthy communities!</u> By focusing on green <u>community-based development,</u> we can ensure that economic revitalization and environmental sustainability go hand-in-hand. We have the technology and the know-how to <u>transform our most polluted areas</u> into thriving, healthy, economically prosperous communities. With <u>smart policies,</u> we can ensure that our <u>kids can grow up healthy</u>, with a clean environment and <u>access to opportunities</u> like education and good-paying <u>union jobs</u>.
4. *Action:*
   Communities around the state that have <u>paid the highest price</u> for our current pollution-based economy are organizing to transform our communities into Healthy Hoods—neighborhoods where <u>community members have a voice in greening our communities from the bottom-up</u>.
5. *Insert Specific Demands or Policy Ask:*
   [INSERT: Local or programmatic demand.]
6. *Universalize the Appeal:*
   <u>Every family deserves to live in a healthy hood.</u> Investing in community-led, green economic development will create a foundation for a <u>healthy California economy</u> that will <u>benefit everyone</u>.

The frame continued to grow and help spread CEJA's campaigns. The following year, in 2014, CSS supported CEJA to apply the Healthy Hoods narrative in their campaign to pass statewide legislation: AB 1330, the Environmental Justice Act. CSS partnered with the Design Action Collective to produce the campaign imagery on the next page.

CEJA members grew the campaign's social media presence using #HealthyHoods as a hashtag that member groups applied to frame a range of related organizing being done by member groups across the state. Over time, CEJA expanded the Healthy Hoods frame to connect with their clean energy and climate campaigns by "powering up Healthy Hoods throughout California."

In the words of CEJA Co-Director Amy Vanderwarker, "The Healthy Hoods narrative has created a cohesive framework to link all of CEJA's programs back to one of the core issues in all the communities where our members work—health and quality of life—while lifting up community leadership, a fundamental value that drives all of our work. It does so in a way that is positive, allowing us to build a solution-oriented approach that has helped us to reach decision-makers and achieve wins."

Members of the Center on Race, Poverty & the Environment attend the CEJA Healthy Hoods rally at the capitol building in Sacramento, California. Photo by Brooke Anderson.

The graphic uses the principles of "show, don't tell" and foreshadowing to present a choice between Toxic Hot Spots or Healthy Hoods. Created in collaboration with Design Action Collective and CSS.

While AB 1330 did not pass, CEJA continued to grow their power and mobilized to achieve even bigger victories. In addition to expanding their organizing, alliance building, and advocacy, CEJA expanded their communications capacity, including hiring the alliance's first ever communications staff person. CEJA staff attended CSS's five-day Advanced Training and participated in the CSS incubated ReFrame Strategic Communications Mentorship (www.reframementorship.org).

CEJA continues to promote bold policies that protect the environment and address the urgent needs of low-income communities of color. In August 2016 their organizing and advocacy helped pass two landmark climate laws. The first, AB 32, the Global Warming Solutions Act, will reduce California's greenhouse gas emissions by 40 percent below 1990 levels by 2030. Its companion measure, AB 197, the Climate Equity and Transparency Act, mandates that future climate-change policies address the health and economic impacts of climate policy on vulnerable populations. Together, these bills will lead to cleaner air, improved public health, and serve as a national model for how to begin equitably addressing the climate crisis.

5.7 Case Study
Our Power: A New Climate Narrative

As movements around the planet mobilize to counter the effects of climate destabilization on their communities, cultures, and ecosystems, a framing battle of global significance is underway. In the climate fight, as with so many other struggles, the heart of the framing battle is naming the real problem, since how we define the problem determines what solutions are needed. To varying degrees, governments and multinational corporations around the world have acknowledged the crisis and are committing to begin addressing it.

But the elite discourse frames the problem through a reductionist lens. The problem is atmospheric carbon, period; thus ignoring the underlying historic issues of equity, economy, and worldview that created an excess of CO_2 in the atmosphere. This simplistic framing (sometimes referred to as "carbon fundamentalism") has not only failed to catalyze structural change, it has perversely justified continuing the same industrial practices that have already pushed the planet to the brink. Increasingly the world's richest countries and companies are co-opting environmental rhetoric to put a PR friendly "green" face on the same old politics of fossil fuel expansion, unlimited economic growth, and corporate exploitation.

Over the past two decades, global resistance efforts have converged into a climate justice movement offering a deeper analysis of the problem.[15] Led by communities on the literal "frontlines"—who have both borne the historic brunt of fossil-fuel pollution and are the most vulnerable to climate disruption—the climate justice movement emphasizes the root causes of climate change and the need for an equitable transition away from fossil-fuel dependency.

Starting in 2009, CSS began supporting North American climate justice leaders in amplifying their frontline perspective in order to shift the climate debate. CSS supported creative **interventions** in the United Nations climate talks and then provided training, strategy consultation, and support for a multiyear alignment process. In 2013, this process birthed the Climate Justice Alliance (CJA) and the Our Power Campaign.

CJA is a unique alliance of 40 community organizations, movement networks, and support organizations on the frontlines of the climate crisis. The member groups are rooted in diverse communities—Indigenous peoples, African American, Latin@, Asian Pacific Islander, and poor white communities—with common experiences of racial and economic oppression and strong traditions of social justice organizing. Proximity to the destructive impacts of fossil fuels has provided these communities with the lived expertise to lead a transformative response to the crisis. The frontlines of the problem are also the frontlines of the solutions.

CJA members knew that in order for their communities to thrive they would need to expand public understanding of the climate crisis beyond a narrow "environmental" frame that isolated the issue from the larger social context. They set out to amplify their own climate advocacy, rooted in the community organizing and social justice values in order to transcend the traditional climate movement's single-issue campaigns, top-down legislative strategies, and reliance on flawed market-based approaches.

To do so, CJA launched a different type of campaign. The Our Power Campaign (OPC) focuses on the frontlines of community-led change and lifts up solutions that address the roots of the climate crisis at the intersections of race, class, and the economy. The campaign's shared narrative aggregates place-based organizing by articulating the common values and transformative visions that unite the different community efforts.

The campaign name uses the double meaning of *power* to speak to both changing energy systems and growing the grassroots people-power of impacted communities.

OPC launched in 2013 with a historic gathering of coal-impacted communities hosted by the Black Mesa Water Coalition on the Navajo reservation. The gathering From the Mesa to the Mountain Top: Climate Justice in Coal Country united communities from across coal's destructive life cycle to share lessons, grow their skills, and strategize how to grow the movement.[16]

CSS provided our story-based strategy expertise to support the alliance's development, including facilitating a process to define the campaign identity and core framing. Working with CJA leaders, CSS identified the need to bring the climate discourse out of the atmosphere and down to the ground where more people can make the connections with their daily lives. This framing helps see the crisis not only as looming catastrophe but also an opportunity: an unprecedented imperative to transform society to be more democratic, just, *and* ecologically sane.[17]

The campaign name uses the double meaning of *power* to speak to both changing energy systems and growing the grassroots people-power of impacted communities. Understanding the two goals as interrelated expands the framing of climate and energy policy to include economy, governance, and the democratic values we want to drive the transition.

The Our Power Campaign narrative builds on the global climate justice movement's work to reframe the problem beyond atmospheric pollution and even beyond fossil fuels. Climate destabilization is not the core problem, rather just one of the most visible symptoms of a deeper problem: the current economic system. The OPC names this problem the "extractive economy" (sometimes described with the more visceral imagery of the Banks and Tanks economy or the Dig-Burn-Dump economy).[18]

By emphasizing the extractive economic model as the problem, the narrative reminds us that ecological disruption and economic impoverishment stem from a common systemic failure. The same pathological drive of corporate capitalism that reduces the life-sustaining systems of the natural world to extractable resources treats human labor as just another commodity to relentlessly exploit.

The Our Power Campaign narrative pairs honesty about the scale of the problem with an approach CSS calls "leading with vision." Compelling narratives need to match well-framed conflicts with clearly foreshadowed solutions. In contrast to environmental narratives that have often foreshadowed only catastrophe, CJA's tagline is "Communities Uniting for a Just Transition." Just Transition[19] is a unifying frame to describe the multifaceted process of moving economic priorities away from the

The People's Climate March in September 2014 brought 400,000 people into the streets of New York City and was led by a massive contingent of CJA allied frontline community members and youth.

Re:Imagining Change

"It Takes Roots to Weather the Storm" was a meme developed at the 2014 CSS's Advanced Training to communicate the Just Transition analysis. It has spread in different versions across the climate justice movement and beyond. Image created for CJA and the Our Power Campaign by Bec Young from Just Seeds. justseeds.org/artists/becyoung

extractive economy and toward supporting local, living economies that are sustainable, resilient, and regenerative.

As part of CJA's strategy to define and promote Just Transition, CJA populates the frame by amplifying the stories of real community-based solutions happening in the Our Power communities around the country. In Richmond, California, campaigns to prevent the expansion of Chevron's toxic oil refinery are complemented with the creation of worker and community-owned solar cooperatives. In Black Mesa, on the Navajo Nation, Just Transition means protecting the land, water, and indigenous sovereignty with solutions like strengthening the traditional wool economy and creating community-owned renewable energy. In Eastern Kentucky, out-of-work miners unite with their neighbors to create a Just Transition away from the dying coal economy toward a more sustainable and equitable future.[20]

Just Transition is place-based and looks different depending on the unique local conditions. United by the OPC, however, each initiative promotes a unified vision, rooted in shared values, aligned strategies, and a common narrative. As the OPC has grown it has succeeded in popularizing Just Transition as a useful movement framework and defining climate justice as a multifaceted struggle to transform the dominant economic model.

One of CJA's parachute banners at the People's Climate March in September 2014.

Along with reframing the conflict and foreshadowing a new vision for the future, the OPC elevates new characters to the center of the story. The traditional climate narrative emphasized charismatic megafauna like polar bears as the victims and highlighted scientists as messengers to communicate heavily data-driven arguments about the severity of the threat. The characters who carry the OPC narrative are from diverse frontline communities: Indigenous peoples speaking to sacred responsibilities and the Rights of Mother Earth; former coal miners talking about the need for economic transition; inner city youth demanding clean air; racial justice and immigrant rights organizers talking about the interconnection of all these struggles. The traditional climate narrative has often featured frontline communities but usually in the role of victims. The OPC narrative flips this drama triangle and positions frontline organizers as heroes leading a just transition and building local, living economies from the ground up.

CJA's strategy to change the story in the climate movement has been working. In September 2014 CJA united with a huge coalition of environmental groups and allied labor unions to organize the People's Climate March in New York City. Over 400,000 people marched, making it the largest climate mobilization in history.

Even more important than its scale was its composition. In order to emphasize the growing leadership of frontline communities in the movement, the march was led by a nearly 40,000-person "Front Lines of Cri-

Re:Imagining Change

sis, Forefront of Change" contingent organized by CJA and allies, with young people holding the lead banner. Instead of the media spotlight focusing on the usual celebrities and leaders of national environmental groups, the coalition highlighted spokespeople from impacted communities amplifying the local solutions emerging from the grassroots climate justice movement.[21] This shift portrays the true depth and diversity of grassroots leadership and challenges the assumption that climate change is just a concern of white, middle-class environmentalists. The following day after the march CJA joined thousands of climate activists to #FloodWallStreet and make the connection that acting for climate justice requires challenging the entrenched power and parasitic practices of the big banks and financial institutions.

One of the campaign's challenges has been how to make the unfamiliar and abstract language of Just Transition more accessible to broader audiences. In the lead-up to the New York march, CSS made this question a focus of a practicum at our annual Advanced Training. With CJA leaders working alongside CSS trainers and organizers from other sectors the group produced an inspiring framing narrative around the message: "It Takes Roots to Weather the Storm." This narrative provides some imagery and a metaphor to describe the pragmatic essence of Just Transition. Roots: organized communities, traditions, and unified people power are essential components of the resilience that climate destabilization requires. There are no shortcuts; the vision and leadership of frontline impacted communities is needed to equitably transition away from fossil fuels. The It Takes Roots meme continues to proliferate through the climate justice movement and beyond.

While continuing local fights against fossil fuels and the extractive economy, CJA is simultaneously promoting energy democracy, food sovereignty, and other initiatives to build local, living economies. They have united with the fossil fuel divestment movement to launch the Reinvest in Our Power Campaign and innovate nonextractive financing models to resource local Just Transition efforts. CJA has amplified frontline voices nationally in organizing around federal energy policies and internationally through the "It Takes Roots" delegation to the 2015 COP-21 United Nations Climate Talks in Paris.[22] In 2016 at their National Convening, CJA adopted an ambitious four-year strategic plan to consolidate and grow. As the plan states, "Together we must and we can further unleash our capacity, stretch beyond what is seen as politically possible . . . and play a critical role in building the world we need." ■

❝ *It's about a fight for the planet's resources, but the fight is taking place through a capture of the mind. We can only liberate our rivers and our seeds and our food, and our educational systems, and redefine and deepen our democracy, by first liberating our minds and decolonizing our minds.*"

–Vandana Shiva

"There are no passengers on Spaceship Earth. We are all crew."

–Marshall McLuhan

VI

Navigating Crisis and Transition: A Call to Innovation

6.1 Beyond Talking Points

Frames emerge from history, and they are connected with institutions. To win, we must take on all of it—the frames, the history, and the institutions. We must have the courage to name what is right and plot a course that connects to everyday lives and transforms them. If we do this, we can reframe our movements in ways that astonish, delight, and liberate.
—From *The Soul of Environmentalism*[1]

There is a growing disconnect between global society's lofty rhetoric of values, rights, and mutual responsibility and the realities unfolding around the jagged edges of the global economy. Global inequality (fueled by elite tax avoidance) is reaching record levels with the richest 1 percent owning more than the rest of the global population combined.[2] While nearly 800 million people, mostly children, go hungry every day,[3] global military spending has doubled since 2001 reaching $1.7 trillion in 2014.[4] Corporate monopolies continue their steady enclosure of nearly all aspects of life: the food we eat, the medicines we rely on, the media we consume, and the mechanics of government. Popular movements rooted in racism, nationalism, fear, and xenophobia are making a public resurgence, including elevating Donald Trump to the president of the United States on a wave of neofascist rhetoric.

Meanwhile, tune in to any serious scientific or long-term policy discussion and you get a different list of ominous symptoms: mass extinction, the erosion of cultural and biological diversity, climate chaos, diminishing fresh water, skyrocketing disease rates linked to pollution,

Fueled by warming seas Typhoon Haiyan hit the Philippines in December 2013, killing over 6,000 people and affecting 11 million more. Many historically poor communities who have never benefited from fossil fuel use are among the most vulnerable to climate disruption.

ocean acidification, collapsing ecosystems, topsoil loss, runaway toxic contamination . . . the list continues beyond most people's ability to absorb the true implications.

These converging trends forecast a troubling future. The ecological crisis is already feeding the historic dynamics of militarism, entrenched corporate power, and the systems of racism and oppression that have shaped Western society, law, and culture. It is tragically predictable that the impacts of environmental disruption—like all structural problems—will follow the well-worn tracks of privilege that divide haves from have-nots and impact people of color, Indigenous peoples, and poor communities first and worst.

Terrifying scenarios foreshadowed: private mercenary armies policing cities devastated by increasingly unnatural disasters. Waves of displaced refugees trapped at militarized borders. Small island nations negotiating relocation plans in the face of rising seas. Drought and extreme weather fueling social breakdown and conflict. Unchecked financial speculation heralding the next economic meltdown. A global rise of fascism, complete with militaristic nationalism, political repression, and racist violence. Food riots. Spiraling resource wars. This version of our future is already here for many communities.

Together, they are warning signs that our global economic and political systems—based on centuries of unchecked industrial extraction, colonial conquest, and exploitation—are pushing our planet's ecological life-support systems perilously close to collapse. By any standard, it is clear we are at an inflection point in human history, a moment that calls for bold and strategic action.

Those of us sounding the alarm need to go beyond talking points and isolated policy proposals. We must unearth the deep roots of our social and ecological problems and unleash collective momentum toward addressing them. Transformation, at the scale we need, will require systematic intervention to shift popular understanding of economy, politics, and our relationship with the natural world.

6.2 The Slow-Motion Apocalypse

We're in a giant car heading toward a brick wall and everyone's arguing over where they're going to sit.
—David Suzuki

Our lifetimes are witness to a *slow-motion apocalypse*—the unraveling of the routines, expectations, and institutions that comfort the privileged and define the status quo. The word "apocalypse" does not simply mean "the end of the world," or only refer to a religious ideology's much prefigured world-ending-cosmic-smack-down. The Greek word *apokalypsis* combines the verb "kalypto" meaning to "cover or to hide," with the prefix "apo" meaning "away." Apocalypse literally means to "take the cover away," or to "lift the veil" and reveal something that has not been seen.[5]

As the veil lifts, the assumptions and narratives that rationalize the status quo are shifting. What has been made invisible, by propaganda and privilege alike, is becoming a glaring truth: global corporate capitalism (increasingly buttressed by neofascist policies) is on a collision course with the planet's ecological limits. And thus, these are indeed apocalyptic times.

Depending on our positioning in the intersecting hierarchies of privilege, the apocalypse is either familiar and ongoing (500 years and counting for Indigenous peoples of the Americas), or just beginning to lap at the walls of more sheltered bastions. As activists, we often dare not speak with full honesty about the systemic crises we face for fear of self-marginalizing, terrifying people, or worse—dousing the essential fires of hope with an immobilizing despair. Alternatively, we fall prey to a different

(Left) The militarized streets of New Orleans in the wake of Hurricane Katrina, September 2005. (Right) Water Protectors from the Standing Rock Sioux Tribe and their allies march as part of the massive nonviolent resistance campaign to uphold Native sovereignty and stop the construction of the Dakota Access Pipeline. Picture courtesy of Dallas Goldtooth and the Indigenous Environmental Network, September 2016.

version of denial: a bleak catastrophism that allows the magnitude of the threat to overshadow any collective agency or transformative potential.

Facing the scale and all of the implications of the crisis requires psychological courage, spiritual fortitude, and a commitment to hold a moral center. The lifting of the veil can release an emotional rollercoaster of anxiety, anger, grief, and despair. Even for those us familiar with the histories and intersections, when we allow ourselves to take it all in—the suffering, the destruction, all that is at risk—added onto ongoing daily struggles, it is easy to be overwhelmed and immobilized.

These dynamics are often at play inside of progressive movements. The undertow of perpetual emergencies traps us in reaction mode, focusing on the metaphorical patient on the triage table while suspending disbelief about the limits of current strategies to actually cure the underlying disease. Denial is a more comfortable alternative to despair, but its impact on the collective political imagination is equally corrosive.

The underlying assumption of many progressives is that *if we just keep doing what we've been doing, and just work harder, it will be enough.* The consequences are a policy paradigm of timid incrementalism incapable of addressing the scope of the overlapping problems. This failure leaves an unnerved public vulnerable to hateful fear-mongering, corporate greenwashing, and phony techno-fix narratives.[6]

In order to build visionary movements, we must have the courage to put forward our own visionary narratives. As the outcome of the 2016 U.S. elections showed, the consequence of failing to do so can be catastrophic.

Re:Imagining Change

6.3 Psychic Breaks

Sometimes a breakdown can be the beginning of a kind of breakthrough, a way of living in advance through a trauma that prepares you for a future of radical transformation.
—Cherríe Moraga

But what happens when the inertia of denial is shattered by unfolding events? As disruptive events ripple through the physical world they dramatically impact our collective narratives and mythologies: conventional wisdom is upended, underlying assumptions are challenged, certainty is dethroned.

In an interconnected, fast-paced media environment, certain shocking events shatter collective expectations and transcend to become unavoidable cultural and political touchstones: 9/11, the 2008 Wall Street meltdown, new manifestations of extreme weather, police killings, mass shootings, Donald Trump becoming president of the United States . . .

These types of seismic events inevitably disrupt the dominant culture's mental maps and can trigger mass **psychic breaks:** moments when status quo stories are no longer adequate and those reliant on conventional wisdom are left searching for new explanations. As a result, the narrative landscape can shift rapidly. The assumptions of a discourse are exposed, new perspectives are unexpectedly elevated, and issues are reframed overnight.

The global mobilization of millions of women and their allies marching against President Trump on his first day in office is a powerful example of effectively harnessing a mass psychic break to stoke the fires of an emerging social movement.[7]

After the 2015 Charleston church massacre, community activist Bree Newsome removed the Confederate flag from outside the South Carolina state capitol saying, "...in order to move into the future we must reckon with the past."[8]

Psychic breaks open new political space and can provide powerful opportunities for new stories to take root in popular consciousness. The devastation of Hurricane Sandy in New York City in 2012 birthed Occupy Sandy, a people-powered disaster relief network that helped tens of thousands across the Northeastern U.S. In 2015, after an avowed white supremacist murdered nine African American people in a church in Charleston, South Carolina, popular outrage and acts of protest, like Bree Newsome's courageous action above, forced removal of the Confederate flag from numerous public sites in a matter of weeks.

In the absence of progressive framing, however, these moments are often hijacked by self-serving power-holders to manipulate trauma and re-entrench traditional power dynamics. Old control mythologies are invoked—the historic scripts of fear and blame, targeting people of color, non-Christians, or LGBTQ people. The post 9/11 psychic break quickly turned to warmongering, hate crimes against Muslim Americans, and the swift passage of the repressive PATRIOT Act. The 2008 financial crisis became an excuse to bailout wealthy investors while ordinary people lost their homes. Community mobilizations to stop racist police shootings are met with calls by white reactionaries for police escalation to restore "law and order." Donald Trump seized on the devastation caused by corporate "free trade" agreements but blamed Mexico and immigrants rather than the multinational corporations (like his) who enriched themselves at everyone's expense.

As the slow-motion apocalypse accelerates, the control mythologies that glue the system together will strain under the pressure and new constituencies will experience psychic breaks. Will the fallout strengthen desperate elites struggling to entrench business-as-usual, or magnify popular demands for social transformation?

The answer will be shaped by the orientation of competing social forces. As this book has outlined, the objective "truth" of such seismic events is no guarantee of a shared narrative or mass response. When control mythologies publically unravel, our movements have a unique opportunity to frame popular understanding and foreshadow more just futures. To leverage these moments and protect against reactionary backlash, our movements must build the capacity to wage the **battle of story** in the midst of upheaval, fracture, and rapid change.

6.4 Turning Moments into Movements

Small acts can make a big difference when there is a background of concern, understanding, and preliminary activism.
—Noam Chomsky

Social movements don't just react to psychic breaks, sometimes we create them and harness the momentum to shift debates and mobilize millions. Story-based strategy is a force multiplier for decentralized and network-based campaigns that employ this type of strategy.[9]

A well-designed narrative can act as a viral structure and facilitate self-organizing. This is the underlying logic that turns a meme into an ongoing mobilization, whether it's Occupy Wall Street reframing economic debates with "We are the 99%," #IdleNoMore galvanizing Native-led resistance across the hemisphere, the ocean of pink "pussy hats" at the 2017 Women's Marches, or the ongoing movement building and deep cultural intervention of #BlackLivesMatter.[10] When movements successfully harness a widely felt psychic break with a compelling and memetic framing narrative, moments of shock, outrage, and uprising can turn into ongoing movements for transformation.[11]

Storytelling is the original media, emerging directly from the human experience to be shared around cooking fires and painted on cave walls. For most of human existence the tools of story were largely limited to the spoken word. Even with the creation of writing, few knew how to write or read, and the role of maintaining the most important stories was a specialized position: elder, priest, teacher, shaman, midwife, griot, bard, minstrel, raconteur. The 20th century brought us the Age of Broadcast

Black Lives Matter organizers have turned moments of tragedy into an ongoing movement to end police shootings and anti-Black racism.

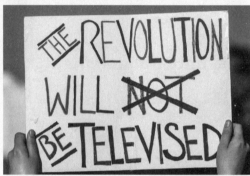

The digital revolution has removed barriers to sharing information but also fragmented audiences, so getting "televised" no longer guarantees reach.

when prominent newspapers, radio, and television curated a common media diet for the masses, while the 21st century has unleashed the disruptive forces of the internet media age defined by the lighting fast churn of personalized digital newsfeeds.

The rapid adoption of social media has radically democratized the role of media, leaving us to navigate shrinking screens and expanding social reach. The old barriers to producing and sharing content have come crashing down: bloggers have become grassroots journalists, activist live streamers have emerged as rival broadcasters and smartphones have transformed eyewitnesses into movement first responders.[12] Meanwhile, the, age-old political tactics of misinformation, propaganda, and deliberate lies have found new niches (and revenue streams) amidst a fragmented and polarized "filter bubble" media environment as designer control memes and "fake news."

The poet and musician Gil Scott-Heron coined the phrase "the revolution will not be televised" in 1970 and it grew to be a widely accepted truism of 20th-century protest and resistance movements. This core insight that power-holders often limit information in order to maintain social control is certainly still true. But today, there are fewer barriers to generating and releasing content, so the proverbial "revolution" will most likely be live tweeted and "televised" in real time through live-streaming mobile apps. But, as empowering as that may feel, amidst the flood of content competing for shrinking attention spans on corporate-controlled digital platforms, getting "televised" online is no longer a guarantee of reaching your audience.

As the production, distribution, and consumption of information morphs, the political terrain of narrative struggle is also transforming. New types of power and contestation are emerging that make narrative even more important than it has been in previous eras.[13] In this increasingly complex and fragmented media environment, it's important not to confuse tactical tools with an actual narrative strategy.

Choosing among the ever-evolving world of media platforms, social networks and applications are important tactical decisions. But a social-media engagement plan should not be mistaken for a comprehensive story-based strategy. From clear cornerstones, to a compelling framing narrative with the right hashtaggable memes, to designing multiple on and offline engagement pathways; effective story-based strategy means addressing the whole narrative and the whole strategy.

Regardless of technology's effect on changing social conditions, one constant is the power of narrative to inspire, mobilize, invite, cajole, reframe, interpret, contest, agitate, and engage ordinary people in fighting for their future.

6.5 Narrating Change

> *People are aware that they cannot continue in the same old way*
> *but are immobilized because they cannot imagine an alternative.*
> *We need a vision that recognizes that we are at one of the great*
> *turning points in human history when the survival of our planet and*
> *the restoration of our humanity require a great sea change in our*
> *ecological, economic, political, and spiritual values.*
> —Grace Lee Boggs

Change versus the status quo is familiar political shorthand for rhetorically uniting the broadest range of constituencies. Even this book has occasionally relied on it as easy code to navigate the mechanics of pan-movement alliances and multisector audiences.

In the fast-changing context of the 21st century, however, the status quo *is* the struggle to manage change. Elites scramble to react to shifting

NEOCLASSICAL
PARADIGM

ECOLOGICAL
PARADIGM

The control mythologies of neoclassical economics must be challenged with the simple reality that human economic systems are contingent on our planet's ecological operating system.[14]

circumstances. Venture capitalists boast of the "creative destruction" unleashed by their "disruptive" business strategies. Institutions of all types evolve or stagnate based on their ability to rapidly adapt. Grassroots movements balance quelling reactionary backlash with opportunities to promote more transformative solutions.

Growing instability means more psychic breaks. As they chip away at old worldviews, many fights are increasingly about who provides the narration for the culture—will it be the elite media, political figures, right-wing Twitter trolls, or progressive movements? Actively narrating the change means building the power and reach to define public interpretation of the shifts happening all around us.

Is the so-called gig economy or "sharing economy" liberating workers from the shackles of routine and unleashing an entrepreneurial future of prosperous flexibility for all? Or is it actually a sharecropping economy creating precarity, poverty, and inequality for the benefit of the 1%? Will the growing visibility of climate disruption fuel efforts to rebalance modern society within ecological limits? Or will it be used to justify dangerous mega-technological experiments like geoengineering as a desperate gamble to preserve the status quo?[15]

If grassroots movements successfully narrate the changes that ordinary people are experiencing in their lives, there is an incredible opportunity to engage public participation in the fight for systemic solutions. But to win these types of macro-framing contests we must collectively prioritize narrative as a key arena of struggle. Given the enormous gap between what's politically possible within our current institutional structures and what's actually necessary, there is an urgent need to articulate alternative visions that dramatically expand the terms of current debate.

As a number of theorists have pointed out, it is easier to imagine the end of the world than it is to imagine the end of this system.[16] Indeed as the escalating crises makes the end of our current world increasingly imaginable, the role of articulating alternatives is growing more urgent. We cannot win what we believe is impossible. We cannot create what we cannot imagine.

In the midst of this historic moment, one of the exciting trends is the growing tendency linking ecological politics with social-justice organizing. New strategies for narrating change that reimagine and combine ecological analysis with demands for racial equity and social justice are emerging. Powerful frames like "just transition" and **"ecological justice"** are spreading and challenging the entrenched assumption of an all-important mythic "economy" that is separate from (and more important than) people and planet.

Visions are taking shape, foreshadowing the multiracial alliances, networks, and grassroots movements that will undertake the grand project of redesigning our society to be sustainable, inclusive, and liberating. Collectively, the work to craft a politics that is commensurate with the scale of the crisis is evolving.

NARRATIVE AND SYSTEMS THINKING

Pioneering environmental scientist and systems thinker Donella Meadows created a famous list of "Leverage points to intervene in a system."[17] The top half of the list is reprinted below in a countdown to the most effective. As she discovered, the most influential points relate to paradigms and are interventions in the realm of worldview and narrative.

6. The structure of information flows (who does and does not have access to information).
5. The rules of the system (such as incentives, punishments, constraints).
4. The power to add, change, evolve, or self-organize system structure.
3. The goals of the system.
2. The mindset or paradigm out of which the system–its goals, structure, rules, delays, parameters–arises.
1. The power to transcend paradigms.

6.6 A Movement of Storytellers

We are an army of dreamers, and that's why we're invincible.
—Subcomandante Marcos, Ejército Zapatista de Liberación
Nacional

As strategists and communicators working in grassroots movements, our task is not just to calculate the best response to public opinion. Our task is to *shape* public opinion to build and support real solutions and structural change.

Winning the battle of the story—and creating more fertile cultural ground for movement building and organizing—will require expanding our skills, our strategies, and our connectivity infrastructure. Every activist's toolbox and every social change organization's approach should include story-based strategy basics: how to analyze dominant culture narratives, reframe issues, and craft effective messages. That's why we wrote this book and why we cofounded the Center for Story-based Strategy.

We have learned that the best way to build this story-based strategy capacity is to grow it from the ground up as part of grassroots social movements. To develop these types of transformative narratives requires story-based strategists who are actively embedded in the frontlines of grassroots struggles. We need a movement of storytellers.

There are no certain paths to the world we deserve, no one blueprint to win the future. This is why our movements must nurture a culture of strategic innovation. Imagine community-led organizations with research and development budgets, street level laboratories, and swarms of creative strategists. In an era of accelerating change, activist culture must evolve to see innovation not as a luxury at the edge of *the work,* but rather

Re:Imagining Change is a call to innovation. What are you doing to change the story for a better future?

Re:Imagining Change

as a necessity that drives *the work*. We must be willing to take risks, fail, and innovate faster. We must reimagine not only a vision for our world, but also a vision of what social change process and practice can look like.

And make no mistake, bold innovations are emerging, especially in response to the rise of the Trump regime. Innovative organizations are stepping beyond single-issue politics to open new political spaces for movement building, test new models, and embrace new organizational forms. Leaders are forging alliances that build unity amongst different constituencies without denying differences or compromising diversity. Story-based approaches are helping bridge historic divides and articulate shared values that effectively communicate the connections between all the issues. But will it be enough to narrate the broader, inviting story of transformation we need to scale our movements?

As Martin Luther King Jr. said, "What is needed is a realization that power without love is reckless and abusive, and that love without power is sentimental and anemic."[18]

Over 35 years ago, social ecologist Murray Bookchin theorized that as capitalism hit the planet's ecological limits, struggling elites would turn toward fascism to maintain social control amidst catastrophic social upheaval and ecological collapse. His stark warning resonates even more deeply today: "If we do not do the impossible, we shall be faced with the unthinkable."[19]

Our generations have the opportunity to lead a path toward ecological reconstruction, reconciliation with history's crimes, a more free, just society, and ultimately, a better world for all. We can transform fear and denial into hope and action, but only if we step into our collective power as story makers and story changers.

The transformational stories of 21st-century change will not be handed down from the meme-makers on high but rather bubble up as collaborative strategies from communities and grassroots movements on the forefront of transition. The new stories will emerge from struggle and celebration, amplify the (s)heroes at the margins, and inspire us to meet the true scale of our problems. Most importantly, they will reveal the creative sparks to do the seemingly impossible: reimagine change and remake our world. ■

Endnotes

Introduction

1. The Zapatista movement is well chronicled but in addition to the actual communiqués and declarations from the EZLN, we recommend two other great books: Jeff Conant's *A Poetics of Resistance: The Revolutionary Public Relations of the Zapatista Insurgency* (AK Press, 2010); and Hilary Klein's *Compañeras: Zapatista Women's Stories* (Seven Stories Press, 2015).

2. Previous to the industrial revolution, atmospheric CO_2 levels were roughly 280 parts per million (ppm). Scientific consensus has identified 350 ppm as the upper safe limit to keep planetary climate in the same relatively stable zone that allowed human civilization to develop over the past 10,000 years. For the latest data from the National Oceanic and Atmospheric Administration's Mauna Loa Observatory, check out https://www.esrl.noaa.gov/gmd/ccgg/trends/weekly.html (unless, of course, the Trump regime shuts it down). To explore the broad implications for life on our planet now that we have overshot our historic ecological limits, see Bill McKibben's book *Eaarth* (Times Books, 2010); or Elizabeth Kolbert's *Field Notes from a Catastrophe* (Bloomsbury, 2015).

3. The statistic comes from a January 2017 report released by Oxfam. The report is available at http://policy-practice.oxfam.org.uk/publications/an-economy-for-the-99-its-time-to-build-a-human-economy-that-benefits-everyone-620170. Six of the world's eight richest billionaires are U.S. citizens.

4. Among the wealth of movement literature about these developments, two that provide overviews and useful frameworks are NetChange's 2016 report *Networked Change: How Progressive Campaigns Are Won in the 21st Century* by Jason Mogus and Tom Liacas, available along with a summary article from the Stanford Social Innovation Review at http://netchange.co/networked-change-in-stanford-social-innovation-review, accessed October 2016; and Greenpeace's Mobilisation Lab's 2015 *Mobilization Cookbook: A Greenpeace Guide to Cooking Up People Powered Campaigns*, which although targeted at the international Greenpeace activist community, is broadly applicable. Available at http://www.mobilisationlab.org/wp-content/uploads/2016/01/The_Mobilisation_Cookbook_2.pdf

I. Why Story

1. For an in-depth exploration of how an understanding of human evolution can inform our understanding of story and art, check out Brian Boyd's *On the Origin of Stories: Evolution, Cognition and Fiction* (Belknap Press, 2009).

2. Lisa Cron, *Wired for Story: The Writer's Guide to Using Brain Science to Hook Readers from the Very First Sentence* (Ten Speed Press, 2012).

3. From "The Secrets of Storytelling: Why We Love a Good Yarn," *Scientific American*, September 18, 2008, at http://www.scientificamerican.com/article/the-secrets-of-storytelling/

4. As reported in the article "Your Brain on Fiction" by Annie Murphy Paul, *New York Times*, March 17, 2012, at http://www.nytimes.com/2012/03/18/opinion/sunday/the-neuroscience-of-your-brain-on-fiction.html?adxnnl=1&pagewanted=all&adxnnlx=1354716276-vBCJNxgtIuIFGnU+PmkBpA&_r=0. Accessed October 2016.

5. For more insights on this research, see "How Stories Change the Brain" by Paul J. Zak, published in *Greater Good*, December 17, 2012, at http://greatergood.berkeley.edu/article/item/how_stories_change_brain. Accessed October 2016.

6. You can read the science behind this, as well as see the video and other similar experiments in Jason Goldman's article, "Animating Anthropomorphism: Giving Minds to Geometric Shapes," *Scientific American*, March 8, 2013, at http://blogs.scientificamerican.com/thoughtful-animal/animating-anthropomorphism-giving-minds-to-geometric-shapes-video/. Accessed October 2016.

7. Walter R. Fisher, *Human Communication as Narration: Toward a Philosophy of Reason, Value and Action* (University of South Carolina Press, 1989).

8. Thoreau's 1849 essay has been reprinted under several titles and is also commonly called *Civil Disobedience* or *On the Duty of Civil Disobedience*.

9. One prominent example was the 2012 song "Same Love," by hip-hop duo Macklemore and Ryan Lewis, which was released during Washington State's Marriage Equality referendum and became globally popular. As of July 2016 the video has been viewed over 157 million times on YouTube.

10. For extensive research and ongoing insights on these trends, check out www.glaad.org. You can also check out CSS's *Stop the Presses* webcast series on communications and innovation at www.storybasedstrategy.org. Season 2.0 specifically dealt with applying a narrative power analysis to scripted television.

11. Evan Wolfson is quoted on p. 107 of the excellent book *This Is an Uprising: How Nonviolent Uprising Is Shaping the Twenty-First Century* by Mark Engler and Paul Engler (Nation Books, 2016). Inevitably, the focus on a single aspect of an issue, such as marriage, overshadowed and marginalized other critical LGBTQ struggles, but it nonetheless provides an indicator for the broader movement's ability to drive dramatic cultural shift.

12. Lawrence Freedman, *Strategy: A History* (Oxford University Press, 2013).

13. "Network society" is a term borrowed from the work of Spanish sociologist Manuel Castells. For Castells's contemporary thinking, check out the 2015 2nd edition of his book *Networks of Outrage and Hope: Social Movements in the Internet Age.* The term "open source campaign" comes from the trailblazing work of the Not1More campaign as they document in their article "The Way We Make Change Is Changing" by Marisa Franco, B. Loewe and Tania Unzueta, available at https://medium.com/organizer-sandbox/how-we-make-change-is-changing-part-i-5326186575e6#.uwb9ij87p. Accessed October 2016.

14. The term "leaderful" has been frequently used as a corrective to the misnomer that directly democratic and more horizontal or networked organizations are "leaderless." For a comparison of the traditional leadership models versus the emerging leaderful paradigm, see "We the Leaders: In Order to Form a Leaderful Organization" by Joseph A. Raelin, in the *Journal of Leadership and Organizational Studies*, 2005, Vol. 12, No. 2. Although the paper is not focused on social change organizations, its 4 Cs of leaderful practice (concurrent, collective, collaborative, and compassionate) echo the best practices of many directly democratic social movements.

15. This definition was created by researchers affiliated with the Arizona State University Center for Strategic Communications and documented in their book *Master Narratives of Islamist Extremists* by Jeffry R. Halverson, H.L. Goodall Jr., and Steven

R. Corman (Palgrave MacMillian, 2013). For a short summary of some of their definitions, check out http://csc.asu.edu/2011/12/08/why-story-is-not-narrative. Accessed October 2016.

II. Narrative Power

1. Turns out that technically the Big Dipper is not actually a constellation; it is an asterism, which means it is a prominent part of another constellation, in this case Ursa Major. Who knew?

2. In his book *Representation: Cultural Representations and Signifying Practices* (Open University/Sage Publications, 1997) cultural studies guru Stuart Hall writes "representation is the production of meaning through language." The concept of representation is central to what Hall calls the "social constructivist approach" within cultural and media studies. This approach argues that meaning is not "fixed" in one objective external reality, but rather created by being represented through human interpretation. Thus representation, through language or any other medium, goes beyond just *depicting* the meaning of reality to actually *creating* that meaning, which is why cultural theorists often say "representation is constitutive."

3. We caution that narrative approaches must be grounded in principles and ethics. For the Center for Story-based Strategy, this means a commitment to transparency, undoing oppression, and accountability to our partners and the communities we serve. Learn more by reviewing CSS's Anti-Oppression Principles at www.storybasedstrategy. org. For another great model of incorporating ethics into narrative development, check out the *Dóchas Code of Conduct on Images and Messages* at http://dochas.ie/images-and-messages, produced by the Irish Association of Non-Governmental Development Organisations, and subsequently adopted by many European civil society organizations.

4. In case you weren't old enough or attentive enough to follow the George W. Bush administration's media manipulations, "We don't want the smoking gun to be a mushroom cloud" was a potent meme that the Bush administration used repeatedly as part of its campaign to convince the U.S. public that Iraq had weapons of mass destruction, in order to justify the illegal invasion of Iraq in 2003. This is an example of using powerful imagery to control the meaning of a story. See Section 3.8 for more insights on imagery.

5. The welfare queen meme has been widely exposed as a right-wing distortion; for more information, see http://www.npr.org/sections/codeswitch/2013/12/20/255819681/the-truth-behind-the-lies-of-the-original-welfare-queen. Republican politician Newt Gingrich frequently referred to President Obama as a "food stamp president" during his 2012 campaign for his party's presidential nomination. You can watch Associated Press footage of him using the term in his stump speech at https://www.youtube.com/watch?v=VXcyX8blbu0. For more insights on unpacking racist codes, check out Drew Westin's work on racial unconsciousness in *The Political Brain: The Role of Emotion in Deciding the Fate of the Nation* (Public Affairs, 2007) and *Talking the Walk: A Communications Guide for Racial Justice* by Hunter Cutting and Makani Themba-Nixon (AK Press, 2006). Both are excellent resources for framing issues of race and racial justice in a U.S. context.

6. For deeper insights into these mechanics, see Francesca Polleta's *It Was Like a Fever: Storytelling in Protest and Politics* (University of Chicago Press, 2006); in particular, her analysis of metonymy and metaphor.

7. We were introduced to this exercise by Sha'an Mouliert in her anti-oppression training at CSS's 2005 *Incite/Insight* national gathering.

8. The Culture Group's influential 2013 report, *Making Waves: A Guide to Cultural Strategy*, offers a helpful two-part definition of culture: 1) Culture as "shared space" or a group's way of life, including the prevailing beliefs, values, and customs of a group; a group's way of life; and 2) the "doing of culture"—the set of practices that contain, transmit or express ideas, values, habits and behaviors between individuals and groups. You can read the report at http://theculturegroup.org. Accessed October 2016.

9. This working definition of culture is informed by a much longer exploration of the concept of culture in Stuart Hall's book *Representation: Cultural Representations and Signifying Practices* (Open University/Sage Publications, 1997).

10. *Framing Public Life: Perspectives on Media and Understanding of the Social World*, edited by Stephen D. Reese, Oscar H. Gandy Jr., and August E. Grant (Routledge, 2001) provides a detailed breakdown on how frames operate.

11. Erving Goffman, *Frame Analysis: An Essay on the Organization of Experience* (Harvard University Press, 1974).

12. George Lakoff is a cognitive linguist, professor at UC Berkeley, and cofounder of (the now shuttered) Rockridge Institute (www.rockridgeinstitute.org). He has written extensively on how frames operate in the brain. For more on conceptual models, check out *Moral Politics: How Liberals and Conservatives Think* (University of Chicago Press, 1996); or for a quick primer, *Don't Think of an Elephant* (Chelsea Green, 2004).

13. For a constructive critique of Lakoff's work and the dangers of disconnecting framing from broader change efforts see, "Thinking About Elephants: Toward a Dialogue with George Lakoff" by William Gamson and Charlotte Ryan, published in the Fall 2005 edition of Political Research Associate's magazine *Public Eye* and available at http://www.publiceye.org/magazine/v19n2/gamson_elephants.html. Accessed October 2016.

14. *Prime Time Activism: Media Strategies for Grassroots Organizing* (South End Press, 1991).

15. You can read more about the controversy stirred up by this blatant example of media bias at http://www.nytimes.com/2005/09/05/business/whos-a-looter-in-storms-aftermath-pictures-kick-up-a-different.html or http://www.salon.com/2005/09/02/photo_controversy. Accessed October 2016.

16. The exact quantity of typical daily advertising exposure has been a popular topic to generalize about for the past several decades. Estimates range from the hundreds to upwards of 20,000 daily advertising messages. You can read reflections on the number from the Choice Behavior Insights unit at advertiser Hill Holiday at http://cbi.hhcc.com/writing/the-myth-of-5000-ads/. Accessed October 2016.

17. According to a report by the research arm of global advertising giant IPG Mediabrands, $493 billion was spent globally on advertising in 2016. Available at http://www.cnbc.com/2016/12/05/global-ad-spend-to-slow-in-2017-while-2016-sales-were-nearly-500bn.html

18. Check out any of Sut Jhally's prolific and influential writing and multimedia output. A particular favorite is his essay and video lecture *Advertising and the End of the World*. The work of Jhally and many other important cultural critics can be found at the Media Education Foundation at http://www.mediaed.org

19. See Duncombe's book, *Dream: Re-Imagining Progressive Politics in an Age of Fantasy* (The New Press, 2007).

20. The origins of branding were drawn to our attention by our colleague Sean A. Witters who explored the issue in his PhD dissertation *The Logic of the Brand: Authorship and Literary Authenticity in the Modern American Novel* (Brandeis University, 2010).

21. Frederick Allen, *Secret Formula: How Brilliant Marketing and Relentless Salesmanship Made Coca-Cola the Best Known Product in the World*. (Harper Collins, 1995) Additionally, some scholars have proposed links between the Santa story and traditional Scandinavian shamanistic practices, particularly the ritual use of the red and white amanita muscaria mushroom, which may be the original source of the now iconic Santa Claus color scheme. See http://www.livescience.com/42077-8-ways-mushrooms-explain-santa.html

22. Barry Silverstein, "A Few Brand Campaigns Are Forever (Well, Almost)," January 17, 2006, at http://www.marketingprofs.com/6/silverstein2.asp?part=2

23. "Culturally obligatory" is a quote from a promotional video produced by the industry and distributed to diamond retailers in which marketing executives describe their intentions to make these new products as "culturally obligatory" as the original diamond engagement ring. In our early years, CSS used to show the video in our trainings to teach organizers about the power and cultural ambitions of corporate marketing. The film is excerpted in the Media Education Foundation's slightly dated but still classic 1998 documentary *Advertising and the End of the World*. You can find it at www.mediaed.org

24. You can read about diamond engagement rings marketed to men at http://www.huffingtonpost.co.uk/2011/12/05/rise-in-demand-for-mangagement-rings-for-men_n_1123209.html and about the right-hand ring campaign at http://www.nytimes.com/2004/01/04/magazine/the-way-we-live-now-1-4-04-consumed-the-right-hand-diamond-ring.html?_r=0. Accessed August 2016.

25. For more info on ongoing efforts to address the problem of conflict diamonds, check out https://www.amnestyusa.org/reports/chains-of-abuse-the-global-diamond-supply-chain-and-the-case-of-the-central-african-republic/. Accessed June 2017.

26. Heidi Cody created the "American Alphabet" in 2000. You can find out more about her work at http://www.heidicody.com. In case you are desperate to figure out a specific letter: A: All B: Bubblicious C: Campbells D: Dawn E: Eggo F: Fritos G: Gatorade H: Hebrew National I: Ice J: Jello (Sugar Free) K: Koolaid L: Lysol M: M&Ms N: Nilla Wafers O: Oreo P: Pez Q: Q-Tips R: Reese's S: Starburst T: Tide U: Uncle Ben's V: V8 W: Wisk X: Xtra Laundry Detergent Y: York Peppermint Patties Z: Zest.

27. This statistic is documented by Oberlin Environmental Science professor David Orr in his essay "Political Economy and the Ecology of Childhood," which is included in the anthology *Children and Nature: Psychological, Sociocultural, and Evolutionary Investigations*, edited by Peter H. Kahn and Stephen. R. Kellert (MIT Press, 2002).

28. In addition to his work as an evolutionary biologist, Richard Dawkins has become a well-known advocate for atheism. Unfortunately, his public statements have repeatedly crossed beyond reasonable critique into fear-mongering and he has developed a track record of overt Islamophobia. You can find out more at http://www.alternet.org/belief/richard-dawkins-islamophobia-just-reached-disturbing-new-heights. Accessed October 2016. Thank you to our colleague Sabiha Basrai for bringing this to our attention!

29. "Memes: Introduction" by Memeticist Glenn Grant at http://pespmc1.vub.ac.be/MEMIN.html and his related Memetic Lexicon http://pespmc1.vub.ac.be/MEMLEX.html. Although both pieces come from the early days of interest in memes in the 1990s, they still provide some novel insights. Accessed Oct 2016.

30. Check out Wikipedia for some useful Cliff Notes on Gramsci at http://en.wikipedia.org/wiki/Antonio_Gramsci. For a deeper look, see Gramsci's original writings compiled in various anthologies of his *Prison Notebooks*.

31. The term "manufacturing consent" was coined by Walter Lippmann in his 1922 book *Public Opinion* and elevated by Noam Chomsky in his work around the propaganda model of news media, which he and Edward S. Herman document in their 1988 book *Manufacturing Consent: The Political Economy of the Mass Media*.

32. Gene Sharp's body of work on strategic nonviolence has been incredibly influential on social movements around the world. A great way to learn about Sharp in the context of broader social-movement strategy and debate is in the book *This Is an Uprising: How Nonviolent Uprising Is Shaping the Twenty-First Century* by Mark Engler and Paul Engler (Nation Books, 2016). CSS thanks Jethro Heiko and Nick Jehlen at the Action Mill for their efforts to integrate the applications of this theory drawn from the Serbian student movement *Otpor* and their "upside down triangle" curriculum into a U.S. context. CSS supported Action Mill in applying this framework with Iraq Veterans Against the War, during the latter part of the Bush administration.

33. In CSS trainings we often include a third type of power, "power-within," to describe the individual will, creative force, psychological or spiritual reserves that shape personal motivation to make change. It is the power we get from believing in ourselves. As with the other types of power, it has a narrative component. This three-fold model of power comes from the feminist and antinuclear movements. It is well articulated in Starhawk's book *Truth or Dare: Encounters with Power, Authority and Mystery* (Harper & Row, 1987).

34. In 2008, researchers Erica Chenoweth and Maria Stephan confirmed that nonviolent uprisings were twice as successful at achieving their stated goals as violent ones. Their research was published in book form as *Why Civil Resistance Works: The Strategic Logic of Nonviolent Conflict* (Columbia University Press, 2011).

35. For a personal account of the Egyptian revolution, see Wael Ghomin's memoir *Revolution 2.0: The Power of the People Is Greater than the People in Power* (Houghton Mifflin-Harcourt, 2012).

36. See *This Is an Uprising: How Nonviolent Uprising Is Shaping the Twenty-First Century* by Mark Engler and Paul Engler (Nation Books, 2016). To learn about applying the insights in the book, check out the Momentum Training Community at https://www.momentumcommunity.org and this review by veteran movement strategist and trainer George Lakey at http://wagingnonviolence.org/feature/using-momentum-to-build-a-stronger-movement/. Accessed December 2016.

37. See Laura Elliff's article "Cooking the History Books: The Thanksgiving Massacre" at http://www.republicoflakotah.com/2009/cooking-the-history-books-the-thanksgiving-massacre/ or United Native America's account and editorial at http://www.unitednativeamerica.com/bureau/bwa_2.html. Accessed October 2016.

38. The phrase was first coined by 19th-century German philosopher Friedrich Nietzsche and expanded upon by Walter Benjamin; now it is a meme with a life of its own and has largely been accepted as conventional wisdom.

39. For information on ongoing organizing of the International Day of Mourning, see United American Indians of New England at http://www.uaine.org. Accessed October 2016.

40. For background on the racist origins and spread of "right to work" laws, check out https://www.facingsouth.org/2012/12/the-racist-roots-of-right-to-work-laws. Accessed August 2016.

41. Voter fraud campaigns have been used across the U.S. These billboards appeared in Milwaukee, Wisconsin in the run-up to the 2012 elections. After community voting rights advocates demanded that Clear Channel, the owner of the billboards, reveal the

"anonymous family foundation" that had placed them, they were removed. For local news coverage of the incident, see http://archive.jsonline.com/news/milwaukee/clear-channel-billboards-on-voter-fraud-to-come-down-kb7a4pj-175165001.html. For more insights into the ongoing use of the voter fraud myth to undermine the right to vote, see the March 2016 article at http://www.motherjones.com/politics/2016/03/voter-fraud-laws-gop-minority-voters-elections. Accessed October 2016.

42. For more information on Judi Bari's inspiring work as a transformative organizer, check out https://www.iww.org/history/biography/JudiBari/1. For some of her visionary political writing, check out her classic essay "Revolutionary Ecology" at http://www.judibari.org/revolutionary-ecology.html. For ongoing work building bridges between labor and the environmental movement and resources to directly challenge the "jobs versus the environment" control myth, check out the Labor Network for Sustainability at http://www.labor4sustainability.org. Accessed October 2016.

43. If you have been involved in social change work you've probably personally experienced the limits of facts alone for persuasion, but it is also something that has been shown repeatedly through experiments. One classic example is a study by Hans-Bernd Brosius and Anke Bathelt, which found that media accounts providing more facts ("base rate data") failed to affect people's understanding of a specific problem, compared to sharing specific stories ("exemplars"). "The Utility of Exemplars in Persuasive Communications," published in *Communication Research*, February 1994, vol. 21 no. 1, 48–78. Check out the abstract at http://crx.sagepub.com/content/21/1/48.abstract

44. Confirmation bias is a widely documented and common type of cognitive bias. "What is confirmation bias? Examples and observations" by Kendra Cherry last updated June 22, 2016, provides a simple overview and references within the psychological literature. Available at https://www.verywell.com/what-is-a-confirmation-bias-2795024. Accessed October 2016.

45. Drew Weston's *Political Brain* (Public Affairs, 2007) examines the biological implications of partisanship and provides useful examples of messaging strategies.

III. Winning the Battle of the Story

1. For more insights on using traditional "media hooks," check out *Spin Works: A Media Guidebook for Communicating Values and Shaping Opinion* by Robert Bray (pages 24–25) available for free download from the Resources section of spinacademy.org. Also *Talking the Walk: A Communications Guide for Racial Justice* by Hunter Cutting and Makani Themba-Nixon (AK Press, 2006) has a section called "Sharpen the Hook" (page 41).

2. We first encountered the term "battle of the story" in the work of the RAND Corporation, a wide-ranging private think tank specializing in military and corporate research. The term was used in an article by RAND analysts John Arquilla and David Ronfeldt, who cowrote *Networks and Netwars: The Future of Terror, Crime, and Militancy* (RAND, 2001).

3. For a chilling look at the PR industry's practices, see the classic *Toxic Sludge Is Good For You: Lies, Damn Lies, and the Public Relations Industry* by John Stauber and Sheldon Rampton (Common Courage Press, 1995).

4. February 15, 2003, was listed in the 2004 *Guinness Book of World Records* as the largest antiwar protest in human history. Estimates range from 6 to 30 million people participating in protests in over 800 cities demanding that the U.S. not invade

Iraq. Given this wide range, it is not clear if it has been surpassed in numbers by various other mobilizations since, although some reports suggest the October 2009 "International Day of Climate Action" organized by 350.org in the lead-up to the United Nation's COP-15 climate talks was larger. You can find out more at https://en.wikipedia.org/wiki/Protests_against_the_Iraq_War. Accessed October 2016.

5. www.nytimes.com/2003/02/17/world/threats-and-responses-news-analysis-a-new-power-in-the-streets.html. Although the exact phrase is not used, the term "second superpower" emerged from a front-page *New York Times* article analyzing the impact of the February 15, 2003 global antiwar protests. The reporter Patrick Tyler described world public opinion as a potential superpower that could rival the power of the U.S. state. The term was then promoted by the antiwar movement (including CSS, which at the time was embedded in national antiwar movement media relations) and then got widely used, including by UN General Secretary Kofi Annan. The term was a powerful enough meme in its own right that it even has its own Wikipedia entry at https://en.wikipedia.org/wiki/Second_Superpower. Accessed October 2016.

6. Quote reported in "Snap Judgments: Did Iconic Images from Baghdad Reveal More About the Media than Iraq?" by Matthew Gilbert and Suzanne Ryan, April 10, 2003, *Boston Globe* (page D1). Available at www.boston.com/news/packages/iraq/globe_stories/041003_snap_judgements.htm. Accessed July 2016.

7. "Baghdad: The Day After" by Robert Fisk, *The Independent*, April 11, 2003, available at www.independent.co.uk/voices/commentators/fisk/robert-fisk-baghdad-the-day-after-114688.html. Accessed July 2016.

8. This additional aspect of the ongoing story of the Pentagon's efforts to manipulate U.S. media coverage of the war was broken in a major multipage exposé by the *New York Times*: "Behind TV Analysts, Pentagon's Hidden Hand" by David Barstow, April 20, 2008.

9. For a deeper exploration of information warfare and a case study of its use against nonviolent protest movements, check out Patrick Reinsborough and Ilyse Hogue's analysis of protests at the 2003 Free Trade Area of the Americas Summit in Miami. The article "Information Warfare in Miami" can be found at www.alternet.org/story/17293/information_warfare_in_miami. Accessed October 2016.

10. CSS identified #BlackLivesMatter as the top social movement meme of the year for 2013, 2014, and 2015, showing that it was a meme that had helped frame a lasting movement.

11. Check out the full movement herstory and get the latest updates on BLM organizing at www.blacklivesmatter.com. For some reflections on BLM as a brand see the September 2016 article "Black Lives Matter, The Brand" at https://www.fastcodesign.com/3062127/black-lives-matter-the-brand

12. Check out the full policy platform "Vision for Black Lives: Policy Demands for Black Power, Freedom and Justice," which was collaboratively assembled by over 50 Black organizations in 2016 at https://policy.m4bl.org

13. For a powerful synopsis of this user-generated campaign, which was a trending topic on Twitter after a routine traffic stop resulted in Sandra Bland's unexplained death in a Texas jail in July 2015, see www.colorlines.com/articles/11-heartbreaking-revolutionary-ifidieinpolicecustody-tweets

14. #SayHerName focused on drawing attention to how anti-Black racism disproportionately affects Black women, especially queer and trans Black women. For more information, see African American Policy Forum at www.aapf.org and their report *Say Her Name: Resisting Police Brutality Against Women.*

15. You can find out more about the installation at notabugsplat.com. It was part of Inside Out a global participatory art project which grew out of French artist JR's large-format photographic street postings, see www.insideoutproject.net. Accessed October 2016.

16. Richard Berman, president of Berman and Company, is notorious for his web of industry front groups that launch attacks on labor unions, environmental groups, and other public interest advocates who stand in the way of his anonymous clients' agendas. For a partial detailing of his shady exploits, check out www.bermanexposed.org or read *Lies, Incorporated: The World of Post-Truth Politics* by Ari Rabin-Havt and Media Matters (Anchor Books, 2016), which refers to Berman's tactics as "asymmetric public policy warfare."

17. This is what some critical theorists have called "epistemic violence," a term popularized by postcolonial theorists, such as Gayatri Spivak, and often associated with the logic of dehumanization and constructing the Other.

18. *Gasland* is a 2010 Academy Award–nominated documentary written and directed by Josh Fox that highlights the negative impacts of hydraulic fracturing (aka fracking) and the gas development boom. The film helped galvanize the anti-fracking movement across the U.S.

19. You can read some press coverage about the action at https://mic.com/articles/154526/a-london-square-is-filled-with-life-jackets-in-memory-of-refugees-who-drowned?utm_source=policymicFB&utm_medium=main&utm_campaign=social#.bX7mRv5cz. Accessed October 2016.

20. This image, although a plausible estimate, is not intended to be precise and is provided only as an example of imagery. To compare the actual 2016 U.S. military budget of $598 billion dollars to military spending around the world, check out https://www.washingtonpost.com/news/worldviews/wp/2016/02/09/this-remarkable-chart-shows-how-u-s-defense-spending-dwarfs-the-rest-of-the-world/. Accessed October 2016.

21. Stacey Malkan's *Not Just a Pretty Face: The Ugly Side of the Beauty Industry* (New Society Publishers, 2007) is an excellent book from a frontline environmental health activist and researcher. Also see the Environmental Working Group's Skin Deep product safety database at www.ewg.org/skindeep

22. www.safecosmetics.org

23. The two proposed laws, SOPA (the Stop Online Piracy Act) and PROTECT IP ACT (Preventing Real Online Threats to Economic Creativity and Theft of Intellectual Property Act), were designed to strengthen copyright protections at the expense of internet freedom. For more insights on the campaign, check out bostonreview.net/world/day-wikipedia-went-dark. To see a gallery of the participating websites, check out https://gigaom.com/2012/01/18/sopa-pipa-protest-gallery/. Accessed August 2016.

24. www.nytimes.com/2012/01/21/technology/senate-postpones-piracy-vote.html?_r=0. Accessed August 2016.

25. For a detailed analysis of CSS's #ChangeTheMcStory video, check out the coverage on Upworthy at www.upworthy.com/if-you-think-15-is-too-much-this-parody-of-mcds-advertising-might-make-you-finally-understand. Accessed June 2017. To find out more about ongoing worker organizing for better wages and the right to unionize, check out fightfor15.org

26. www.news-medical.net/news/2006/10/23/1500-animal-species-practice-homosexuality.aspx. Accessed January 2017.

27. CSS's F.R.A.M.E.S model was partially inspired by Chip and Dan Heath's SUCCESS model of what makes an idea "sticky" as documented in their book *Made to Stick* (Random House, 2009). http://www.penguinrandomhouse.com/books/77687/made-to-stick-by-chip-heath-and-dan-heath/9781400064281/

28. The quote is associated with Geoffrey Crowther, editor of *The Economist* magazine from 1938 to 1956, who offered it as advice to young journalists. Referenced in "The Case against Globaloney" at http://www.economist.com/node/18584204

29. You can find a partial list of Occupy sites and protest locations at en.wikipedia.org/wiki/List_of_Occupy_movement_protest_locations. Accessed October 2016.

30. Check out the Boston based Design Studio for Social Intervention's groundbreaking work at www.ds4si.org

31. There is a wealth of literature on the mechanics and significance of Occupy Wall Street. We particularly recommend the writings of CSS co-conspirator Jonathan Matthew Smucker, who dedicates a chapter to it in his book *Hegemony How-To: A Roadmap for Radicals* (AK Press, 2017). You can read a range of perspectives from Occupy movement organizers in several anthologies including, *Occupying Wall Street: The Inside Story of an Action That Changed America* by Writers for the 99% (Haymarket Books, 2012) and *We Are Many: Reflections on Movement Strategy from Occupation to Liberation*, edited by Kate Khatib, Margaret Killjoy, and Mike McGuire (AK Press, 2012).

IV. Points of Intervention

1. You can learn more about Wes's multifaceted work as both progressive commentator and Buddhist teacher at www.wesnisker.com or https://en.wikipedia.org/wiki/Wes_Nisker

2. For a detailed account of this historic occupation, check out Kari Lydersen's book *Revolt on Goose Island: The Chicago Factory Takeover and What It Says about the Economic Crisis* (Melville House, 2009). In 2016 the workers won additional compensation from a bankruptcy court. See inthesetimes.com/working/entry/18802/republic-windows-doors-factory-occupation-bankrupcty-ue-union. Accessed September 2016.

3. The action was organized by Puente Movement (www.puenteaz.org) and other community-led organizations with support from the Ruckus Society (www.ruckus.org). It was part of the broader Alto Arizona campaign to challenge the human rights crisis created by the passage of SB 1070. Thanks to dedicated community organizing Sheriff Arpaio was voted out of office in November 2016.

4. You can find out more about this historic day of action at www.democracynow.org/2012/11/26/wal_mart_worker_uprising_protests_held. In Feb 2015 the OUR-Walmart campaign won a pay raise for 500,000 workers. You can find out more about Walmart workers' ongoing organizing at forrespect.org. Both sites accessed October 2016.

5. To see the "markets campaign" model in action, check out the work of the Rainforest Action Network (www.ran.org) or Stand.earth (formerly Forest Ethics) (www.stand.earth).

6. First Nations directly impacted by the Tar Sands have been resisting their expansion for decades. Allies from climate groups like 350.org and other environmental and social justice organizations joined them in the fall of 2011 to target Obama under the umbrella of Tar Sands Action. You can learn more about the mechanics of the Keystone campaign in the Beautiful Trouble module beautifultrouble.org/case/tar-sands-action/. Unfortunately, as this book goes to print the Trump administration is threatening revive the project and attempt to undo this movement victory, so the KXL may become a major flashpoint again. You can support the important work of the Indigenous Environment Network at www.ienearth.org

7. You can find out more about the SWEAT Coalition at www.sweatny.org. For updates on campaigns around the country to stop wage theft, check out www.wagetheft.org. To see how the wage theft reframing began to get covered by mainstream media, check out www.nytimes.com/2014/09/01/business/more-workers-are-claiming-wage-theft.html. For a great description of wage theft as a meme that is also a review of the first edition of this book, check out "Storytelling as Organizing: How to Rescue the Left from its Crisis of Imagination," Adam Kader, January 10, 2011, *In These Times* magazine at www.inthesetimes.com/working/entry/6824/. Accessed August 2016.

8. There Is No Alternative (TINA) is a phrase coined by British Prime Minister Margaret Thatcher in the early 1980s as part of her austerity campaign of shredding the British welfare system, instituting mass privatization, and challenging organized labor. Her economic policies became a model for much of the neoliberal reforms that have caused destruction and misery around the world.

9. The strategy of creating alternatives that both prefigure radically different possibilities and directly resist the status quo is a long-standing practice of transformative social movements around the world. The pithy meme of "visionary and oppositional" comes from our friends (and partners on the 2030 Scenarios project) at the Movement Generation Justice and Ecology Project. Check out their great 2017 manual *From Banks and Tanks to Cooperation and Caring: A Strategic Framework for a Just Transition*, available for free download in either English or Spanish at movementgeneration.org/justtransition

10. You can read about a real life example of this type of action that happened in Providence, Rhode Island, in 1989 in Beautiful Trouble's Daycare Center Sit-in Case Study, which is in both the print copy of the book and online at beautifultrouble.org/case/day-care-center-sit-in/. Accessed October 2016.

11. CSS did this project in partnership with the Movement Generation Justice and Ecology Project (movementgeneration.org) and the Occidental Arts and Ecology Center (oaec.org) to use these different scenarios as a tool to bridge the gap between our current movement strategies and the scale of the emerging ecological crisis. The multiphase experimental project identified key trends, articulated new strategies, and engaged movement leaders in an ongoing dialogue around strengthening our campaigns for resilient communities and ecological justice.

12. For more info on the action, including an archive of media coverage, see www.turnyourbackonbush.org. Accessed Oct 2016.

13. Read a full account of the action at www.buzzfeed.com/meredithtalusan/the-trans-woman-who-heckled-president-obama-last-summer-refu?utm_term=.vokbQmgAA#.taroA4XRR. Accessed October 2016.

14. Read the *LA Weekly*'s coverage of the action at www.laweekly.com/news/donald-trumps-walk-of-fame-star-gets-a-baby-border-wall-photos-7157242. See Plastic Jesus's latest creative provocation at www.plasticjesus.net. Both sites accessed October 2016.

15. For a full account of the organizing that led up to the action and the consequences, check out John Carlos's book, written with Dave Zirin, *The John Carlos Story: The Sports Moment that Changed the World* (Haymarket Books, 2011).

16. You can read about this framework in-depth in Duncombe's 2007 book *Dream*, available for free download at www.stephenduncombe.com/dreampolitik/. You can find an abbreviated version in the *Beautiful Trouble* book/web toolbox at beautifultrouble.org/theory/ethical-spectacle/

17. CSS is proud to have partnered with IVAW to lead strategy sessions, train members and support mobilizations. Support their important work at www.ivaw.org

18. Find out more about Earthworks' campaigns at www.earthworksaction.org. CSS has supported Earthworks by providing story-based strategy training to the Stop the Frack Attack gathering of communities impacted by the expansion of oil and gas extraction around the U.S.

19. See a rundown of some of the actions at www.huffingtonpost.com/2014/10/29/carry-that-weight-columbia-sexual-assault_n_6069344.html; and for broader analysis on the impact of the actions, see www.rollingstone.com/politics/news/how-carry-that-weight-is-changing-the-conversation-on-campus-sexual-assault-20141201

20. Check out www.robinhoodtax.org to find out more about the international campaign.

21. Check out CSS's Stop the Presses Podcast (Season Two and others) for an ongoing examination of social change engagement through scripted television and other pop culture moments. Another great resource is the 2016 *#PopJustice* reports from Liz Manne Strategy, which explores the intersection of social justice and pop culture strategies at popjustice.org

22. If you are unfamiliar with methane's incredibly destructive role in destabilizing the climate, check out www.scientificamerican.com/article/how-bad-of-a-greenhouse-gas-is-methane/. Accessed October 2016.

23. You can see the image in action along with other creative interventions and tactical media from that era at www.counterproductiveindustries.com. Accessed October 2016.

24. The campaign run by the U.S.-based Rainforest Action Network was exposing PepsiCo's use of conflict palm oil which continues to destroy the Indonesian rainforest. Find out the latest about the campaign at www.ran.org/inpepsishands. Accessed October 2016.

25. In 2014, as part of their Save the Arctic campaign, Greenpeace released a brand-busting 90-second video called *LEGO: Everything is NOT Awesome* (repurposing a theme song from the recent LEGO feature film) which depicted an Arctic made entirely of LEGO pieces slowly getting submerged beneath oil. The campaign successfully convinced LEGO to end its long-standing partnership with Shell Oil due to their efforts to drill for oil in the Arctic. You can read coverage of LEGO's decision and see the infamous video, which received over 6 million views at www.theguardian.com/environment/2014/oct/09/lego-ends-shell-partnership-following-greenpeace-campaign. Accessed October 2016.

26. Although Kalle Lasn and *Adbusters* magazine have popularized the terminology, the creation of the term "culture jamming" is credited to the American experimental band Negativland who used the term to describe manipulating media samples as a form of media critique. You can read more about the origins of the term and the practice in Mark Dery's 1993 essay "Culture Jamming: Hacking, Slashing and Sniping in the Empire of Signs," which can be found online at project.cyberpunk.ru/idb/culture_jamming.html. Accessed December 2016.

27. CSS and some colleagues from the Echo Justice Initiative (Jen Soriano of Lionswrite Communications and Stephen Boykewich of Prescient Media) partnered on the Bank versus America mobilization with six national alliances of grassroots racial and economic justice groups, including National Domestic Workers Alliance, Jobs With Justice, Pushback Network, Grassroots Global Justice, Right to the City, and National Day Laborer Organizing Network. CSS's recent Advanced Training had workshopped the mobilization scenario and produced a powerful guerrilla theater action to move the Bank versus America narrative. CSS's on-the-ground strategy team helped stage the action outside the shareholder's meeting and amplify the voices of spokespeople from around the country who had been directly impacted by BofA.

V. CHANGING THE STORY

1. See Rex Weyler's *Greenpeace: The Inside Story* (Rodale, 2005).
2. For a deeper discussion of Greenpeace's use of "image events," see *Image Politics: The New Rhetoric of Environmental Activism* by Kevin Michael DeLuca (Guildford Press 1999).
3. For info on current campaigns to protect whales, check out www.greenpeace.org/usa/oceans/save-the-whales/, as well as the ongoing work of the Sea Shepherd Conservation Society at www.seashepherd.org. Both sites accessed Sept 2016.
4. For more information on Rural Vermont, check out their website at www.ruralvermont.org. For critical analysis about the impacts of biotechnology on local economies and biodiversity, check out the ETC Group's resources at www.etcgroup.org/issues/genomics-biotechnology.
5. The full scale of Monsanto's sinister strategy to cover up genetic contamination is still not known. The practice was first revealed to the world by the courageous resistance of a Canadian farmer named Percy Schmeiser who sounded the global alarm and fought Monsanto in court. You can learn about his case in the 2009 documentary *Percy Schmeiser: David Versus Monsanto* from director Bertram Verhaag. A trailer for the film is available at https://www.youtube.com/watch?v=RAuOo5qFUXo. Accessed October 2016.
6. This historic law set a deadline of July 1, 2016, for all GE labeling to go into effect in Vermont. Even though the law covered only one state, many of the largest food manufacturers committed to the labeling nationally. The biotech industry responded with a massive lobbying campaign to get the federal government to overrule the Vermont law. In a perverse twist reminiscent of the 2005 veto of the Farmer Protection Act, mere days before the law would go into effect the U.S. Congress passed an industry-authored bill that preempted Vermont's law and dramatically diluted the labeling standards. Food Safety advocates dubbed the bill the Denying Americans the Right to Know (DARK) Act and committed to fight to repeal it. Regardless of the setback numerous national food manufacturers including Campbell's and Mars committed to continue labeling their products. To find out more about the ongoing campaign, check out www.ruralvermont.org/vtrighttoknowgmo/
7. Data provided by BCC Research, see www.bccresearch.com/pressroom/fod/global-bottled-water-market-reach-$195-billion-2018. Accessed October 2016. For more information about the destructive nature of the bottled water industry and updates on global campaigns for the human right to water, see Corporate Accountability International at www.thinkoutsidethebottle.org
8. See http://ciw-online.org
9. www.ciw-online.org/about.html
10. Student/Farmworker Alliance (SFA) is an exemplary model of an effective network of youth leaders organizing in accountable relationship with a directly impacted community through a worker-led alliance. SFA was an organizational partner of CSS's S.T.O.R.Y. (Strategy Training Organizing Resources for Young Leaders) youth leadership initiative. CSS supported SFA in developing their message and media capacity, provided story-based strategy trainings, facilitating strategy and alliance building sessions, and helped develop their overall story and visual brand. Visit them at www.sfalliance.org
11. www.allianceforfairfood.org. Accessed September 2016.
12. For more insights on the campaign, see David Solnit's 2005 article "Taco Bell Boycott Victory—A Model of Strategic Organizing: An interview with the

Coalition of Immokalee Workers" at http://truth-out.org/archive/component/k2/item/56758:david-solnit--taco-bell-boycott-victory. Accessed September 2016.

13. To find out more about the EJ movement, check out the "Principles of Environmental Justice" that were drafted and adopted at the 1991 First National People of Color Environmental Leadership Summit. These principles continue to be a guiding vision for communities organizing for environmental justice around the world, see www.ejnet.org/ej/principles.html

14. CEJA's member organizations are the Asian Pacific Environmental Network, Center for Community Action and Environmental Justice; Center on Race, Poverty and the Environment; Communities for a Better Environment; Environmental Health Coalition; and PODER: People Organizing to Demand Environmental and Economic Rights. In 2015 they expanded their alliance to include four partner organizations: Leadership Counsel for Justice and Accountability, Physicians for Social Responsibility Los Angeles, Pacoima Beautiful, and CAUSE: Central Coast Alliance United for a Sustainable Economy.

15. For a grounding in the politics and vision of the global climate justice movement, check out the "Bali Principles for Climate Justice," at www.ejnet.org/ej/bali.pdf and the "10 Principles for Just Climate Change Policies" in the U.S. at www.ejnet.org/ej/climatejustice.pdf

16. The gathering and the work of the Black Mesa Water Coalition (http://blackmesawatercoalition.org) are profiled in the short film *Our Power* produced by Kontent films and available on the Our Power Campaign website at www.ourpowercampaign.org/our_power_convening_2013

17. For a fuller articulation of this argument and useful analysis of the climate crisis, see Naomi Klein's 2014 book *This Changes Everything: Capitalism versus the Climate.*

18. Much of CJA's framing, although honed by CSS, comes from fellow CJA member Movement Generation Justice & Ecology Project, which has done the trail-blazing work to articulate a whole Strategy Framework for Just Transition. Check out their analysis and resources at www.movementgeneration.org

19. "Just Transition" is a term with a long history in the labor movement and in alliance building between communities living on the fence lines of toxic industries and the workers in those same industries. At the core of the concept is the principle that when economic transitions occur to end dangerous industrial processes like extracting, processing, or burning fossil fuels, the transition should happen in a just way that supports the workers and communities who are economically and culturally impacted. In the words of one of the pioneering efforts in the field (and a member group of CJA), the Just Transition Alliance: "Just Transition is a principle, a process and a practice." See www.jtalliance.org

20. CJA's member groups are anchoring the Our Power Campaign in each of these regions. In Richmond, California, the work is led by Asian Pacific Environmental Network (http://apen4ej.org) and Communities for a Better Environment (www.cbecal.org). On Black Mesa it is the Black Mesa Water Coalition http://blackmesawatercoalition.org. In Eastern Kentucky the work is led by Kentuckians for the Commonwealth www.kftc.org. See details on all the Our Power Communities around the U.S. on the CJA website at www.ourpowercampaign.org

21. In our role as a CJA member, CSS provided extensive message development, spokesperson training, and on-the-ground support to amplify voices from the frontlines.

22. The "It Takes Roots" delegation to the 2015 COP-21 United Nations Climate Talks in Paris unified Climate Justice Alliance with Grassroots Global Justice Alliance and the Indigenous Environmental Network to create a shared voice of North American frontline communities. You can read a full account of the delegation in the We Are

Mother Earth's Red Line report at http://ggjalliance.org/we-are-mother-earths-red-line.

VI. Navigating Crisis and Transition: A Call to Innovation

1. From "The Soul of Environmentalism: Rediscovering Transformational Politics in the 21st Century" by Michel Gelobter, Michael Dorsey, Leslie Fields, Tom Goldtooth, Anuja Mendiratta, Richard Moore, Rachel Morello-Frosch, Peggy M. Shepard, and Gerald Torres (May 27, 2005) at community-wealth.org/content/soul-environmentalism-reconsidering-transformational-politics-21st-century. This paper was written by Environmental Justice leaders to respond to an earlier controversial paper, "The Death of Environmentalism." You can read the paper and about some of the controversy surrounding it at grist.org/article/doe-intro/

2. For details see Oxfam's January 2016 report *An Economy for the 1%* documenting global wealth inequality and the role that tax havens play in hiding $7.6 trillion. Report available at www.oxfam.org/en/research/economy-1. Accessed October 2016.

3. The exact number in 2015 was 795 million people living in hunger, or approximately one out of every nine people on the planet according to *The State of Food Insecurity in the World 2015* from the Food and Agriculture Organization of the United Nations at www.fao.org/news/story/en/item/288229/icode/

4. This statistic on military spending is provided by the Stockholm International Peace Research Institute (sipri.org, inactive May 2017), which also documents that the U.S. controlled about 33 percent of the global arms trade in 2015. Accessed October 2016.

5. Edward F. Edinger, *Archetype of the Apocalypse: Divine Vengeance, Terrorism, and the End of the World* (Open Court, 1999). Until his death in 1999 Edinger was one of the leading Jungian analysts in the U.S.

6. The techno-fix narrative is a common control myth that appears across issues. The familiar template dismisses the need to address imbalances of power, historic inequities, or structural issues; because the solution (regardless of the problem) is technology. Police cameras will end institutional racism, automation will magically address economic disparity, "clean" coal and geoengineering the planet will let the U.S. stabilize the climate while still burning fossil fuels. Whatever the problem, techno-fix narratives simplify complex problems to present technology (regardless of whether the technology in question even exists) as the panacea that will save us.

7. Women's marches happened in over 500 U.S. cities (and many more around the world) mobilizing over 3.3 million people—making them among the largest demonstrations in U.S. history, see vox.com/2017/1/22/14350808/womens-marches-largest-demonstration-us-history-map. Accessed January 2017.

8. To see media coverage of this action and read more of Bree Newsome's own words, see washingtonpost.com/news/post-nation/wp/2015/06/29/why-bree-newsome-took-down-the-confederate-flag-in-s-c-i-refuse-to-be-ruled-by-fear/?utm_term=.e4526b7503c6. Accessed October 2016, inactive May 2017.

9. For a useful dissection of contemporary campaigning, including the dynamics of framing and narrative in distributed campaigning, see NetChange's 2016 report *Networked Change: How Progressive Campaigns Are Won in the 21st Century* by Jason Mogus and Tom Liacas. Available along with a summary article from the Stanford Social Innovation Review at netchange.co/networked-change-in-stanford-social-innovation-review. Accessed October 2016.

10. Occupy Wall Street may have faded from its 2011 discourse defining peak but occupywallst.org continues to highlight ongoing projects. For more information on

Idle No More, see idlenomore.ca; for Black Lives Matter, see blacklivesmatter.com. Both accessed October 2016.

11. Bill Moyer, in his classic book *Doing Democracy: The Map Model for Organizing Social Movement* (New Society, 2001), uses the term "trigger events." Mark and Paul Engler provide an excellent account and expansion of the concept in their book *This Is an Uprising: How Nonviolent Revolt Is Shaping the Twenty-First Century* (Nation Books, 2016).

12. The year 2015 marked a new turning point—the first time the majority of digital media consumption occurred on mobile rather than desktop—creating a growing expectation of continuous internet access regardless of time, location, or circumstance. Documented by comScore the global media analytics company in their March 2016 whitepaper, "2016 US Cross-Platform Future in Focus" as reported by *Wireless Week* at wirelessweek.com/news/2016/03/death-desktop-65-digital-media-consumed-mobile

13. For insights into the emerging concept of "new power," see the *Harvard Business Review*'s 2014 article "Understanding New Power" by Jeremy Heimans and Henry Tims, at hbr.org/2014/12/understanding-new-power. You can also check out the Tumblr site thisisnewpower.com for ongoing commentary.

14. This image is from kickitover.org, where you can find various resources to challenge the control myths of neoclassical economics. Another helpful resource is Anat Shenker-Osorio's book *Don't Buy It: The Trouble with Talking Nonsense About the Economy* (Public Affairs, 2012).

15. For more information about geoengineering and the fight to prevent techno-fix initiatives and disaster profiteering from impeding real efforts to address the climate crisis, check out the work of the ETC group at www.etcgroup.org/issues/climate-geoengineering. Accessed November 2016.

16. The best-known articulation of this sentiment, "It is easier to imagine the end of the world than the end of capitalism," is often attributed to Fredric Jameson. Before that version of the remark became widely quoted, Jameson had written, "It seems to be easier for us today to imagine the thoroughgoing deterioration of the earth and of nature than the breakdown of late capitalism; perhaps that is due to some weakness in our imaginations." Jameson, *The Seeds of Time* (Columbia University Press, 1994), xii.

17 Donella Meadows died in 2001, but her writing is available at the Donella Meadows Institute. You can read the full list of 12 leverage points at donellameadows.org/archives/leverage-points-places-to-intervene-in-a-system/. Accessed October 2016.

18. The quote comes from his August 1967 speech *Where Do We Go from Here?* The full text is available at www.stanford.edu/group/King/publications/speeches/Where_do_we_go_from_here.html

19. The quote comes from Murray Bookchin's 1982 book *The Ecology of Freedom: The Emergence and Dissolution of Hierarchy.* For some context of Bookchin's life and legacy, check out Damian White's article "Murray Bookchin's New Life," *Jacobin* magazine, July 2016 at jacobinmag.com/2016/07/murray-bookchin-ecology-kurdistan-pkk-rojava-technology-environmentalism-anarchy. Accessed January 2017.

Glossary

action logic – the explicit or implicit narrative that is illustrated by a specific action; how an action makes sense politically to an outside observer. (See **meta-verb**.)

advertising – the manipulation of collective desire for commercial/political interests; an interlocking system of manufactured images, narratives, and cultural codes that provides the propaganda vehicles, psychological drivers, and dream life of modern consumerism. (See **branding**.)

apocalypse – the Greek word *apokalypsis* combines the verb "kalypto," meaning to "cover or to hide," with the prefix "apo," meaning "away." Apocalypse literally means to "take the cover away," or to "lift the veil" and reveal something that has not been seen.

assumption – something that is accepted as true without proof; hypothesis that is taken for granted. Underlying assumptions are one of the elements of story and represent what you have to believe in order to believe the story is true.

battle of the story – 1. the political contest to define meaning and frame an issue, event, or situation for a popular audience; 2. a social change narrative with the goal of persuading people who aren't necessarily already in agreement with the social change effort. (See **story of the battle**.)

branding – the processes and symbolic demarcations to endow an object (product), idea, or person with specific narrative and emotional qualities; a common expression of narrative power and a foundational concept for the contemporary social context of commodification and consumerism.

brand-busting – a tactic to pressure corporate decision-makers by linking the company's public image or brand with the injustices they are perpetrating.

change agent – a person who embraces their own power as a catalyst; a term for anyone who is engaged in some form of social change work.

change the story – a catch phrase to describe the complex process of shifting the dominant public understanding of an issue or situation.

control mythology – the web of powerful narratives, beliefs, and underlying ideas (often emerging from historical processes of domination and shaped by powerful interests) that maintain the status quo and marginalize, co-opt, or limit collective imagination of alternatives and social change. Often distilled into highly replicable control myths that spread prejudices and power-holder bias. Sometimes described as **hegemony**.

culture – (from the Latin *cultura*, stemming from *colere*, meaning "to cultivate") refers to patterns of human activity including ways of living, arts, beliefs, customs, and practices that are passed down through the generations. A matrix of shared mental maps that define collective meaning.

culture jamming – a technique to subvert dominant culture narratives, such as corporate advertising or control mythologies, by co-opting slogans and images and recontextualizing them to create (usually subversive) new meanings.

defector syndrome – when a social change effort marginalizes itself by exhibiting dissent using symbols and language designed to communicate alienation from and rejection of the target audience.

direct action at the point of assumption – action with the goal of intervening in dominant narratives by targeting underlying assumptions and changing the story. Often used to shift popular understanding and reframe issues.

discourse – the entirety of public debate around a specific topic, including the full range of conflicting narratives, ideas, stories, messages, and contested viewpoints; for example, "climate discourse" or "racial justice discourse"; although the definitions and parameters of any given discourse are inevitably contested and shift over time.

drama triangle – a common narrative structure that casts characters in the roles of villain, victim, or hero. Examining how these relationships are defined in a story is a key form of **narrative power analysis**.

earth-centered – 1. a political perspective that situates oneself, a vision of society and social change strategy in the broader context of the earth's ecological operating systems including cultural and biological diversity, natural cycles and planetary boundaries; 2. a politicized acceptance of the sacredness of living systems.

ecological justice – an emerging frame to describe holistic, community-led responses to the ecological crisis that combine a vision of respect and restoration of natural systems with advocacy for justice in all its forms. (See **earth-centered**.)

elements of story – the five components of a story that can be used to apply a narrative power analysis: conflict, characters, imagery, foreshadowing, and underlying assumptions.

frame – the larger story that shapes understanding of information, experiences, and messages; the structure and boundaries of a narrative that defines point of view and power. Frames operate as preexisting narrative lenses in our minds.

framing narrative – the distilled narrative that communicates all the aspects of a campaign's framing; the public face of a story-based strategy.

hegemony – a concept developed in the 1930s by Antonio Gramsci to describe how powerful interests and institutions don't just rule society with coercion and violence, but also control society through shaping cultural norms, priorities, and "common sense." This multifaceted, intergenerational cultural process limits the terms of the debate and legitimizes existing power relationships. (See **control mythology**.)

information warfare – as defined by the U.S. military in the 1996 Chairman of the Joint Chiefs of Staff Instruction Number 3210.01: "Actions taken to achieve information superiority by affecting adversary information, information-based processes, and information systems." It includes the realm of psychological operations and the manipulation of narrative and public opinion for military purposes.

intervention – an action meant to change the course of events; interference or interaction with a previously existing social relationship, institution, system, structure, space, audience, or narrative.

meme – (rhymes with dream) a unit of self-replicating cultural information (i.e. idea, slogan, melody, ritual, symbol) that spreads virally from imagination to imagination and generation to generation. Coined by evolutionary biologist Richard Dawkins in 1976 as analogous to "gene"; from a Greek root meaning "to imitate." Glenn Grant defines it as "a contagious information pattern." A meme operates as a container, capsule, or carrier for a story.

message – (from the Latin *mittere*, "to send") the information, concept, or specific content a communicator is sending to their audience, often distilled to sound bites in order to spread in the contemporary media environment.

meta-verb – the overarching verb that embodies the narrative and distills the logic of a action or intervention, i.e. resist, disrupt, transform, expose, etc. (See **action logic**.)

movement – a critical mass of people who share ideas and values, organize themselves in large groupings, networks, and social blocs of individuals and/or organizations, take collective social action, and build alternative institutions to create social change.

narrative – (from the Proto-Indo-European root *gnō-*, "to know") an account of events, sequenced over time and space, often one that is fluid and meaningful enough to include multiple stories within it; a fundamental cognitive structuring process for the human mind to make meaning and relate with the world.

narrative cornerstones – the foundations of a story-based strategy, such as goals, target, audience, and constituency, which will inform the narrative that needs to be developed.

narrative filters – the existing stories and assumptions people have about the world that screen out new information that doesn't fit with their existing mental frameworks.

narrative logic – the quality of coherence when all the elements of a story make sense together, reinforce the intended meaning, and effectively communicate the desired message. (See **action logic**.)

narrative power – a multifaceted and fluid form of power expressed through stories, particularly through the processes that socially construct specific stories as "the truth." (See **power** and **narrative power analysis**.)

narrative power analysis – an analytical framework for assessing the interactions between narrative and relationships of power. The approach is grounded in the recognition that since the human brain uses stories to understand the world, all power relations have a narrative dimension. It can be used deconstructively to examine existing narratives and stories, as well as constructively to create new ones.

narrowcasting – targeting information to a specific audience rather than the general public; the term emerged as a contrast to traditional broadcasting.

people-power – the term originates from the 1986 mass uprising when the people of the Philippines nonviolently overthrew their authoritarian government. It has come to mean any movement or social change strategy that recognizes that dominant institutions rely on mass consent and that the removal of popular consent can lead to dramatic social changes.

point of intervention – a place in a system, be it a physical system or a conceptual system (ideology, cultural assumption, etc.), where action can be taken to effectively interfere with the system in order to change it. Examples include *point of production* (factory), *point of destruction* (oil well), *point of consumption* (retail store), *point of decision* (corporate headquarters), and *point of assumption* (intervening in an existing narrative, making alternatives visible).

popular culture – as defined in the 2016 report *#PopJustice Volume #1: Social Justice and the Promise of Pop Culture Strategies*: "The elements of culture capable of sustaining and perpetuating themselves based on endorsement and participation by large groups of people through their own agency." The roots of the term relate to the culture of "the common people" in contrast with the "high culture" of elites.

power – a dynamic set of relationships between people, institutions, and ideas characterized by the (often unequal) distribution of controlling influence. Defined by British philosopher Bertrand Russell as "the ability to produce intended effects" and Rev. Martin Luther King Jr. as "the ability to achieve purpose." Some social change practitioners differentiate between *power-over* (coercive power) and *power-with* or *power-together* (collaborative power) and *power-within* (personal, internal power). All power relations have a narrative dimension. (See **narrative power**.)

power-holder – an individual who possesses influence within a specific power structure. This person is sometimes known as a "decision-maker," and is often an effective target for a campaign.

psychic break – the process or moment of realization whereby a deeply held dominant culture narrative comes into question, oftentimes stemming from a revelation that a system, event, or course of events is out of alignment with previous expectations or core values.

racism – we find the definition provided by the People's Institute for Survival and Beyond to be particularly useful: "Racism is race prejudice plus power. Historically in the U.S. it has been the single most critical barrier to building effective coalitions for social change. Racism has been consciously and systematically erected, and it can be undone only if people understand what it is, where it comes from, how it functions, and why it is perpetuated."

radical – a problem-solving approach that focuses attention on addressing the root cause of problems rather than the symptoms. Also a change agent who adopts this approach.

reframing – the process of shifting popular understanding of an issue, event, or situation by changing the terms for how it is understood. (See **change the story** and **frame**.)

social change – the multifaceted process of acting to transform society's power relationships including decision-making, social processes, material conditions, institutional power, economic distribution, narratives, and culture.

spectacle – a concept coming from the work of the radical French artist-philosopher-revolutionary Guy Debord to describe "a social relation between people that is mediated by images."

story – a fundamental unit of human communication, an account of events, relayed from a specific point of view, usually with a beginning, middle, and end. (See **narrative** and **elements of story**.)

story-based strategy – an approach that places an analysis of narrative power and effective storytelling at the center of social change strategy; a participatory methodology with frameworks and tools to craft more effective social change narratives, challenge assumptions, change the story around specific issues and contest meaning in dominant culture narratives.

story of the battle – a social change narrative that focuses on mobilizing an audience of people who already share political assumptions with the communicator, rather than persuading others. (See **battle of the story**.)

strategy – a premeditated and systematic plan of action to achieve a particular goal. Strategy is inseparable from analysis and requires reflection and flexibility to adapt to emergent situations.

Further Reading

Adams, Maurianne, Pat Griffin, and Lee A. Bell, eds. *Teaching for Diversity and Social Justice: A Sourcebook for Teachers and Trainers.* New York: Routledge, 1997.

Adamson, Joni, Mei M. Evans, and Rachel Stein, eds. *The Environmental Justice Reader: Politics, Poetics, and Pedagogy.* Tucson: University of Arizona Press, 2002.

Albert, Michael. *Parecon: Life after Capitalism.* New York: Verso Books, 2004.

Alexander, Michelle. *The New Jim Crow: Mass Incarceration in the Age of Colorblindness.* New York: The New Press, 2010.

Alinsky, Saul. *Rules for Radicals.* New York: Vintage, 1995.

Allen, Theodore W. *The Invention of the White Race: Racial Oppression and Social Control.* New York: Verso Books, 1993.

Ancel, Judy, and Jane Slaughter. *A Troublemaker's Handbook 2: How to Fight Back Where You Work—and Win!* Lincoln: Labor Notes, 2005.

Anzaldúa, Gloria. *Borderland/La Frontera: The New Mestiza.* San Francisco: Aunt Lute Books, 1987.

Arquilla, John, and David Ronfeldt. *Networks and Netwars: The Future of Terror, Crime and Militancy.* RAND, 2001.

Berry, Wendell, Daniel Kemmis, and Courtney White. *The Way of Ignorance: And Other Essays.* New York: Counterpoint, 2006.

Blackmore, Susan. *The Meme Machine.* New York: Oxford University Press, 2000.

Boal, Augusto. *Theatre of the Oppressed.* New York: Theatre Communications Group, 1985.

Boggs, Grace Lee. *The Next American Revolution: Sustainable Activism for the Twenty-First Century.* Berkeley: University of California Press, 2011.

Bookchin, Murray. *Post-Scarcity Anarchism.* New York: Penguin Group (USA) Incorporated, 2004.

———. *The Ecology of Freedom: The Emergence and Dissolution of Hierarchy.* Oakland: AK Press, 2005.

Boyd, Andrew, and Dave Oswald Mitchell. *Beautiful Trouble: A Toolbox for Revolution.* New York: OR Books, 2012.

Bracken, Len. *Guy Debord: Revolutionary*. Venice: Feral House, 1997.

Brafman, Ori, and Rod A. Beckstrom. *The Starfish and the Spider: The Unstoppable Power of Leaderless Organizations*. New York: Portfolio, 2006.

Bray, Robert. *SPIN Works! A Media Guidebook for Communicating Values and Shaping Opinion*. San Francisco: Independent Media Institute, 2000.

Bringing Down a Dictator. Dir. Steve York. DVD. 2001–2002.

Brodie, Richard. *Virus of the Mind: The New Science of the Meme*. New York: Integral Press, 2004.

brown, adrienne maree. *Emergent Strategy: Shaping Change, Changing Worlds*. Oakland: AK Press, 2017.

brown, adrienne maree, and Walidah Imarisha, eds. *Octavia's Brood: Science Fiction Stories from Social Justice Movements*. Oakland: AK Press, 2015.

Campbell, Joseph. *Myths to Live By*. New York: Bantam, 1984.

Castells, Manuel. *Communication Power*. New York: Oxford University Press, 2009.

——. *Networks of Outrage and Hope: Social Movements in the Internet Age*. Cambridge: Polity, 2015.

Century of the Self. Dir. Adam Curtis. DVD. 2007.

Chenoweth, Erica, and Maria J. Stephan. *Why Civil Resistance Works: The Strategic Logic of Nonviolent Conflict*. New York: Columbia University Press, 2011.

Chisom, Ronald, and Michael Washington. *Undoing Racism: A Philosophy of International Social Change*. 2nd edition. New Orleans: People's Institute Press, 1997.

Chomsky, Noam. *Media Control: The Spectacular Achievements of Propaganda*. New York: Seven Stories Press, 2004.

Collins, Chuck, and Felice Yeskel. *Economic Apartheid in America: A Primer on Economic Inequality and Insecurity*. New York: The New Press, 2005.

Conant, Jeff. *A Poetics of Resistance: The Revolutionary Public Relations of the Zapatista Insurgency*. Oakland: AK Press, 2010.

Control Room. Dir. Jehane Noujaim. DVD. 2004.

Cron, Lisa. *Wired for Story*. Berkeley: Ten Speed Press, 2012.

Cutting, Hunter, and Makani Themba-Nixon. *Talking the Walk: A Communications Guide for Racial Justice*. Chicago: Consortium Book Sales & Distribution, 2006.

Dawkins, Richard. *The Selfish Gene*. New York: Oxford University Press, 2006.

Distin, Kate. *The Selfish Meme: A Critical Reassessment*. New York: Cambridge University Press, 2004.

Duarte, Nancy. *Resonate: Present Visual Stories that Transform Audiences.* Hoboken: John Wiley & Sons, 2010.

Dunbar-Ortiz, Roxanne. *An Indigenous Peoples' History of the United States.* Boston: Beacon Press, 2014.

Duncombe, Stephen. *Cultural Resistance: A Reader.* New York: Verso Books, 2002.

———. *Dream: Re-Imagining Progressive Politics in an Age of Fantasy.* New York: New Press, 2007.

During, Simon, ed. *The Cultural Studies Reader.* New York: Routledge, 1999.

Duvall, Jack, and Peter Ackerman. *A Force More Powerful: A Century of Nonviolent Conflict.* New York: Palgrave Macmillan Limited, 2001.

Edinger, Edward. *Archetype of the Apocalypse: A Jungian Study of the Book of Revelation.* Edited by George R. Elder. Boston: Open Court Company, 1999.

Engler, Mark, and Paul Engler. *This Is an Uprising: How Nonviolent Revolt Is Shaping the Twenty-First Century.* New York: Nation Books, 2016.

Eisler, Riane. *The Chalice and the Blade: Our History, Our Future.* New York: Harper San Francisco, 1988.

Ferreira, Eleonora C., and Joao P. Ferreira. *Making Sense of the Media: A Handbook of Popular Education Techniques.* New York: Monthly Review Press, 1996.

A Force More Powerful. Dir. Steve York. DVD. 2000.

Foucault, Michel. *The Foucault Reader.* Edited by Paul Rabinow. New York: Pantheon, 1988.

Frank, Thomas. *The Conquest of Cool: Business Culture, Counterculture, and the Rise of Hip Consumerism.* Chicago: University of Chicago Press, 1997.

Freire, Paulo. *Pedagogy of Hope: Reliving Pedagogy of the Oppressed.* London: Burns & Oates, 1997.

———. *Pedagogy of the Oppressed.* New York: Continuum, 1997.

Giroux, Henry A., Colin Lankshear, and Michael Peters. *Counternarratives.* New York: Routledge, 1996.

Gladwell, Malcolm. *Blink: The Power of Thinking Without Thinking.* New York: Back Bay, 2007.

———. *The Tipping Point: How Little Things Can Make a Big Difference.* New York: Back Bay, 2002.

Goffman, Erving. *Frame Analysis.* New York: Harper Colophon, 1974.

Goodwyn, Lawrence. *The Populist Moment: A Short History of the Agrarian Revolt in America.* New York: Oxford University Press, 1978.

Gottlieb, Robert. *Forcing the Spring: The Transformation of the American Environmental Movement.* New York: Island Press, 2005.

Gramsci, Antonio. *The Antonio Gramsci Reader: Selected Writings, 1916–1935.* Edited by David Forgacs and Eric J. Hobsbawm. New York: New York University Press, 2000.

Hall, Stuart. *Representation: Cultural Representations and Signifying Practices (Culture, Media and Identities).* Thousand Oaks, CA: Sage Publications, 1997.

Halverson, Jeffry R., H.L. Goodall Jr., and Steven R. Corman. *Master Narratives of Islamist Extremism.* New York: Palgrave MacMillian, 2011.

Hanne, Michael. *The Power of Story.* New York: Continuum Books, 1994.

Hardisty, Jean. *Mobilizing Resentment: Conservative Resurgence from the John Birch Society to the Promise Keepers.* New York: Beacon Press, 2000.

Hardt, Michael, and Antonio Negri. *Empire.* Cambridge, MA: Harvard University Press, 2001.

——. *Multitude: War and Democracy in the Age of Empire.* New York: Penguin Press HC, 2004.

Hartman, Harry. *Marketing in the Soul Age: Building Lifestyle Worlds.* New York: Hartman Group, 2001.

Heath, Chip, and Dan Heath. *Made to Stick: Why Some Ideas Survive and Others Die.* New York: Random House, 2007.

Herman, Edward S., and Noam Chomsky. *Manufacturing Consent: The Political Economy of the Mass Media.* New York: Pantheon, 1988.

Hoffer, Eric. *The True Believer: Thoughts on the Nature of Mass Movements.* New York: HarperCollins, 1989.

Holloway, John. *Change the World Without Taking Power: The Meaning of Revolution Today.* New York: Pluto Press, 2005.

hooks, bell. *Feminism Is for Everybody: Passionate Politics.* Cambridge, MA: South End Press, 2000.

——. *Feminist Theory: From Margin to Center.* Edited by Manning Marable. Cambridge, MA: South End Press, 2000.

Horton, Myles, and Paulo Freire. *We Make the Road by Walking: Conversations on Education and Social Change.* Edited by Brenda Bell. New York: Temple University Press, 1990.

Horton, Myles, Judith Kohl, and Herbert R. Kohl. *The Long Haul: An Autobiography.* New York: Teachers College Press, Teachers College, Columbia University, 1998.

Horwitz, Claudia. *The Spiritual Activist: Practices to Transform Your Life, Your Work, and Your World.* New York: Penguin, 2002.

Huxley, Aldous. *Brave New World.* New York: Harper and Row, 1932.

Hyde, Lewis. *The Gift: Creativity and the Artist in the Modern World.*
New York: Vintage, 2007.

———. *Trickster Makes This World: Mischief, Myth, and Art.* New York:
Canongate Books, 2008.

INCITE! Women of Color Against Violence, eds. *The Revolution Will
Not Be Funded: Beyond the Non-Profit Industrial Complex.* Cambridge, MA: South End Press, 2007.

Jasper, James M. *The Art of Moral Protest: Culture, Biography, and
Creativity in Social Movements.* Chicago: University of Chicago
Press, 1998.

Joseph, Peniel E. *Waiting 'Til the Midnight Hour: A Narrative History of
Black Power in America.* New York: Owl Books, 2007.

Kahn, Si. *Organizing: A Guide for Grassroots Leaders.* Silver Spring, MD:
NASW Press, 1991.

Kaufman, Cynthia. *Ideas for Action: Relevant Theory for Radical Change.*
Oakland: PM Press, 2016.

Kelley, Robin D. *Freedom Dreams: The Black Radical Imagination.*
Boston: Beacon Press, 2002.

King, Martin Luther Jr. *A Testament of Hope: The Essential Writings and
Speeches of Martin Luther King, Jr.* Edited by James M. Washington.
Grand Rapids: Zondervan, 1991.

Kivel, Paul, and Howard Zinn. *Uprooting Racism: How White People Can
Work for Racial Justice.* New York: New Society Publishers, 2002.

Klein, Naomi. *No Logo: Taking Aim at the Brand Bullies.* New York:
Picador, 2000.

———. *The Shock Doctrine: The Rise of Disaster Capitalism.* New York:
Metropolitan Books, 2007.

———. *This Changes Everything: Capitalism vs. the Climate.* New York:
Simon & Schuster, 2014.

Korten, David C. *The Great Turning: From Empire to Earth Community.*
New York: Berrett-Koehler, Incorporated, 2007.

———. *The Post-Corporate World: Life after Capitalism.* New York:
Berrett-Koehler, Incorporated, 1999.

———. *Change the Story, Change the Future: A Living Economy for a
Living Earth.* New York: Berrett-Koehler, Incorporated, 2015.

Lakey, George. *Strategy for a Living Revolution.* Grossman, 1973.

Lakoff, George. *Moral Politics: How Liberals and Conservatives Think.*
New York: University of Chicago Press, 2002.

———. *Thinking Points: Communicating Our American Values and Vision:
A Progressive's Handbook.* New York: Farrar, Straus & Giroux, 2006.

Lasn, Kalle. *Culture Jam: The Uncooling of America.* New York: Harper-
Collins, 1999.

Lee, Martha F. *Earth First! Environmental Apocalypse*. Syracuse University Press, 1995.

Leiss, William, Stephen Kline, and Sut Jhally. *Social Communication in Advertising: Persons, Products and Images of Well-Being*. Boston: Methuen & Company, Limited, 1986.

Lorde, Audre. *Sister Outsider: Essays and Speeches*. New York: Crossing Press, 2007.

Lui, Meizhu, Barbara Robles, and Betsy Leondar-Wright. *The Color of Wealth: The Story Behind the U.S. Racial Wealth Divide*. New York: The New Press, 2006.

Luntz, Frank. *Words That Work: It's Not What You Say, It's What People Hear*. New York: Hyperion Press, 2007.

Lynch, Aaron. *Thought Contagion: How Belief Spreads Through Society*. New York: Basic Books, 1996.

Malkan, Stacy. *Not Just a Pretty Face: The Ugly Side of the Beauty Industry*. New York: New Society, 2007.

Mander, Mary S., ed. *Framing Friction: Media and Social Conflict*. New York: University of Illinois Press, 1998.

Marcos, Subcomandante I. *Our Word Is Our Weapon: Selected Writings of Subcomandante Marcos*. Edited by Juana Ponce de Leon. New York: Seven Stories Press, 2004.

Martinez, Elizabeth, and Angela Y. Davis. *De Colores Means All of Us: Latina Views for a Multi-Colored Century*. Cambridge, MA: South End Press, 1998.

Marx, Karl, and Friedrich Engels. *The Communist Manifesto*. Edited by Gareth S. Jones. New York: Penguin Group, 2002.

McKenzie-Mohr, Doug, and William Smith. *Fostering Sustainable Behavior: An Introduction to Community-Based Social Marketing*. New York: New Society, 2000.

McLuhan, Eric, Frank Zingrone, and Marshall McLuhan, eds. *The Essential McLuhan*. New York: Basic Books, 1996.

McMurtry, John. *The Cancer Stage of Capitalism*. New York: Pluto Press, 1998.

Meadows, Donella H. *Thinking in Systems: A Primer*. White River Junction, VT: Chelsea Green Publishing, 2008.

Moraga, Cherríe, and Gloria Anzaldúa, eds. *This Bridge Called My Back: Writings by Radical Women of Color*. New York: Kitchen Table Women of Color Press, 1983.

Moyer, Bill. *Doing Democracy: The MAP Model for Organizing Social Movements*. New York: New Society, Limited, 2001.

Mumby, Dennis K., ed. *Narrative and Social Control: Critical Perspectives*. Minneapolis: SAGE Publications, 1993.

Notes from Nowhere Collective. *We Are Everywhere: The Irresistible Rise of Global Anti-Capitalism*. New York: Verso Books, 2003.

Nunberg, Geoff. *Talking Right: How Conservatives Turned Liberalism into a Tax-Raising, Latte-Drinking, Sushi-Eating, Volvo-Driving, New York Times-Reading, Body-Piercing, Hollywood-Loving, Left-Wing Freak Show*. New York: Public Affairs, 2006.

Orwell, George. *1984*. New York: Signet Classic, 1949.

Parry, Alan, and Robert E. Doan. *Story Re-Visions: Narrative Therapy in the Postmodern World*. New York: Guilford Press, 1994.

Payne, Charles M. *I've Got the Light of Freedom: The Organizing Tradition and the Mississippi Freedom Struggle*. Berkeley: University of California Press, 2007.

The Persuaders. Dir. Barak Goodman and Rachel Dretzin. DVD. 2003.

Polletta, Francesca. *It Was Like a Fever: Storytelling in Protest and Politics*. Chicago: University of Chicago Press, 2006.

Poo, Ai-jen. *The Age of Dignity: Preparing for the Elder Boom in a Changing America*. New York: The New Press, 2015.

The Power of Nightmares. Dir. Adam Curtis. DVD. 2007.

Rabin-Havit, Ari, and Media Matters for America. *Lies Incorporated: The World of Post-Truth Politics*. New York: Anchor Books, 2016.

Rampton, Sheldon, and John Stauber. *Trust Us, We're Experts! How Industry Manipulates Science and Gambles with Your Future*. New York: Jeremy P. Tarcher, 2002.

———. *Weapons of Mass Deception: The Uses of Propaganda in Bush's War on Iraq*. New York: Jeremy P. Tarcher, 2003.

Ray, Paul H., and Sherry R. Anderson. *The Cultural Creatives: How 50 Million People Are Changing the World*. New York: Three Rivers Press, 2001.

Reese, Stephen D., Oscar H. Gandy, Jr., and August E. Grant. *Framing Public Life: Perspectives on Media and Our Understanding of the Social World*. New York: Routledge, 2003.

Roberts, Kevin. *Lovemarks: The Future Beyond Brands*. New York: PowerHouse Books, 2005.

Rubin, Jerry. *Do It!* New York: Simon and Schuster, 1970.

Rushkoff, Douglas. *Media Virus! Hidden Agendas in Popular Culture*. New York: Random House, 1994.

Ryan, Charlotte. *Prime Time Activism: Media Strategies for Grassroots Organizing*. Cambridge, MA: South End Press, 1991.

Sachs, Jonah. *Winning the Story Wars: Why Those Who Tell (and Live) the Best Stories Will Rule the Future*. Cambridge, MA: Harvard Business Review Press, 2012.

Sharp, Gene. *The Politics of Nonviolent Action.* 3 vols. Edited by Marina Finkelstein. Boston: Porter Sargent, 1974.

Sharp, Gene, Joshua Paulson, and Christopher Miller. *Waging Nonviolent Struggle: 20th Century Practice and 21st Century Potential.* Boston: Porter Sargent, 2005.

Shenker-Osorio, Anat. *Don't Buy It: The Trouble with Talking Nonsense about the Economy.* New York: Public Affairs, 2012.

Shepard, Benjamin, and Ronald Hayduk, eds. *From ACT UP to the WTO: Urban Protest and Community Building in the Era of Globalization.* New York: Verso Books, 2002.

Shirky, Clay. *Here Comes Everybody: The Power of Organizing Without Organizations.* New York: Penguin Press, 2008.

Shoemaker, Pamela J., and Stephen D. Reese. *Mediating the Message in the 21st Century: A Media Sociology Perspective.* New York: Routledge, 2014.

Simmons, Annette. *The Story Factor: Inspiration, Influence, and Persuasion Through the Art of Storytelling.* New York: Basic Books, 2006.

Smith, Paul C., and Robert A. Warrior. *Like a Hurricane: The Indian Movement from Alcatraz to Wounded Knee.* New York: New Press, 1996.

Smucker, Jonathan Matthew. *Hegemony How-To: A Roadmap for Radicals.* Oakland: AK Press, 2017.

Solnit, David B., ed. *Globalize Liberation: How to Uproot the System and Build a Better World.* New York: City Lights Books, 2004.

Stauber, John, Sheldon Rampton, and Mark Dowie. *Toxic Sludge Is Good for You: Lies, Damn Lies and the Public Relations Industry.* Monroe, ME: Common Courage Press, 1995.

Storey, John. *Inventing Popular Culture: From Folklore to Globalization.* Grand Rapids: Blackwell Limited, 2008.

Sun Tzu. *The Art of War.* Trans. Thomas Cleary. Minneapolis: Shambhala Publications, 1989.

Swimme, Brian. *The Universe Is a Green Dragon.* Santa Fe: Bear and Company Publishing, 1984.

Szanto, Andre, ed. *What Orwell Didn't Know: Propaganda and the New Face of American Politics.* New York: Public Affairs, 2007.

Takaki, Ronald T. *A Different Mirror: A History of Multicultural America.* New York: Back Bay, 1994.

Taleb, Nassim N. *The Black Swan: The Impact of the Highly Improbable.* New York: Random House, 2007.

Tarrow, Sidney, Robert H. Bates, and Ellen Comisso. *Power in Movement: Social Movements and Contentious Politics.* New York: Cambridge University Press, 1998.

Tong, Rosemarie. *Feminist Thought: A More Comprehensive Introduction.* New York: Perseus Books Group, 1989.

Wallack, Lawrence, Lori Dorfman, David Jernigan, and Makani Themba. *Media Advocacy and Public Health: Power for Prevention.* Minneapolis: SAGE Publications, 1993.

Westen, Drew. *The Political Brain: The Role of Emotion in Deciding the Fate of the Nation.* New York: Public Affairs, 2007.

Weyler, Rex. *Greenpeace: The Inside Story.* Rodale International Ltd., 2005.

Yes Men. *The Yes Men: The True Story of the End of the World Trade Organization.* Boston: Disinformation Company Limited, 2004.

Zerubavel, Eviatar. *The Elephant in the Room: Silence and Denial in Everyday Life.* New York: Oxford University Press, Incorporated, 2007.

Zimbardo, Philip G. *The Lucifer Effect: Understanding How Good People Turn Evil.* New York: Random House, 2007.

Zinn, Howard. *A People's History of the United States.* New York: Harper Perennial, 1980.

Gratitude and Acknowledgments

Although this book was written by Patrick Reinsborough and Doyle Canning, many of these ideas, methods, and tools emerged from the collaboration and shared imagination of a huge community of creative change-makers, beginning with the original *smart*Meme collective members James John Bell, Doyle Canning, J. Cookson, Ilyse Hogue, and Patrick Reinsborough. Over the years, many aligned practitioners have engaged with this work and helped shape it: members of CSS staff and extended collective members, the ever-growing circle of story-based strategy associates and trainers, our partners in grassroots organizations and alliances, fellow movement support intermediaries, community leaders, and thinkers. Our own understanding and the story-based strategy methodology have benefited from all of this co-creative energy.

Special thanks to the amazing crew who currently staff the Center for Story-based Strategy and continue to innovate this approach: Christine Cordero, Rona Fernandez, Felicia Perez, Bernice Julie Shaw, Megan Swoboda, and Ratema Uch. Additionally we have learned so much over the years from collaborating and co-training with so many members of the CSS trainers and associates networks including: Myla Ablog, Celia Alario, Saa'un Bell, Autumn Brown, Danielle Coates-Connor, Tori Cress, Gopal Dayaneni, Maryrose Dolezal, Ashley Downend, Nijmie Dzurinko, Hannah El-Silimy, Hector Flores, Liana Foxvog, Reuben Hayslett, Nene Igietseme, Trina Jackson, Katie Joaquin, Hannah Jones, Nadia Khastagir, Cris Lagunas, sujin lee, Maria Elena Letona, Terry Marshall, Kiara Nagel, Bekah Mandell, Shana McDavis-Conway, Mariana Mendoza, Nupur Modi-Parekh, Lenina Nadal, Joseph Phelan, Rosi Reyes, Amaad Rivera, Raeanne Young, and Diana Pei Wu.

We also offer gratitude to our colleagues at *smart*Meme Studios, all past and present *smart*Meme and CSS board members, participants in our S.T.O.R.Y. young leaders program, all of the participants in our national and regional convenings, including *incite/insight*, Invoking the Pause, our numerous training-for-trainers events, and our annual Advanced Practitioner's Training which has been going strong since 2011. We'd also like to extend our appreciation to everyone involved in the production of the earlier editions of this book, including Libby Modern, Jen Angel, Antonia Juhasz, Cynthia Suarez, Nick Jehlen, Jessica Hoffman, Joshua Kahn-Russell, and Justin Francese.

Many people worked hard to make this edition possible, including current Center for Story-based Strategy staff as well as CSS board members Amara Possian and Gilda Hass, who played a critical role in helping navigate the book's birth pangs; Jonathan Matthew Smucker, who wrote a great foreword; John Yates, who designed the cover; our "rock on" publishing team at PM Press; Jess Clarke, Christine Joy Ferrer, and Merula Furtado from the Reimagine Workers Collective who provided their fantastic copyediting and layout talents on a reduced budget to give the book its look and feel. Additionally this edition benefited from feedback from our partners and allies—thank you to everyone who provided comments, including: Sabiha Basrai, Kay Cuajunco, Reuben Hayslett, Jennifer Krill, Hannah Jones, Hilary Lewis, Yuki Kidokoro, Terry Marshall, Shanelle Matthews, Alan Septoff, Jonathan Mathew Smucker, Craig Tucker, and Amy Vanderwarker. Zara Zimbardo deserves special credit for her multi-faceted feedback and support for the project.

We offer shout-outs to our cousin organizations and community of innovators: Kenny Bailey and crew at the Design Studio for Social Intervention for the vision of "an imagination lab for social justice"; Andrew Boyd and all our collaborators on the Beautiful Trouble book and website which created a potent compilation of movement theory, strategy, and tactics; Jonathan Matthew Smucker and Beyond the Choir for getting us beyond the "story of the righteous few"; Movement Generation for launching a new phase of earth-centered movement building with their ecological justice framework; David Solnit for helping us go beyond "(disem)PowerPoint"; the Ruckus Society for reminding us that actions speak louder than words; Progressive Communicators Network for their stewardship of relationships and practices to align the field; all our colleagues in the Echo Justice Initiative, including the Center for Media Justice, Praxis Project, Community Media Workshop, Lionswrite Communications, and Movement Strategy Center; Terry Marshall and the Intelligent Mischief crew for pushing the movement to "hack social change"; Margi Clarke and the veteran movement consultants at Road-Map for helping *smart*Meme grow into its next organizational phase and become CSS; Joseph Phelan and Jen Soriano for working with CSS to incubate and launch the much-needed and long-awaited ReFrame

Communications Mentorship; and all the hundreds of organizational partners, alliances, and networks who have collaborated to bring the methodology to life while continuing to do the daily work of building transformative movements for change.

We offer respect to our elders, community of peer practitioners, and like-minded visionaries and radicals in the movement and in the academy; our 5,000+ training alumni; and the over 300 social change organizations with which CSS has had the pleasure of partnering. We also would like to acknowledge the generous support of all those people who have financially supported CSS's efforts, including our original funders at the Compton Foundation, the Panta Rhea Foundation, the Hull Family Foundation, the Foundation for Global Community, the Ben & Jerry's Foundation, the Solidago Foundation, and the ongoing funders who have been instrumental in sustaining and scaling CSS's work: including Chorus Foundation, Ford Foundation, Overbrook Foundation, Solidago Foundation, Surdna Foundation, Unitarian Universalist Veatch Program at Shelter Rock, and the Whitman Institute. Most importantly, we want to express our deepest gratitude to all of CSS's members and supporters who have given generously to fund the ongoing work. Thank you.

In 2002 when our work began as an experimental inquiry into transformative narrative and social change strategy, we never could have imagined the 15-year political journey that would grow into the Center for Story-based Strategy. We continue to be in awe of the incredible cast of characters—staff, board, associates, partners, allies, and supporters—who continue to make CSS a vibrant and innovative movement hub.

We give a shout-out of solidarity and respect to the growing community of story-based strategists, both the incredible change agents associated with the Center for Story-based Strategy, and more broadly, the next generation of innovators, makers, artists, activists, poets, campaigners, rebels, organizers, and pragmatic dreamers who are already finding new ways to change the story.

Finally, we would like to thank our beloved friends, families, companer@s, mentors, ancestors, and loved ones. Your faith and support keeps our hearts brimming with hope, curiosity, love, and gratitude. Each one of you has taught us something. Your inspired work is the force of progress that will change our world. Thank you, and let us walk, sing, dream, and struggle together! Onward!

About the Center for Story-based Strategy

The Center for Story-based Strategy (CSS) is a national movement build-ing organization dedicated to harnessing the power of narrative for social change. CSS provides multifaceted support to leading climate, econom-ic, and social justice groups to amplify organizing, integrate messaging with movement building, and strengthen the capacity of our movements to change the story in order to win real solutions. CSS was founded as the *smart*Meme Strategy and Training Project in 2002.

CSS has trained over 5,000 organizers and activists from over 300 organizations to craft shared narratives, frame issues, strengthen alli-ances, and win campaigns. Groups rooted in Indigenous communities, communities of color, and frontline communities bearing the brunt of climate change have participated in trainings on story-based strategy and worked in partnership with CSS. CSS has done trainings across the United States, Canada, the United Kingdom, and other countries.

At the core of CSS's work is the deeply-held belief that, as a society, we must shift away from the old extractive, profit-based economy to a new, regenerative, life-sustaining economy that is fair and just. CSS believes that while transition to a new economy is inevitable due to the limits of the earth's natural resources, a just transition is not. CSS strives to bring about a just transition to a new economy that benefits all. Visit us online and get involved at www.storybasedstrategy.org.

About the Authors

Patrick Reinsborough is a strategist, organizer, and creative provocateur with over 25 years of experience in movements for peace, ecological sanity, democracy, indigenous rights, and economic, racial, and global justice. He cofounded the Center for Story-based Strategy (formerly *smart*Meme) in 2002 to explore the intersection of movement building, the ecological crisis, and strategies to shift cultural narratives. He has trained thousands of grassroots activists and partnered with hundreds of high-impact organizations to build alliances, reframe issues, and win local, national, and global campaigns. Patrick has provided crucial capacity building to the frontlines of social change, from amplifying the voices of Indigenous leaders at the United Nations climate talks to supporting visionary worker organizing to training leaders in Occupy Wall Street, the migrant rights, and climate justice movements. His approach draws from a range of innovative strategies, including brand-busting, distributed organizing, markets campaigning, mass protest, nonviolent direct action, and alliance building. Patrick believes that when our movements dream big, build unity across difference, and unleash collective imagination we are on the path to the future we deserve. He lives with his family in Oakland, CA. Follow him on Twitter at @RadicalWhispers and find out about his latest projects at www.patrickreinsborough.com.

Doyle Canning is cofounder of the Center for Story-based Strategy. She is a strategist, narrative architect, and accomplice in social, racial, and ecological justice movements. She cut her teeth working as a grassroots organizer in rural Vermont, building a movement of white working-class communities against corporate control of agriculture that won the nation's first GMO labeling laws. Doyle was struck in the head by a tear gas canister at the Seattle WTO protests and has been an integral part of social movements ever since, from popular protests against neoliberal globalization to the movement opposing the Iraq invasion to Occupy Wall Street and global climate justice networks. Doyle is dedicated to expanding the political imagination, disrupting outdated models, and building powerful, progressive movements with strategic nonviolence and story-based strategies. She is a consultant, speaker, trainer, and coach, and she is adding to her tactical arsenal by pursuing a JD degree at the University of Oregon School of Law. She is a fellow at the Wayne Morse Center for Law and Politics and cofounder of the grassroots network United FRONT (Families Resisting and Organizing Nonviolently Together). She enjoys growing food and flowers, practicing yoga, and biking with her two young children in a Dutch cargo bike. Follow her adventures at www.doylecanning.com.

PM Press was founded at the end of 2007 by a small collection of folks with decades of publishing, media, and organizing experience. PM Press co-conspirators have published and distributed hundreds of books, pamphlets, CDs, and DVDs. Members of PM have founded enduring book fairs, spearheaded victorious tenant organizing campaigns, and worked closely with bookstores, academic conferences, and even rock bands to deliver political and challenging ideas to all walks of life. We're old enough to know what we're doing and young enough to know what's at stake.

We seek to create radical and stimulating fiction and non-fiction books, pamphlets, T-shirts, visual and audio materials to entertain, educate, and inspire you. We aim to distribute these through every available channel with every available technology—whether that means you are seeing anarchist classics at our bookfair stalls; reading our latest vegan cookbook at the café; downloading geeky fiction e-books; or digging new music and timely videos from our website.

PM Press is always on the lookout for talented and skilled volunteers, artists, activists, and writers to work with. If you have a great idea for a project or can contribute in some way, please get in touch.

PM Press
PO Box 23912
Oakland CA 94623
510-658-3906
www.pmpress.org

FRIENDS OF PM

These are indisputably momentous times—the financial system is melting down globally and the Empire is stumbling. Now more than ever there is a vital need for radical ideas.

In the many years since its founding—and on a mere shoestring—PM Press has risen to the formidable challenge of publishing and distributing knowledge and entertainment for the struggles ahead. With hundreds of releases to date, we have published an impressive and stimulating array of literature, art, music, politics, and culture. Using every available medium, we've succeeded in connecting those hungry for ideas and information to those putting them into practice.

Friends of PM allows you to directly help impact, amplify, and revitalize the discourse and actions of radical writers, filmmakers, and artists. It provides us with a stable foundation from which we can build upon our early successes and provides a much-needed subsidy for the materials that can't necessarily pay their own way. You can help make that happen—and receive every new title automatically delivered to your door once a month—by joining as a Friend of PM Press. And, we'll throw in a free T-shirt when you sign up.

Here are your options:
- $30 a month: Get all books and pamphlets plus 50% discount on all webstore purchases
- $40 a month: Get all PM Press releases (including CDs and DVDs) plus 50% discount on all webstore purchases
- $100 a month: Superstar—Everything plus PM merchandise, free downloads, and 50% discount on all webstore purchases

For those who can't afford $30 or more a month, we have Sustainer Rates at $15, $10, and $5. Sustainers get a free PM Press T-shirt and a 50% discount on all purchases from our website.

Your Visa or Mastercard will be billed once a month, until you tell us to stop. Or until our efforts succeed in bringing the revolution around. Or the financial meltdown of Capital makes plastic redundant. Whichever comes first.

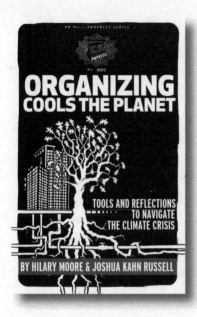

Organizing Cools the Planet
TOOLS AND REFLECTIONS TO NAVIGATE THE CLIMATE CRISIS

Joshua Kahn Russell and
Hilary Moore
$6.95
ISBN: 978-1-60486-443-4
8.5x5.5 • 64 Pages

Organizing Cools the Planet offers a challenge to all concerned about the ecological crisis: find your frontline. This booklet weaves together stories, analysis, organizing tools, and provocative questions, to offer a snapshot of the North American Climate Justice movement and provide pathways for readers to participate in it. Authors share hard lessons learned, reflect on strategy, and grapple with the challenges of their roles as organizers who do not come from "frontline communities" but work to build a movement big enough for everyone and led by the priorities and solutions of low-income people, communities of color, Indigenous, youth, and other constituencies most directly impacted by the crisis. Rooted in the authors' experiences organizing in local, national, and international arenas, they challenge readers to look at the scale of ecological collapse with open eyes, without falling prey to disempowering doomsday narratives. This booklet is for anyone who wants to build a movement with the resiliency to navigate one of the most rapid transitions in human history.

"In an atmosphere heavy with doomsday predictions and fear, this pamphlet is a breath of fresh air. Joshua Kahn Russell and Hilary Moore weave together stories and organizing tools to create a vision for practical transition amid the climate crisis. Organizing Cools the Planet confronts pressing questions of our time."
—Roxanne Dunbar-Ortiz, Founding Director,
Indigenous World Association

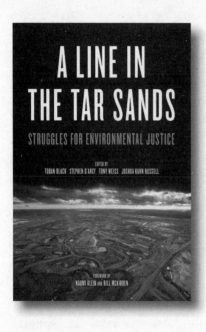

A Line in the Tar Sands
STRUGGLES FOR ENVIRONMENTAL JUSTICE

Edited by Joshua Kahn Russell, Stephen D'Arcy, Tony Weis, Toban Black • Foreword by Naomi Klein and Bill McKibben

$24.95
ISBN: 978-1-62963-039-7
9x6 • 392 Pages

The fight over the tar sands in North America is among the epic environmental and social justice battles of our time, and one of the first that has managed to quite explicitly marry concern for frontline communities and immediate local hazards with fear for the future of the entire planet.

Tar sands "development" comes with an enormous environmental and human cost. But tar sands opponents—fighting a powerful international industry—are likened to terrorists, government environmental scientists are muzzled, and public hearings are concealed and rushed.

Yet, despite the formidable political and economic power behind the tar sands, many opponents are actively building international networks of resistance, challenging pipeline plans while resisting threats to Indigenous sovereignty and democratic participation. Including leading voices involved in the struggle against the tar sands, A Line in the Tar Sands offers a critical analysis of the impact of the tar sands and the challenges opponents face in their efforts to organize effective resistance.

Contributors include: Angela Carter, Bill McKibben, Brian Tokar, Christine Leclerc, Clayton Thomas-Muller, Crystal Lameman, Dave Vasey, Emily Coats, Eriel Deranger, Greg Albo, Jeremy Brecher, Jess Worth, Jesse Cardinal, Joshua Kahn Russell, Lilian Yap, Linda Capato, Macdonald Stainsby, Martin Lukacs, Matt Leonard, Melina Laboucan-Massimo, Naomi Klein, Rae Breaux, Randolph Haluza-DeLay, Rex Weyler, Ryan Katz-Rosene, Sâkihitowin Awâsis, Sonia Grant, Stephen D'Arcy, Toban Black, Tony Weis, Tyler McCreary, Winona LaDuke, and Yves Engler.

The editors' proceeds from this book will be donated to frontline grassroots environmental justice groups and campaigns.

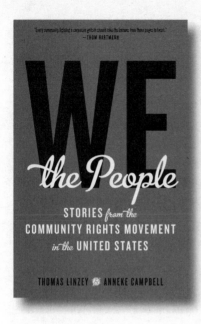

"Every community fighting a corporate goliath should take this lesson to their pages to heart."
—THOM HARTMANN

WE
the People

STORIES *from the*
COMMUNITY RIGHTS MOVEMENT
in the UNITED STATES

THOMAS LINZEY & ANNEKE CAMPBELL

We the People
STORIES FROM THE COMMUNITY RIGHTS MOVEMENT IN THE UNITED STATES

Thomas Linzey and
Anneke Campbell
$14.95
ISBN: 978-1-62963-229-2
8.5x5.5 • 192 Pages

We the People offers powerful portraits of communities across the United States that have faced threats from environmentally destructive corporate projects and responded by successfully banning those projects at a local level. We hear the inspiring voices of ordinary citizens and activists practicing a cutting-edge form of organizing developed by the nonprofit law firm, the Community Environmental Legal Defense Fund (CELDF). Their methodology is an answer for the frustrations of untold numbers of activists who have been defeated time and again by corporate political power and legal entitlement.

Instead of fighting against what we don't want, this book can teach us to create from the ground up what we do want, basing our vision in local control and law. By refusing to cooperate with the unjust laws that favor corporate profit over local sustainability, communities can show the way forward, driving their rights into state constitutions and, eventually, into the federal Constitution.

In communities from New Hampshire to Oregon, new forms of local organizing have sprung up to fight fracking, mining, dumping of toxic waste, and industrial agriculture, among other environmental assaults. These communities have recognized that the law has "legalized" the damaging actions of corporations, while providing no recourse against harm, and they have therefore decided to create a new system of law that makes local control and sustainability legal. Starting small, this process has spread from rural Pennsylvania to larger cities and towns, and has resulted in the creation of state networks seeking to amend state constitutions.

This work is about finishing the American Revolution by giving up the illusion of democracy and forging a system of true self-governance. In addition, this is about recognizing in law, for the first time in history, that nature possesses legally enforceable rights of its own.

Against Doom
A Climate Insurgency Manual
Jeremy Brecher
$12.95
ISBN: 978-1-62963-385-5
8x5 • 128 pages

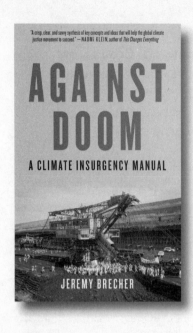

Before the election of Donald Trump the world was already speeding toward climate catastrophe. Now President Trump has jammed his foot on the global warming accelerator. Is there any way for the rest of us to put on the brakes?

Climate insurgency is a strategy for using people power to realize our common interest in protecting the climate. It uses mass, global, nonviolent action to challenge the legitimacy of public and corporate officials who are perpetrating climate destruction.

A global climate insurgency has already begun. It has the potential to halt and roll back Trump's fossil fuel agenda and the global thrust toward climate destruction.

Against Doom: A Climate Insurgency Manual tells how to put that strategy into action—and how it can succeed. It is a handbook for halting global warming and restoring our climate—a how-to for climate insurgents.

"In *Against Doom*, Brecher has provided the climate movement with two essential tools: a moral framework for the struggle against fossil fuels, and an actual plan for victory. By blending sober social movement analysis with the fire of grassroots activism, this book shows that there is a genuine, and winnable, case against the fossil fuel economy—a case to be argued in the streets as well as the courtroom. It's an essential volume for anyone committed to social change in the fight against climate change."

—Joseph Hamilton, Climate Defense Project

Organize!
BUILDING FROM THE LOCAL FOR GLOBAL JUSTICE
Edited by Aziz Choudry, Jill Hanley, and Eric Shragge
$24.95
ISBN: 978-1-60486-433-5
9x6 • 336 Pages

What are the ways forward for organizing for progressive social change in an era of unprecedented economic, social, and ecological crises? How do political activists build power and critical analysis in their daily work for change?

Grounded in struggles in Canada, the United States, Aotearoa/New Zealand, as well as transnational activist networks, *Organize!: Building from the Local for Global Justice* links local organizing with global struggles to make a better world. In over twenty chapters written by a diverse range of organizers, activists, academics, lawyers, artists, and researchers, this book weaves a rich and varied tapestry of dynamic strategies for struggle. From community-based labor organizing strategies among immigrant workers to mobilizing psychiatric survivors, from arts and activism for Palestine to organizing in support of Indigenous Peoples, the authors reflect critically on the tensions, problems, limits, and gains inherent in a diverse range of organizing contexts and practices. The book also places these processes in historical perspective, encouraging us to use history to shed light on contemporary injustices and how they can be overcome. Written in accessible language, *Organize!* will appeal to college and university students, activists, organizers and the wider public.

Contributors include: Aziz Choudry, Jill Hanley, Eric Shragge, Devlin Kuyek, Kezia Speirs, Evelyn Calugay, Anne Petermann, Alex Law, Jared Will, Radha D'Souza, Edward Ou Jin Lee, Norman Nawrocki, Rafeef Ziadah, Maria Bargh, Dave Bleakney, Abdi Hagi Yusef, Mostafa Henaway, Emilie Breton, Sandra Jeppesen, Anna Kruzynski, Rachel Sarrasin, Dolores Chew, David Reville, Kathryn Church, Brian Aboud, Joey Calugay, Gada Mahrouse, Harsha Walia, Mary Foster, Martha Stiegman, Robert Fisher, Yuseph Katiya, and Christopher Reid.

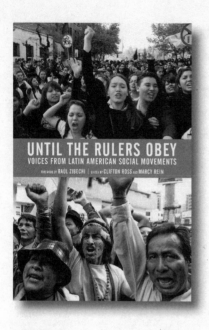

Until the Rulers Obey
VOICES FROM LATIN AMERICAN SOCIAL MOVEMENTS
Edited by Clifton Ross
and Marcy Rein
Foreword by Raúl Zibechi
$29.95
ISBN: 978-1-60486-794-7
9x6 • 528 Pages

Until the Rulers Obey brings together voices from the movements behind the wave of change that swept Latin America at the turn of the twenty-first century. These movements have galvanized long-silent—or silenced—sectors of society: indigenous people, campesinos, students, the LGBT community, the unemployed, and all those left out of the promised utopia of a globalized economy. They have deployed a wide range of strategies and actions, sometimes building schools or clinics, sometimes occupying factories or fields, sometimes building and occupying political parties to take the reins of the state, and sometimes resisting government policies in order to protect their newfound power in community.

This unique collection of interviews features five dozen leaders and grassroots activists from fifteen countries presenting their work and debating pressing questions of power, organizational forms, and relations with the state. They have mobilized on a wide range of issues: fighting against mines and agribusiness and for living space, rural and urban; for social space won through recognition of language, culture, and equal participation; for community and environmental survival. The book is organized in chapters by country with each chapter introduced by a solidarity activist, writer, or academic with deep knowledge of the place. This indispensable compilation of primary source material gives participants, students, and observers of social movements a chance to learn from their experience.

Contributors include ACOGUATE, Luis Ballesteros, Marc Becker, Margi Clarke, Benjamin Dangl, Mar Daza, Mickey Ellinger, Michael Fox, J. Heyward, Raphael Hoetmer, Hilary Klein, Diego Benegas Loyo, Courtney Martinez, Chuck Morse, Mario A. Murillo, Phil Neff, Fabíola Ortiz dos Santos, Hernán Ouviña, Margot Pepper, Adrienne Pine, Marcy Rein, Christy Rodgers, Clifton Ross, Susan Spronk, Marie Trigona, Jeffery R. Webber, and Raúl Zibechi.

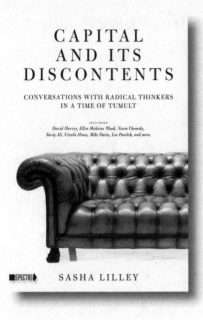

Capital and Its Discontents

CONVERSATIONS WITH RADICAL THINKERS IN A TIME OF TUMULT

Edited by Sasha Lilley

$20.00
ISBN: 978-1-60486-334-5
9x6 • 296 Pages

Capitalism is stumbling, empire is faltering, and the planet is thawing. Yet many people are still grasping to understand these multiple crises and to find a way forward to a just future. Into the breach come the essential insights of *Capital and Its Discontents*, which cut through the gristle to get to the heart of the matter about the nature of capitalism and imperialism, capitalism's vulnerabilities at this conjuncture—and what can we do to hasten its demise.

Through a series of incisive conversations with some of the most eminent thinkers and political economists on the Left—including David Harvey, Ellen Meiksins Wood, Mike Davis, Leo Panitch, Tariq Ali, and Noam Chomsky—*Capital and Its Discontents* illuminates the dynamic contradictions undergirding capitalism and the potential for its dethroning. The book challenges conventional wisdom on the Left about the nature of globalization, neoliberalism, and imperialism, as well as the agrarian question in the Global South. It probes deeply into the roots of the global economic meltdown, the role of debt and privatization in dampening social revolt, and considers capitalism's dynamic ability to find ever new sources of accumulation—whether through imperial or ecological plunder or the commodification of previously unpaid female labor.

The Left luminaries in *Capital and Its Discontents* look at potential avenues out of the mess—as well as wrong turns and needless detours—drawing lessons from the history of post-colonial states in the Global South, struggles against imperialism past and present, the eternal pendulum swing of radicalism, the corrosive legacy of postmodernism, and the potentialities of the radical humanist tradition. At a moment when capitalism as a system is more reviled than ever, here is an indispensable toolbox of ideas for action by some of the most brilliant thinkers of our times.

The Traffic Power Structure

Planka.nu
$12.00
ISBN: 978-1-62963-153-0
8x5 • 96 Pages

The Traffic
Power Structure

Planka.nu

"Scandinavia might seem an unlikely
breeding ground for a subway revolution."
—*The Wall Street Journal*

The modern traffic system is ecologically unsustainable, emotionally stressful, and poses a physical threat to individuals and communities alike. Traffic is not only an ecological and social problem but also a political one. Modern traffic reproduces the rule of the state and capital and is closely linked to class society. It is a problem of power. At its core lies the notion of "automobility," a contradictory ideal of free movement closely linked to a tight web of regulations and control mechanisms. This is the main thesis of the manifesto *The Traffic Power Structure*, penned by the Sweden-based activist network Planka.nu.

Planka.nu was founded in 2001 to fight for free public transport. Thanks to creative direct action, witty public interventions, and thought-provoking statements, the network has become a leading voice in Scandinavian debates on traffic. In its manifesto, Planka.nu presents a critique of the automobile society, analyzes the connections between traffic, the environment, and class, and outlines its political vision. The topics explored along the way include Bruce Springsteen, high-speed trains, nuclear power, the security-industrial complex, happiness research, and volcano eruptions. Planka.nu rejects demands to travel ever-longer distances in order to satisfy our most basic needs while we lose all sense for proximity and community. *The Traffic Power Structure* argues for a different kind of traffic in a different kind of world.

The book has received several awards in Sweden and has been hailed by Swedish media as a "manifesto of striking analytical depth, based on profound knowledge and a will to agitation that demands our respect" (*Ny Tid*).

"We could build a Berlin Wall around the metro stations, and they would still try to find ways to get around it."
   —Jesper Pettersson, spokesperson for Stockholm's Public Transport Services